Praise for *The New Power U*

'*The New Power University* offers a practical and in
higher education. It makes a compelling case for a
broad participation and greater impact. A must-re

Jeremy Heimans and Henry Timms, co-au...

'The world demands new models for higher education that are relevant in the face
of seismic societal change and take on the moral and practical requirement for
inclusivity. Jonathan Grant shows us a path for getting there, leveraging the New
Power of collective participation, distributed and networked governance, and radical
transparency to build the New Power University. Critically, Grant puts a stake in
the ground with social responsibility inherent in the mission of every university and
universities as active advocates for social good. Grant is masterful in bringing the
reader from the hallowed history to the essential transformation, writing with clarity
and insight, provoking us to both think and act.'

Susan Marquis, Frank and Marcia Carlucci Dean,
Pardee RAND Graduate School; Vice-President,
Innovation, RAND Corporation

'There can be no doubt – the university needs to be rethought, and urgently, or it
will lose the confidence of the governments and the public. Jonathan Grant knows
this problem intimately. With *The New Power University*, he has made an enormous
contribution to pushing the debate forward. He has done it with elegance, and most
important, a highly persuasive argument. Those who don't agree about the need for
change really need to read this book.'

John Ralston Saul, author of The Collapse of Globalism

'*The New Power University* is a compelling vision statement on the role of the
university in 21st-century society, *and* a blueprint for universities of the future that
must respond to the demands of a new generation of learners and academics.'

'Funmi Olonisakin, Vice-President and Vice-Principal
International, King's College London

'Jonathan Grant transformed innovation, engagement and impact for King's
College London. Now in *The New Power University* he poses a challenge for every
tertiary institution – what is the public purpose of your university, and how can it
accept social responsibility as a core part of its mission? This is an important and
provocative contribution to new thinking and new practices.'

Glyn Davis, former Vice-Chancellor, University of Melbourne

'This book is very timely and extremely thoughtful. We need a debate about what universities can offer in our volatile and challenged world. Jonathan Grant has provided a clear set of signposts highlighting how universities in the 21st century are not only relevant but desperately needed. Do read this book.'

Mary Stuart, Vice-Chancellor, University of Lincoln

'Even before COVID-19, universities around the world were facing a wave of change. Now that has become a tsunami. In *The New Power University*, Jonathan Grant examines the trends and urges the shedding of old shibboleths in order to embrace a new future. Insightful and engaging, this book will spur and shape the urgent debates learning communities need to have and resolve to avoid being left behind.'

Julia Gillard, former Prime Minister and Minster for Education of Australia; Chair-elect of the Wellcome Trust

'This is a timely vision for how universities can rediscover their purpose and renew the social contract that provides their licence to operate. *The New Power University* is essential material for anyone wondering what universities are for and how they can help provide the answers to the most pressing challenges of our times.'

Jo Johnson, Chairman of Tes Global; former Minister of State for Universities, Science, Research and Innovation

'We are entering a new world and in *The New Power University*, Jonathan Grant sets out a vision of how universities can be leaders rather than followers at a time of societal change. He builds on his longstanding leadership in defining the broad service and civic leadership that universities must aspire to, to set out a blueprint as to how universities can transform themselves and in so doing make their most effective contribution broadly. This is a must-read for anyone interested in the transformative power of higher education.'

Ed Byrne, former President, King's College London; co-author of The University Challenge

'As we navigate through these increasingly complex times, we must re-imagine what universities are for. In this provocative and stimulating book, Jonathan Grant not only identifies the challenges that universities face today, but sets out a radical agenda for change. An essential text for everyone involved in higher education.'

Sally Davies, Master of Trinity College Cambridge and former Chief Medical Officer England

The New Power University

Pearson

At Pearson, we have a simple mission: to help people make more of their lives through learning.

We combine innovative learning technology with trusted content and educational expertise to provide engaging and effective learning experiences that serve people wherever and whenever they are learning.

From classroom to boardroom, our curriculum materials, digital learning tools and testing programmes help to educate millions of people worldwide – more than any other private enterprise.

Every day our work helps learning flourish, and wherever learning flourishes, so do people.

To learn more, please visit us at **www.pearson.com/uk**

The New Power University

The social purpose of higher education in the 21st century

Jonathan Grant

Pearson

Harlow, England • London • New York • Boston • San Francisco • Toronto • Sydney
Dubai • Singapore • Hong Kong • Tokyo • Seoul • Taipei • New Delhi
Cape Town • São Paulo • Mexico City • Madrid • Amsterdam • Munich • Paris • Milan

PEARSON EDUCATION LIMITED
KAO Two
KAO Park
Harlow CM17 9NA
United Kingdom
Tel: +44 (0)1279 623623
Web: www.pearson.com/uk

First edition published 2021 (print and electronic)

ISBN: 978-1-292-34942-8 (print)
          978-1-292-34944-2 (PDF)
          978-1-292-34943-5 (ePub)

British Library Cataloguing-in-Publication Data
A catalogue record for the print edition is available from the British Library

Library of Congress Cataloging-in-Publication Data
Library of Congress Control Number 2020924652

10 9 8 7 6 5 4 3 2 1
25 24 23 22 21

Cover design by At the Pop

Print edition typeset in 11/14pt Electra LT Std by SPi Global
Printed by Ashford Colour Press Ltd, Gosport

NOTE THAT ANY PAGE CROSS REFERENCES REFER TO THE PRINT EDITION

*With love and thanks to Lucila, Almarina and Noah
for all their support, patience and comradery.*

Contents

Author's acknowledgements

Countless people have supported me in writing this book. Sometimes, they did this by not realising it; other times, I reached out to people asking for a conversation, a coffee and, on occasion, a beer. Other times, I was seeking a specific piece of information, fact check or a request to critically review some text. In the Preface, I explain how three people – Ed Byrne, Louise Gough and Ross Pow – have been instrumental in shaping a number of ideas I put forward in the book. I also acknowledge my attempts to adopt some new power values in writing the book – in building, as I wrote, a network or social movement of people, who I could bounce ideas off, stimulate my thinking and help me illustrate my ideas by example. I began by formalising this as an international sounding board but, as I progressed through the book, that started to be more amorphous, with the network growing in unpredictable directions. In a small way, I hope this network will be the beginning of a social movement around the New Power University. Below, I try to name all of those I have interacted with on this journey – in doing so, I should stress that the ideas I present are mine and, in acknowledging their contribution, I am not implying in any way that they support the case I make, but hope that they do! Needless to say, any mistakes are mine and mine alone.

I would like to begin by thanking those people who reviewed, on behalf of my publisher Pearson, the proposal for this book. Their engaged and critical comments helped me resolve a number of early tensions: Sarah Beart; Charles Clarke; Glyn Davis; Verity Firth; Phil Harvey; Nick Hillman; Tom Kennie; and Debbie McVitty.

As noted, at the outset, I established an international sounding board. The board contributed in two ways. First, I would post draft text for them to review as I was writing. Second, I would ask individuals for specific examples or to fact check something I had written: Hamad Al Ibrahim; James Asfa; Anne-Marie Canning; Derek Douglas; Shaun Ewen; Diana Iancu; Andrew Macleod; 'Funmi Olonisakin; Amar Parikh; Benedict Wilkinson; and Cynthia María Villarreal Muraira.

The third group of people are those that I reached out to as I went along – often through a contact of a contact. They often helped me develop some specific idea through examples and their lived experiences: Jamie Agombar; Liz Allen; Carlos Andradas Heranz; Holly Andrew; Jen Angel; Ant Bagshaw; Hajera Begum; Deborah Bull; Richard Burridge; Angel Calderon; Pedro Chacón Fuertes; Tina Crawford; Veronica Daly; Bobby Duffy; Margaret Gardner; James Green; David Guest; Mitra Gusheh ; Josephine Hansom; Kirstie Hewlett; Susannah Hume; Benjamin Hunt; Kiven James Kewir; Daniel Jones; Shitij Kapur; Danielle Kemmer; Anna Laverty; Mark Lester; Tania Lima; Jessica Marcos; Sonja Marjanovic; Nicole Mennell; Molly Morgan Jones; Ed Newell; Kialee Nyiayaana; Emma Palmer; Vanessa Patel; Sara Pedersen; Tamson Pietsch; Alexandra Pollitt; Ben Quash; John Ralston Saul; Julian Skyrme; Emily Spencer; Klaudia Stanoch; Martin Stewart-Weeks; Alitse Stovicek; Lucy Strang; Kat Thorne; Robyn Kingler-Vidra; Alan Wager; Mary Walsh; Jessica Weereratne; and Tom Woolf.

The last group are those who reviewed the final draft, including a fabulous team at Pearson who supported me brilliantly throughout: Felicity Baines; Ed Byrne; Melanie Carter; Glyn Davis; Liz Elliott; Laurie Forcier; Andrew Jaspan; 'Funmi Olonisakin; Sarah Owens; Joanna Pyke; Richard Stagg; Marc Stears; Andy Ware; and Chris White.

Finally, I dedicate this book to my amazing partner, Lucila Sanz, and our two inspiring kids, Almarina Grant Sanz and Noah Grant Sanz. Without their support this book would never have come about.

By my counting, that is nearly a hundred people. Thank you to each and every one of you.

About the author

Jonathan Grant was formerly Vice-President and Vice-Principal (Service) at King's College London. Service is King's award-winning and unique commitment to social responsibility and covers a range of activities including social reform, research impact, service-led learning, volunteering and environment sustainability.

Jonathan joined King's in 2014 to set up the Policy Institute and was its Director until 2017 when he stepped down to 'hold the pen' on developing King's Strategic Vision 2029. He continues to work on a part-time basis at the Policy Institute, where he is Professor of Public Policy and leads several research projects. He also runs Different Angles, a small consultancy business that focuses on the social impact of research and universities.

Jonathan's research interests are in biomedical and health R&D policy, research impact assessment, the use of research and evidence in policy and decision making, and the social purpose of universities in the 21st century.

Prior to joining King's, Jonathan was President of RAND Europe between June 2006 and October 2012. Before joining RAND in 2002, he was Head of Policy at the Wellcome Trust.

Preface

From time to time, a generation is faced with some very big choices. We are currently living through one of these times. Failures in globalism, the rise of populism, existential pressures around climate and resources, embedded racism and inequities, the shift from the analogue world to the digital one and, most recently, a devastating global pandemic, all contribute to a potentially overwhelming sense of systemic change. History suggests that there are long-term economic cycles where a number of innovations – social and physical – come together to reset society. We saw this with the introduction of the steam engine preceding the industrial revolution and we are witnessing a similar revolution today with the ubiquitous application of networked technologies. At these moments of change – these 'in-between times' – the future can go one of two ways, with the potential for the world to follow a more negative and destructive path (as we saw in the 1930s), or take a more humanitarian and sustainable turn (as I, personally, hope will occur today).

The choices that universities make at this time will play a critical role in determining which path we all take together as a society. On the one hand, universities might choose to stand back and largely be passive bystanders, remote from the world around them. On the other, universities will each embark on a deliberate evolution of their public purpose, in the same way that such adaptations have happened over millennia. This book will argue that the latter transformation is an urgent change that is both necessary and needed. Necessary as the social contract, under which universities have their licence to operate from politicians and public alike, is broken. Needed as the external environment they exist within is at a moment of flux which both threatens and invites opportunity.

In calling for this change, I make the case that the next step in the long history of universities is through embracing the concepts of 'new power'. New power is an idea originally put forward by Henry Timms and Jeremy Heimans in 2018[1] that captures and explains some of the tensions I have felt throughout my career. New power is a set of values that focuses on participation, networks governance and radical transparency. It combines approaches like crowdsourcing and social media campaigns with social movements, leading to new structures and business models as such Airbnb and Uber, campaigns like Black Lives Matter and MeToo, and other mass-participation events such as crowd-sourcing the analysis of UK politician expenses by *The Guardian* newspaper. As such, it contrasts with 'old power' institutions that tend to have formal structures, centralised power and a managerial practice. It provides, in my view, a way to refresh and renew that social contract between universities and society. Universities are instinctively old power institutions where power is 'jealously guarded, closed, inaccessible and leader-driven'.[2] As Timms and Heimans describe it, old power is a currency that is traded, while new power is a current that connects.

In this book, I use the framing of new power and its associated practices to reimagine what the social purpose of the university should be in the 21st century. In doing so, I illustrate how the New Power University can resolve the very real tensions in the trade-offs that shape its purposes, including social vs economic goods, universalism vs elitism, collectivism vs competition, autonomy vs system dependence. All of this gets to the 'soul' of the New Power University. As such, this book is both a warning against the complacency of the old power, and a voice for the many who see opportunity and necessity for radical change in universities.

The book is split into four parts. I open Part One by introducing the case for the New Power University, by using three ideas that frame my central argument, namely that universities need to change and change rapidly if they are to adapt to the 21st century. I then locate this argument by briefly recounting the history of the evolving purpose of universities, suggesting that the New Power University is the next step on that journey.

Part Two has three chapters that explore the three missions of a university: learning, research and social responsibility. I argue that these three missions are of equal weight and mutually reinforce one another. The introduction of

---

[1] Timms and Heimans (2018).

[2] https://www.theguardian.com/politics/2018/apr/20/new-power-jeremy-heimans-social-media.

'social responsibility' as a mission of the university will be explored and justified, acknowledging that not everyone will agree with this articulation (but
noting that many universities were, actually, founded on this principle).

Part Three describes the people that make up the New Power University –
that is the students, academic faculty and professional staff, and various wider
communities which, collectively, give universities their licence to operate and
enable them to deliver their purpose. This Part will examine their motivations,
expectations, values and skills and how these are changing and will need to
change.

Part Four will develop the thinking around missions and people and explore
the conduct of the New Power University. I will argue that the existing organisational structures of the university are no longer fit for purpose and that this
has implications on approaches to governance. The final chapter will make
the case that the New Power University can no longer 'sit on the fence' on the
contested political and social issues of the day and has to become an advocate
on issues that matter to its communities.

Overall, my argument is a mix between a critique of the current managerialism that defines contemporary old power universities, a manifesto for the future
New Power University and a provocation to stimulate the higher education
sector into rapid change, to ensure that the institution of the university survives
and flourishes through the 21st century. I know that the ideas put forward will
delight and disgust my colleagues in equal measure. There are ideas that, I suspect, will be enthusiastically embraced and others that will be rapidly repelled.
That is fine – but a debate is desperately needed so I would be delighted for
these ideas to be challenged and shaped as part of that deliberation.

I do ask the reader to try and avoid 'cherry picking' the ideas that you
instinctively agree with and rejecting those you don't. In writing the book, I
have tried to apply the ideas and values of new power systematically and have,
consequently, ended up in places that I did not anticipate when I began the
journey.

There are also a number of gaps in the case I make for the New Power University, some of which I touch on but don't elaborate and others I avoid. The
first group includes topics such as the relationship between further and higher
education, the role of technical universities, research-led teaching, diversity
and inclusion, and the regulation of universities. The second group includes
three substantive issues that I consciously do not address. First, I have avoided
the critical topic of financing universities. I have done this for three reasons.
First, I strongly believe that, with any enterprise, you have to start by deciding

on purpose (putting in place your 'value proposition' in management-speak) before you work out how to finance that, either on a not-for-loss or for-profit basis. Second, models for financing vary by jurisdiction and, thus, it is a very difficult topic to address in a single chapter of a book (and, indeed, is worthy of a tome in its own right). Third, while not directly addressing the issue of costs, much of this book is about value – the value of education, the value of research and the value of being socially responsible.

The second gap is that I disproportionately draw on examples from the UK, Australia and North America. This means that my arguments are anchored in an Anglo-Saxon model of higher education, reflecting my lived experience. Where possible, I have reached out to colleagues beyond this cultural and geographical boundary but stress, from the outset, that this was not systematic, but rather used as a way of informally testing and challenging some of the ideas I present.

Finally, I have avoided any detailed commentary of the impacts of the COVID-19 pandemic on higher education. Part of this is pragmatic – I was about half-way through the book when the pandemic took hold in Western Europe in March 2020, and I wanted to avoid both having to undertake a significant rewrite or making this book about COVID-19. More substantively, I would contend that, while the arguments I put forward pre-date the pandemic, the impact of COVID-19 both amplifies and accelerates my arguments. As universities begin to navigate the post-COVID world, they will, by necessity, implement some of the ideas I put forward in this book. That said, in the Postface, I do provide a very brief reflection on the implications of the COVID-19 pandemic on the New Power University.

In keeping with the new power topic of this book, I established a global sounding board of friends and colleagues to bounce ideas off, shape my thinking and to share examples from around the world. For me, this has been one of the most rewarding aspects of this project: through my network, I have been able to meet and connect with individuals from across the world. They have enthusiastically engaged in the process and reviewed some of my earlier drafts. Their generosity in time and ideas is fully acknowledged. I have already mentioned these incredible people in the Acknowledgements, but I want to highlight the contribution of three individuals. The first is my former boss and former President and Principal of King's College London, Ed Byrne. Ed inadvertently put me on the path that led to this book by asking me to 'hold the pen' in formulating a new strategy for King's in 2015. It was through this project that I really engaged with the idea of what universities are for and began to be increasingly uncomfortable with the status quo but optimistic about the potential for change.

The resultant strategy, *Vision 2029*,[3] was co-produced through an open consultative approach with over 1,000 colleagues at King's, but two individuals were central to that process, and thus central to the ideas put forward in this book. The first is Louise Gough, with whom I have worked closely at King's, first on *Vision 2029* and then on implementing our commitment to service (more in Chapter 5). We spent many an hour debating and shaping numerous ideas that are developed in this book. The second is Ross Pow, from Power of Numbers,[4] who helped Louise and me facilitate the consultative workshops at King's and then take the ideas from those discussions into *Vision 2029*. When I began to think about writing this book, I asked if Ross would be kind enough to help me out both in brainstorming the structure and content of each chapter and in reviewing my early drafts. He generously agreed to do this, and I am indebted for his input.

Needless to say, while all these conversations and exchanges have stimulated my thinking, I am responsible for any mistakes or misunderstandings and the involvement of these amazing people is not necessarily an endorsement for the New Power University.

---

[3] https://www.kcl.ac.uk/aboutkings/strategy.

[4] https://www.powerofnumbers.co.uk.

Part One

The role of the university in the 21st century

Old power works like a currency. It is held by few. Once gained, it is jealously guarded . . . New power operates differently, like a current. It is made by many. It is open, participatory, and peer driven. It uploads, and it distributes. Like water or electricity, it's most forceful when it surges.

Henry Timms and Jeremy Heimans (2018)

Throughout this book, I want to challenge conventional thinking about the question: what *is* the public purpose of a university in the 21st century. Being able to answer this question with clarity and precision is an essential first step in addressing the current, and largely deserved, negative reputation in some parts of the world that universities are elitist out-of-touch institutions that are exploiting students, their parents and broader society through worthless and expensive degrees and irrelevant esoteric research. I set the scene by introducing the concept of new power and why it is an idea of our time, relevant to universities today and in the near future. In doing so, I examine how the public purpose of the university has evolved, identifying four phases over a long history of a thousand years, and make the case that a new era is about to begin – that of the New Power University.

Chapter 1

Foundations for the New Power University

The idea for the New Power University comes from three books that link the past to today and provide an optimistic outlook for tomorrow

Three ideas, taken from three books, have shaped my thinking over the past few years and led me to the view that universities need to change rapidly and radically if they are to survive the 21st century. These books, very different in context and style, share a common thread that links the past to today and provides an optimistic outlook for tomorrow. It is that thread that I try to apply to universities, in the UK and around the world.

The first book is *The Collapse of Globalism* by John Ralston Saul. From this comes the idea of living in an 'in-between time' when one system is fading to be replaced by another. This moment of flux brings profound challenges and risks. It also offers a unique opportunity to make choices about the future that is not given to every generation. We are currently living in such a moment.

During this 'in-between time', we experience powerful negative forces which undermine, even directly attack, the value of knowledge, the role of the expert and the purpose of learning.

The second book, *Darkness Over Germany* by Amy Buller, warns against acquiescence to these threats. Buller tells the stories of a number of Germans that she had met and got to know in visiting the country in the 1930s and, through these encounters, provides an analysis of how National Socialism took hold. The lesson being that academics, and others with a stake in the future of the university, must not retreat and hide but instead resist and take an active role in shaping a better future.

The third book, *New Power* by Henry Timms and Jeremy Heimans, gives us cause for optimism. It describes the advent of a new way of organising and mobilising which opens new opportunities for how to tackle the big issues we face at a global, national and local level. It is an alternative to the 'old power' way of doings things and could be seen as a threat to universities. Examples of old power that have been disrupted by new power include video rental stores, newspapers, legal and financial services, shopping and campaigning, to name a few. Looked at another way, new power has the potential to bring the energy and engagement to ensure that the university is transformed into something that can flourish through the 21st century and beyond.

We are living in one of the 'in-between times'

John Ralston Saul is a Canadian commentator, philosopher and author. I first met John a few years ago when he approached the president of King's with a curious tale. John did his PhD at King's[5] in the world-famous war studies department in the 1970s. The subject of his PhD was De Gaulle's modernisation of France and, in particular, the relationships between the military and civil leadership following the Algerian War of Independence. As well as looking at historical archives, his research used interviews with a number of military officers, some of whom would have been working undercover in the Algerian War. All of this may sound a bit cloak and dagger, but it is pretty typical of the type of PhD that war studies students worked on at the time and still do so today.

The twist to the tale is that John then went on to write a novel inspired by his research. *The Birds of Prey* is a political thriller that was published in 1977 and describes what happens when a plane carrying the French Chief of Staff explodes over Réunion Island in the Indian Ocean. Just before publication of the novel, John realised that, if someone read his PhD thesis alongside

---

[5] Saul (1973).

The Birds of Prey, they could infer the identity of some of the protagonists. So, John stole the thesis from the King's library by hiding it under his jacket while his brother distracted the librarian. Some 50 years later, John decided that, with the passing of time, the risk of being identified no longer mattered and approached King's to return his stolen thesis. In January 2016, King's hosted a ceremony to welcome back the stolen thesis – probably a university first – and has recently awarded John an honorary doctorate.

In getting to know John, I came across his book *The Collapse of Globalism*. I read it in the summer of 2016, as part of my sense-making introspection of the Brexit referendum result in the UK. *The Collapse of Globalism* was first published in 2005, predating the global financial crash by a number of years. While the main focus of the book is what he sees as the inevitable evils of globalisation, he introduces an interesting observation early on. He talks about how there is a shift going on between two systems – globalism and an as yet undefined successor. He calls this an 'in-between time' and asks:

What about our life in such an in-between time? I described this as a vacuum – an interregnum between two unreasonable certainties. If we use it as a short positive moment of uncertainty when choice is privileged, well then it becomes possible to emerge into a less ideological and more humanitarian era.[6]

The idea that systems change is not new. As Paul Mason describes in his book *PostCapitalism*, there are a number of economic theories that look at cycles of boom and bust. It is at the inflection points in these cycles that we experience Saul's 'in-between times'. Surely, we are living in one of these? The confidence of global liberalism is being challenged by the rise of populism, as evidenced by the election of Donald Trump in the USA, Matteo Salvini in Italy and Jair Bolsonaro in Brazil, as well as the EU referendum in the UK. This is not a political point. Rather, it is emphasising the changing nature of politics and, more importantly, the changing outlook of the communities that politicians represent.

One of the theories that Mason highlights is the Kondratieff Wave, developed by Russian Nikolai Kondratieff in the 1920s. Kondratieff's work is not without its critics and, indeed, he was executed for his views in Stalin's Great Purge in 1938. A Kondratieff Wave is a long-term economic cycle that results from technological innovation. Mason identifies four such waves. The first

---

[6] Saul (2005), p. 6.

resulted in the steam engine and ran between 1790 and 1848. The second wave, between 1848 and the mid-1890s, was characterised by the spread of railways, the telegraph and ocean-going steamboats that resulted in a truly global economy. The third wave was based on electrification and lasted from the 1890s through to 1945. Heavy industry, the telephone and mass production were the key technologies. The fourth wave, starting after the Second World War and running up until the 2008 global financial crisis, was characterised by transmitters, synthetic material, mass consumerisation and the emergence of automation.[7]

Mason argues that we are at the beginning of a fifth Kondratieff Wave that probably overlaps with the fourth, beginning in the 1990s and driven by network technology, mobile communications and the ubiquity of the internet and social media. This is nicely illustrated in Figure 1.1, taken from a blog by Riddhi Sheth Dash, that plots stock market performance over time, suggesting that we are entering the sixth Kondratieff Wave following the global financial crash in 2008.[8] Irrespective of whether we are entering a fifth or sixth wave, the fact is that, as we transition from one to another, there is inevitably great change in the way that we go about our day-to-day business. Some of these changes can be positive, but others can be negative.

Take dating. 'Singles in America' (SIA) is an annual survey funded by dating website Match.com and explores attitudes and behaviours of around 5,000 single people in the USA aged between 18 and 70.[9] In its latest 2019 survey, SIA reports that over half of all singles in the USA have created an online dating profile, and that 26% of respondents had found their last date online (compared to, for example, 16% through work and 9% through friends). The emergence of this new way of connecting with a partner is supported by longitudinal research from the Stanford sociologist Michael Rosenfeld.[10] In the 1940s, about one in four couples met a romantic partner through the family and a further quarter via friends. By the 1990s, 35% of couples were now meeting via friends with 15% via the family. But, at that time, a new match-making method was beginning to make an appearance with 2% of couples meeting online. This was the beginning of a revolution in new power romance – by the 2010s, one in five Americans (20%) met their spouse online and today it is nearly 40%.

---

[7] Mason (2015), p. 47.

[8] https://medium.com/@riddhishethdash/what-are-the-innovations-that-are-predicted-to-unlock-economic-growth-in-the-6th-wave-5f195345e1e9.

[9] https://www.singlesinamerica.com/#DATING.

[10] Rosenfeld, et al. (2019).

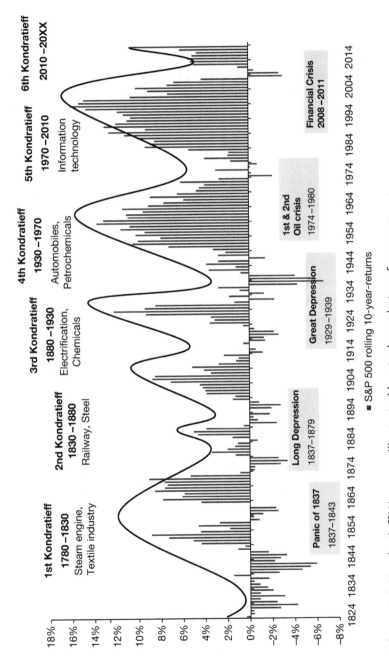

Figure 1.1 Kondratieff Waves, as illustrated by stock-market performance

Source: Allianz GI Global Capital Markets & Thematic Research Data as of December 2019.

But, just as the internet and social media has sparked romance for many lucky people, it has also had a number of negative consequences. Cases of online bullying, the posting of racist, anti-Semitic and misogynistic messages (often behind the coward's veil of anonymity) are reported on a daily basis. Combined with the spread of, so-called, fake news and its corrosive impact on democratic debate, it is perhaps not surprising that new-age Luddites hark back to a pre-internet era. But this friction is exactly what Saul is challenging us to exploit in ensuring that we create a 'short positive moment of uncertainty' for good.

History warns us not to retreat and hide

Sadly, history tells us that we cannot take this positive moment of uncertainty for granted. Dark, unimaginable negative events can arise from those moments, one of those in-between times. It is one of these that is described by Amy Buller who, in 1943, published a book called *Darkness Over Germany*, recently republished with the subtitle *A Warning from History*.

By all accounts, Buller was a fascinating woman. She was brought up in South Africa, returning to England in 1911 at the age of 20. She then sparked a lifelong interest in Germany by travelling around the country just before the outbreak of the First World War in 1914. She returned to London to study – and graduate – from Birkbeck College which, in those times, was unusual, being one of a handful of women. She was a deeply religious woman, converting to Anglo-Catholicism from a Baptist upbringing and joined the Student Christian Movement (SCM) in 1918. It was here that she met her mentor William Temple, who went on to become the Archbishop of Canterbury. She was an active participant in SCM-sponsored discussion groups and debates, cementing her intellectual credentials with her appointment as warden to the University of Liverpool's only female student residency, University Hall.

By the time Hitler became Chancellor in Germany in 1933, Buller had been on a number of study visits to Germany and, over the next couple of years, she convened a number of Anglo-German roundtables in both Germany and the UK. These meetings were attended by leading intellects of the German and British establishment and allowed Buller to earn a degree of respect and trust with both the German and British authorities. This is not to suggest that she was an apologist for the Nazis – she clearly was not. She was, though, very connected to both the German and British establishments and desperate to find ways to prevent a war breaking out. For her, the best way of doing this was through dialogue and conversations.

The prologue to *Darkness Over Germany* describes how she told stories of her encounters with Germans to groups of students in Liverpool who were on fire-fighting duty after war had broken out. She then decided to write down these stories 'to emphasise the need for youth and those who plan the training of the youth to consider carefully the full significance of the tragedy of a whole generation of German youth, who having no faith, made Nazism their religion'.[11] She recalls and documents her conversations with students, teachers, professors, ambassadors and even military officers. Each chapter is an oral history in its own right and, taken together, the chapters illustrate how fascism can take hold in a society.

Buller's main argument is almost theological – perhaps not surprising given her own convictions. She sees Nazism as a quasi-religion that created a higher purpose and meaning, especially for the unemployed and under-utilised young people of the time. In reading the book, I drew another lesson – perhaps shaped by contemporary politics – and that is how the middle classes acquiesced to the Nazis.

I say this with some caution for two reasons. First, it is easy with historical hindsight to be critical of people not taking a stance against the Nazis. We know millions of people were killed because of their opposition to Hitler. Whether I would have the courage of opposition under such circumstances is something I don't know and, in all honesty, doubt. The second reason for my nervousness is the risk of trivialising the sheer horror of the Nazi regime by making comparisons with the rise of populism today.

That said, there are enough similarities to at least make us stop and think. Universities are not immune from the popular attacks on institutions as a quick Google search of front-page newspaper headlines will illustrate. The challenge against reasoned thinking – the core value of university – is evident in contemporary debates on climate change, on vaccinations and, I would argue, the economic and social impact of Brexit in the UK. This was again a theme that Buller draws out:

> **You will find it is not essential to them to know what is the scientific explanation of these problems in detail, for they say what is essential, is that our experience is the basic experience of historic reality.**[12]

---

[11] Buller (1943), p. 2.
[12] Buller (1943), p. 152.

In response to these attacks – whether legitimate or not – it is all too easy to retreat, to avoid the issue, to not get involved: to acquiesce. This may be understandable, but it is also a dangerous strategy as Buller points out in a chapter about 'one of the most remarkable Germans I have ever met. He was a professor of philosophy . . . '. She introduces this chapter with the observations:

> **I sometimes think that Hitler would never have made the progress he had if German teachers in schools and universities as well as in the church had not so often been purely academic and remote from life and in particular from the life of the young.**[13]

It is the risk of becoming 'remote from life' that is my biggest concern for universities at the current time. This is the key lesson from *Darkness Over Germany*.

As a postscript, it is worth noting that *Darkness Over Germany* had an immediate impact when it was published in 1943 and has had a lasting legacy in the UK ever since. Queen Elizabeth (later the Queen Mother) read the book following a recommendation from the Bishop of Litchfield, Edward Woods. The Queen was interested in the questions that Buller had explored in her book – the rise of National Socialism, its impact on young people and how Nazism was allowed to take hold in such a powerful and important country such as Germany. This led to a meeting in Buckingham Palace in March 1944. King George VI and Queen Elizabeth were so impressed by Buller and her book that they offered to help establish a residential educational foundation where young people could discuss ethical and social issues. To support this endeavour, the King granted the foundation the use of Cumberland Lodge, in Windsor Great Park, and the Queen Mother became an active Patron until her death in 2002. An article in the *Church Times* in May 2017 described Buller, who died in 1974, as remarkable: 'Driven by a religious quest, and a vision for empowering people intellectually, morally, and spiritually, she captured the attention and support of church leaders, senior academics, politicians and the royal family. Through these networks, she saw to it that her vision became a reality at Cumberland Lodge.'[14] Buller's legacy was to start a social movement.

---

[13] Buller (1943), p. 136.

[14] https://www.churchtimes.co.uk/articles/2017/5-may/features/features/a-warning-from-history.

Giving people permission to dance: unleashing the energy of new power

There is a fabulous TED talk video by Derek Sivers, 'How to start a movement'.[15] It opens with a clip of someone at a festival dancing by themselves on a grassy hill. Half-naked and quite probably stoned, this sole figure is soon joined in the dance by a second person and then, shortly after, a third. As the three-minute clip rolls by, the stream of new dancers grows exponentially so that, by the end, the hilltop is covered in people dancing.

Sivers' point is that it takes the first and second followers to create a movement – not the 'lone nut', as Sivers describes the first dancer. But, as Sivers also acknowledges, it 'takes guts' to be the lone nut, the first mover. Not only do you open yourself to ridicule (and he was not a great dancer!) but you are saying to everyone else that it's OK to follow you. You give them permission to dance.

This idea of giving people permission to dance is found in Henry Timms' and Jeremy Heimans' book *New Power*, first published in 2018. If *Darkness Over Germany* invokes the threat of a 'negative moment of uncertainty', then *New Power* provides the antidote to turn this into a 'positive moment of uncertainty'.

While Timms and Heimans don't use the dancing metaphor in their book, they do develop their thinking around how to start a social movement. Central to this is the idea of *assuming* permission – in effect, opening up the possibility of any one of us being the first dancer on the hill. Assuming permission is the critical difference between 'new power', which is empowering and self-organising, and 'old power', which is transactional in nature. Think of the MeToo movement, Black Lives Matter, Extinction Rebellion and even popular online games such as Fortnite. All have created communities that can exercise their power in novel ways.

While the idea of social movement is not new, what is new is the widespread use of social media. Take Fortnite, for example. My 13-year-old son was outraged when Epic Games released an unpopular update. He was not alone and, within 24 hours, a Twitter storm ensued, connecting young people around the world in their collective disdain. Epic Games quickly relented and released a patch that reversed the change.

---

[15] https://www.ted.com/talks/derek_sivers_how_to_start_a_movement?langu1.2age=en.

Timms and Heimans summarise these new forms of power nicely in this quote:

> **Old power works like a currency. It is held by few. Once gained, it is jealously guarded . . . New power operates differently, like a current. It is made by many. It is open, participatory, and peer-driven. It uploads, and it distributes. Like water or electricity, it's most forceful when it surges.**[16]

The new power in the Fortnite example was made up of participatory gamers (young, online and connected with a shared interest). They exercised their new power by uploading their views on a peer-to-peer platform in an open and critical way. This surge of concern through Twitter was such that it forced a multibillion-dollar business to do a quick U-turn.

In considering the difference between old and new power institutions, Timms and Heimans explore their differing values, as summarised in Figure 1.2.

For anyone who has worked – or even studied – in a university, it is hard to argue that they are not the guardians of old power values and, with some exceptions, really struggle with new power values. Could a battle between old

Old power values	New power values
Managerialism, institutionalism, representative governance	Informal, opt-in decision making; self-organisation; networked governance
Exclusivity, competition, authority, resource consolidation	Open source collaboration, crowd wisdom, sharing
Discretion, confidentiality, separation between private and public spheres	Radical transparency
Professionalism, specialisation	Do-it-ourselves, 'maker culture'
Long-term affiliation and loyalty, less overall participation	Short-term, conditional affiliation; more overall participation

Figure 1.2 Old and new power values

Source: Henry Timms and Jeremy Heimans

---

[16] Timms and Heimans (2018), p. 2.

and new power determine the public purpose of universities of the future? Universities have been around for centuries and the main reason for that is they have evolved their public purpose to address the values and expectations of the time. So, I have to be careful not to over-hype this change. At the same time, it is clear that universities are old power institutions. Indeed, it is difficult to come up with better examples of old power. King's College London, where I did my PhD and currently work, was founded in 1829 by the old power establishment of the Duke of Wellington (then prime minister) and the Archbishop of Canterbury with the support of King George IV.

More evidence of this comes from the academic strikes in the UK during the spring of 2018. The dispute was notionally around proposed pension reforms and occurred on many campuses in the UK, making headline news at the time. From my conversations with colleagues, it was clear that, beyond a focus on pensions, they had a broader concern about what they described as 'the creeping marketisation and managerialism of higher education'.[17] That word 'managerialism' was not one I had come across before but was bandied about with anger and passion. And it was a fair criticism. Being part of the senior management team at King's at the time, I can remember spending days with colleagues crafting email messages from the president in an attempt to communicate our position as an employer on deeply complex and technocratic issues such as the methods for valuing pension deficits. Meanwhile, the highly informed academic staff were communicating in real-time on Twitter, Instagram and other forms of media. By the time our message landed in email inboxes, it was obsolete and, consequently, came across as being managerial and at times inflammatory. A striking example of new power!

This surge of new power in universities – whether from students or staff – is not confined to the UK. In South Africa, the #FeesMustFall movement is an example of an effective student-led protest that began in 2015 and led to a freeze in fees, underwritten by the government. In the USA, we have seen a number of examples of students protesting – sometimes violently – against speakers who, in their view, propagate hate speech.

I should stress from the outset that new power is not a utopian paradigm that will solve all the ills of the university. Timms and Heimans themselves make the point that many institutions operate by moving between both new and old power values, effectively blending both sets of values. As we will see in Chapter 7, President Trump is a master of this – 'the old-power pseudo

---

[17] Naidoo and Williams (2014).

autocrat with new-power grassroots support' – as a reviewer of *New Power* commented in *The Guardian*.[18] It is this blended space to which I suspect most universities will evolve as they navigate the changing dynamics of the 21st century. But, by setting out an extreme position for the New Power University, it may be possible to resist some of the inertia and conservatism that inhibits university reform today. At first glance, there is also a risk to my argument in saying that new power values – which largely arise from social movements – are not applicable to institutions such as universities. But, in reading *New Power*, I do not consider this to be significant as there are a number of organisations that have successfully merged the two and are referred to in places throughout this book – Airbnb and Uber being two obvious examples. Both align nicely with the new power values set out in Figure 1.2, both are established institutions in their own right, and neither are without their critics. Nevertheless, in applying new power values to the purposes of the university, and to the people that make up the university, I am making an assumption that these values are as applicable to institutions as they are to social movements.

Towards the New Power University

There is a strong temptation on the part of universities to resist the values that new power is based on. But that would be a mistake. Instead, at this moment of uncertainty during a potentially threatening 'in-between time', new power can be used to reshape and energise the public purpose and mission of universities into the future. Then you can start to engage with the possibilities for a radical new proposition for higher education.

With the New Power University, you will see the emergence of peer-to-peer online education where students teach each other, enabled by an expert facilitator (not knowledge holders in the traditional academic model).

You will see research and research methods that are based on local, national and international problems that are informed by the lived experiences of communities, where knowledge is free to access and openly shared (not hidden in academic publications and behind paywalls).

You will see universities committing to their social purpose by reforming their procurement policies to support local and social enterprises, divesting

---

[18] https://www.theguardian.com/books/2018/jun/10/new-power-how-changing-21st-century-by-henry-timms-and-jeremy-heimans-review.

their endowments for social good, and being global leaders in setting an example for the fight against the climate crisis (not contributing to emissions through extensive global travel).

You will see a university with a radically different form of networked governance, structures and systems, an activist institution that is comfortable in campaigning for social good, and one that leads the way in addressing some of the greatest challenges of the 21st century.

You will see the New Power University.

Chapter 2

The university's public purpose

The public purpose of the university has evolved over time

Enter the coordinates 37.992784, 23.707410 into Google Maps and you will be taken to a park a few kilometres north of downtown Athens in Greece. It is here in the 6th century BC that legend tells us the mythical hero Academus (or Hecademus) bequeathed a place that was cultivated by the Ancient Greeks to relax, host festivals, debate ideas and compete in athletic events. Sadly, today, according to TripAdvisor, Plato's Academy Park is a bit of a disappointment. Rating an average score of three out of five, one visitor commented: 'The sad remains of what was once the first university of western world is in Athens' outskirts . . . You can get there through a dirt road . . . it needs a very big fantasy to allucinate [sic] what once these places were . . . it is so important that I suggest anyway to visit it.'

Academy Park, as it is now known, marks the birthplace of the university, at least in the Western tradition.[19] Plato began to teach there in around 387 BC and its name has given rise to the words 'academy', 'academic' and 'academia'. Historians are keen to point out that Plato's Academy would have been

---

[19] There is evidence from ancient Egypt and Mesopotamia that c. 3000 BC scholars both undertook research and teaching and were affiliated with institutions of learning (see: www.dailyhistory.org. How_did_universities_develop%3F).

Figure 2.1 Raphael's *The School of Athens*, 1509–11
Source: MShieldsPhotos/Alamy Stock Photo

a very different experience than that captured by the renaissance painter Raphael, in *The School of Athens*, and, by extension, today's image of a university (see Figure 2.1). Nevertheless, what Plato gave us was the idea of a physical space for critical and reasoned thought and reflection. And this has probably been the enduring public purpose of the university over the subsequent 2,500 years.

While it was only at the turn of the first millennia that we started to see the formation of universities in the image created by Raphael, over the next thousand years, the number of these grew exponentially across Europe. The first group – Bologna, Oxford, Cambridge, Paris, Salamanca – were founded in the 11th and 12th centuries, often within an ecclesiastical tradition. Fast forward to the 19th century, and the founding of the University of Berlin in 1809 by William Humboldt saw a move to a more secular mission, focused on the professions and, critically, the inclusion of research.

The third shift in the public purpose of the universities occurred 50–70 years later with the establishment of the land grant universities in the USA and the 'redbrick' universities of the United Kingdom. These institutions added the idea of social responsibility to their missions, in the form of creating skills and commerce for local people. The final phase – which has dominated higher education since the 1980s in the UK and Anglo-world – is what Stefan Collini, author of the provocative book *What Are Universities For?*, called the HiEdBizUK university. For them, the public purpose is as much economic as it is social.

In the same way that rock sediments are formed, with each layer settling on what went before, each of these four phases have built on each other. By the beginning of the 21st century, a typical university was likely to say 'yes' to all of these public purposes. Exploring the reasons behind this evolution, and the pros and cons of these changes, will lead us to see why it is essential for this adaptation to continue; and why the New Power University should be the next step of this millennia-long journey.

The purpose of Europe's first university was to educate immigrants

Imagine a group of young immigrants being harassed by the local population and authorities. The persecution was so unfair that, if one of their number committed a misdemeanour or crime, then they would all be punished. As with the majority of immigrant communities, these young people were clever, entrepreneurial and idealistic. Responding to the xenophobia they experienced, they started to organise into communities – or guilds – identified by their nationalities (*nationes* as they were called) and used their collective new power as a means of protection against the old power authorities in the city.

Being entrepreneurs, once these guilds began to establish themselves, their members were keen to do more. They began to hire teachers from local schools to educate them in law, theology and what today we would call the liberal arts. These societies became known as *universitas scholarium*, which loosely translates as an incorporated group of scholars or students. Then they began to merge together to form a larger association or *studium*, a centre for study. This is the story of how Italy's University of Bologna, Europe's oldest university, was founded in the latter part of the 11th century.

There are two noteworthy features of this tale. The first is that the university was founded by students for students using the methods of community organising. Second, the etymology of 'university' derives from the idea of being incorporated or being part of a collective movement. It is also a strange footnote to history that, based on this story, the more accurate word to describe the university was actually 'studium', suggesting that we should be referring the Studium of Cambridge, Bologna, etc. or even the new power studium.

Following Bologna, you saw the establishment of a number of universities in 11th- and 12th-century Europe, including Paris in France, Oxford and Cambridge in England, and Salamanca in Spain. Each university was founded for different reasons using different models. Paris (or The Sorbonne, as it is sometimes known after its founder) followed Bologna's model of having four faculties of Arts, Law, Medicine and Theology and also adopted the 'nationes' model by organising students into regional and linguistic groups, becoming, arguably, the dominant university of the middle ages. By contrast, Cambridge University was founded after some Oxford University academics were wrongly hanged for the death of a local woman, resulting in their colleagues fleeing the city. At the time, it was tradition for a pardon to be granted by the Church to all scholars, irrespective of the misdemeanour, but, on this occasion, this did not occur because of a dispute between the Church and the King. Some of the Oxford academics arrived in Cambridge – which already had a scholarly reputation due to its neighbouring Cathedral town of Ely – and ended up staying there, even when it became safe to return to Oxford.

Each of these individual universities' histories are fascinating in their own way but, for our purposes, are off-script. The key point to take away is the new power foundations of Europe's first university – Bologna – and the loosely ecclesiastical purpose of the early modern university which, in Figure 2.2, I have called the 'Confessional University' after Pietsch (2019). As she describes, although these universities 'continued to train clergy, they also took on the function of providing moral education to the lay ruling class and to those who served in stated and religious bureaucracies. It was also this version of the university that was mostly exported to the Americas by the colonizing European power and peoples.'[20] This concept of the 'Confessional' University builds on the concept of the 'Clerisy' that was proposed by Coleridge in the 19th century to describe a class of people who embodied the culture and learning of a country.[21] While the Clerisy included theologians, it also embraced non-sectarian thinkers, some but not all of whom may have resided in universities. The second key point is the subsequent growth in universities: as illustrated in Figure 2.2, by 1250, there were 15 universities in Europe, by 1500, there were just under 100 universities and, by 1800, around 250.

---

[20] Pietsch (2019), p. 3.

[21] Knights (1978).

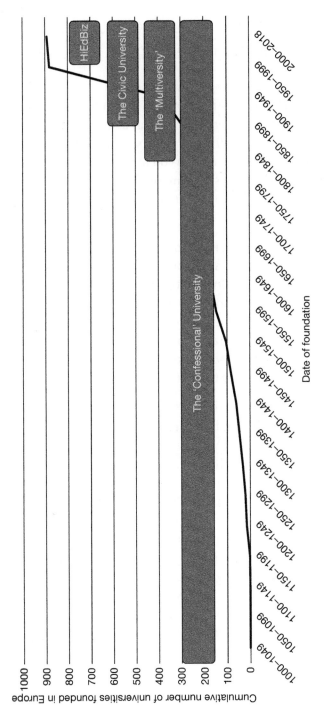

Figure 2.2 One thousand years of the evolving public purpose of the university in Europe[22]

22 The cumulative line is based on a list of foundation dates of universities in Europe. I have superimposed the four phases based on my analysis of the data and as described in this chapter. I have used the term multiversity from 1800 onwards, as explained in the text, the combining of education and research missions only really began at the end of the century.

In the 19th century, a university's mission expanded to include research to create new knowledge

In Europe, in the first half of the 19th century, we begin to see the establishment of institutions that would be recognisable today as the idea of a university. Two key philosophies, developed 40 years apart, set up a teaching–research tension that is still evident 200 hundred years on in many western higher education systems. This is, perhaps, best summarised by De Vries and Slowey (2012) in a concluding chapter in a book, *State and Market in Higher Education Reforms*:

> **At the risk of oversimplification, Humboldt's memorandum of 1810, 'On the Spirit and Organizational Framework of Intellectual Institutions in Berlin', emphasized the role of universities in research and the creation of new knowledge, underpinned by notions of self-formation or self-realization. In contrast, in the middle of that century, Newman's 'The Idea of a University' emphasized the pastoral dimension, with a student-based approach to teaching and an emphasis on the moral dimension and socialization (for the elite).[23]**

Wilhelm von Humboldt (1767–1835) was a liberal politician and educationalist in Prussia who proposed the establishment of the University of Berlin to King Frederick III in 1809. As David Willetts points out in *A University Education*, 'he advocated a university which did not just train the elite but promoted research and an understanding of national culture to strengthen Prussia and catch up with the Industrial Revolution in the United Kingdom'.[24] As such, Humboldt is seen as the father of the modern research-based university.

In contrast, some 40 years later, the recently canonised and, thus, now Saint John Henry Newman (1801–90) delivered a series of lectures that he subsequently published in 1852 in *The Idea of a University*. In its preface, Newman makes the case that 'it is the diffusion and extension of knowledge rather than the advancement of knowledge' that is the core public purpose of a university, otherwise, 'if its object were science and philosophical discovery, I do not see why a university should have students'.[25]

---

[23] De Vries and Slowey (2012), p. 215.

[24] Willetts (2017), p. 20.

[25] As cited by Crow and Dabars (2015), p. 78. Original source is Newman (1852/2008), p. 3.

Importantly, given Newman's religious journey from being an ordained Anglican to a Roman Catholic, he also made it clear that university education should not follow ecclesiastical tradition, noting that 'if certain branches of knowledge were excluded, those students of course would be excluded'.[26] This is a radically inclusive observation when set against today's debate about 'decolonising' the curriculum and the nature of taught knowledge (a topic I return to in Chapter 3).

The research focus of Humboldt and the teaching tradition of Newman then came together in 1876 in the founding of Johns Hopkins University, in Baltimore, USA. Michael Crow, in his 2015 book *Designing the New American University*, describes how Johns Hopkins 'would conjoin in a single institution the Oxbridge model of the residential undergraduate education . . . with advanced scientific research characteristic of the German academic institution'.[27] It would go on to become the model for numerous American institutes of higher education thereafter.

Clark Kerr, in his 1963 book *The Use of the University*, famously coined the phrase 'multiversity' to describe this dual mission of education and research. As Clare Donovan noted in a recent essay, 'the term "multiversity" denotes a group of elite research universities in the United States, which he [Kerr] viewed as located at the heart of national and international economic growth and social, political and cultural development . . . [Kerr] defined the key features of the multiversity as plurality in terms of having multiple purposes, centres of power and clienteles, and inconsistency through embracing many truths, being comprised of several different communities, and serving conflicting interests both internally and externally.'[28]

This form of historical path dependency is a key theme that Glyn Davis, former vice-chancellor of The University of Melbourne, develops in his book *The Australian Idea of a University*. Davis argues that the foundation of The University of Sydney (1850) and The University of Melbourne (1853) created a blueprint for subsequent Australian universities that is still dominant today – something he sees as a risk to the sector as there is a lack of diversity in the provision of higher education. Prior to the founding of Sydney in 1850, aspiring students had to go back to Britain to get a university education. One of those, William Wentworth, who studied at Cambridge, went on to become

---

[26] Newman (1852/2008), p. 38.

[27] Crow and Dabars (2015), p. 76.

[28] Donovan (2016), pp. 1–2.

a successful barrister and politician on his return to Sydney. He believed that the 'new colony needed new professionals'[29] and, as such, needed a university. He acknowledged the Oxbridge model did not translate well into the colonial context and, with others, set about exploring alternative models. As Davis points out – citing the work of Horne and Sherington (2012) – 'this embodied three fundamental values . . . they should not be beholden to religious beliefs; access should be decided by merit alone, tested through public examination; and financial support should not just come from the government but from public spirited citizens.'[30] It was from this set of values that the 'Australian idea of the university arose in an urban setting and remains metropolitan in character – a campus in the city, focused on educating local students into the professions, tied to the life of the surrounding town', as Davis summarised.[31]

As with the US 'multiversity', the Australian idea of a university and, subsequently, universities throughout the Anglo-speaking world and beyond have had to address 'conflicting interests' (in Kerr's language) between two major purposes: research on the one hand and education on the other. The problem arises because, in much of the western world, the income from educating (overseas) undergraduates subsidises the research activity of a university. At the same time, the profile of a university's research activity drives its reputation through global league tables. Since the quality of research is usually measured by how it is cited and used internationally, the incentives for university academics are neither focused on education nor on the impact that their research has locally. This is what I will call the old power university paradox, which will be explored throughout this book and which can only be resolved through new-power thinking.

To take a slight diversion and unpick this observation a bit further, there are two major providers of league tables globally – THE and QS. In both, 60% of the ranking is made up of an assessment of research of which a third (QS) to a half (THE) is based on research citations. Citations are a classic old power instrument as they simply measure the visibility of academic research to academic researchers. They do not the assess the accessibility of research to the general public nor the impact of research to beneficiaries. I fully appreciate it would be easy to dismiss this as a statistical quirk, but league tables matter as they are used by international students to help inform them which universities

[29] Davis (2017), p. 39.

[30] Davis (2017), p. 40.

[31] Davis (2017), p. 58.

to apply to (as they understandably have limited knowledge of foreign universities' reputations, especially those not in the top 50 with global brands). The consequence of this is that, today, the old power universities want to do well in these leagues tables as part of their marketing strategies to attract international students; they want to attract international students as, typically, they will pay twice, sometimes three times, as much as domestic students in tuition fees; and universities want those premium tuition fees as they need to subsidise loss-making research activities, which drive those league tables.

It is this cycle that the New Power University will need to break. One approach to do this would be to develop alternative league tables that value new power education, research and social responsibility.[32] An alternative would be for the old power universities to have the confidence not to play this game and focus on what matters to them – their public purpose. Part of that thinking involves eroding the research–education dualism to include social responsibility as part of a university's mission. That said, it is worth acknowledging that the intensive promotion of university rankings comes from commercial organisations that profit from creating competition between universities and informing choices made by fee-paying international students. In other words, while it is a game that universities do not have to play, they are acting rationally in playing it, even if they have limited influence over the rules of the game.

Social responsibility towards local communities becomes increasingly important in the 20th century

A few years ago, I visited half a dozen universities in Pennsylvania, in the United States, as part of a study tour. These included large institutions, downtown community colleges and a small Catholic liberal arts college situated in a wooded campus. Two universities have lodged in my memory since: the little-known Widener University and the better-known University of Pennsylvania.

Widener University was a former military college located in Chester, Pennsylvania, the one-time 'murder capital of the USA'. In 2003, the incoming president of Widener University, James T. Harris III, described the city as 'a community . . . that in the last census [2000] had one out of four citizens

---

[32] Douglas, *et al.* (2020).

living below the poverty line; where the median family income is half that of the rest of the country; and a community where the school district was placed under the authority of the state'.[33] Harris goes on to describe the university's response as being a 'campus . . . with many fences surrounding it, and the culture has been to ingrain in the students, faculty, and staff that once you leave the campus you should not feel safe and the community is not a welcoming place'.

Harris rejected this approach. He believed that universities had a role in 'taking the lead in fostering economic and social justice' and refocused Widener on this mission throughout his tenure. On visiting in 2015, I have a vivid memory of being taken on a tour around Chester, witnessing the community physiotherapy project, a law clinic and a relatively newly founded Charter School. The image of the 'many fences' being metaphorically demolished and rebuilt through these worthwhile, mutually beneficial community projects has stuck with me ever since.

In contrast, the University of Pennsylvania is well-known – a high-ranking university located in the heart of Philadelphia with a pedigree that goes back to Benjamin Franklin. Again, located in a historically poor and violent part of the city, the University of Pennsylvania has actively gone out of its way to work closely with local communities in ensuring that it is a valued partner. This activity is channelled through the Netter Center, which brings together the university – with its assets of space, people and money – with the wider community to help address local issues such as poverty, health and education.[34]

The University of Pennsylvania's commitment to working with and supporting local communities was nicely captured by its president, Amy Gutmann, in her 2004 inaugural address where she set out the Penn Compact, which identifies inclusion, innovation and impact as the key mission of the university.

One explanation for this focus of US universities on community engagement, social responsibility or 'service', as it is often referred to in US parlance, might be the rise of the so-called 'land grant' universities. The 1862 Morrill Act endowed US federal land to support the establishment of public universities in each state. It followed the American Civil War and was seen as a way, in today's

---

[33] Harris and Karkavy (2003), p. 152.

[34] https://www.nettercenter.upenn.edu/about-center/our-mission. [Accessed 11 November 2019.]

language, of nation building and reunification. As illustrated in the following extract,[35] the explicit aim was largely the spread of knowledge and development of skills to the benefit of local populations beyond the wealthier classes:

> **Without excluding other scientific and classical studies and including military tactics, to teach such branches of learning as are related to agriculture and the mechanic arts, in such manner as the legislatures of the States may respectively prescribe, in order to promote the liberal and practical education of the industrial classes in the several pursuits and professions in life.**

Source: extract from Morrill Act 1862

This Act, and its subsequent expansion in 1890, had a profound impact on US higher education, establishing a third public purpose of US universities – that of service – in addition to the Humboldtian and Newmanian missions of research and teaching. Crow, the current President of the land-grant Arizona State University, talks about 'the utilitarian predication of the land-grant institutions'[36] in *Designing the New American University*. I believe that it can be argued that even institutions like Widener University and the University of Pennsylvania, neither of which were land-grant institutions, have both embraced this idea of service and the 'utilitarian predication' characteristic in the founding of the land-grant universities.

As Gavazzi and Gee (2018) argue in their book, *Land-grant Universities for the Future*, it is easy to underestimate the impact the Morrill Act had on US higher education. That said, and, as they comment, 'The time is exactly right for a robust national conversation on the land-grant institution and its community-focused mission for the twenty-first century, with a special emphasis on its servant university orientation. Said slightly differently, how do we reclaim the mantle of the people's university?'[37] I would suggest part of that answer is through the New Power University.

While there is a long history of social responsibility of US universities to their local communities, I would not wish to suggest that this has been remiss elsewhere around the world. A focus on service is also evident in places such

---

[35] https://www.law.cornell.edu/uscode/text/7/304. [Accessed 11 November 2019.]
[36] Crow and Dabars (2015), p. 85.
[37] Gavazzi and Gee (2018), p. 157.

as Canada and South America.[38] The so-called 'redbrick' universities in the UK, established in the major industrial cities during the 19th century, were also founded on a civic mission. They include the universities of Liverpool, Manchester, Leeds and Birmingham, to name a few. Often founded by local business leaders and politicians, they sought to ensure there was a skilled workforce to support the expansion and rising status of these great cities.

More recently, there has been a rediscovery of the civic mission of the university in the UK. While it is easy to relate this to the fall-out of the Brexit referendum, it is also worth noting that John Goddard published a seminal pamphlet, 'Re-inventing the civic university', for Nesta on the topic in 2009. That said, the view that universities were on the 'wrong side' of the Brexit debate – that is they supported remaining in the European Union – has led to further soul-searching and re-energised the commitment to the civic university that I will pick up again in Chapters 5 and 8.

The purpose of the 21st-century university, HiEdBiz, is to drive the economy

The Cambridge historian Stefan Collini coined the term 'HiEdBizUK' in a critical essay written in response to a 2003 UK Government White Paper, *The Future of Higher Education*. Originally published in the *London Review of Books*, the essay was reproduced in his book *What Are Universities For?* HiEdBizUK is a contraction of 'Higher Education Business UK', a phrase that seeks to capture what he sees as rampant managerialism within the university sector (the very thing that, subsequently, incensed UK academics in their strikes about pensions).

Collini starts his essay by citing the following extract from the introduction of the White Paper:

> **We see a higher education sector which meets the needs of the economy in terms of trained people, research and technology transfer. At the same time it needs to enable all suitably qualified individuals to develop their potential both intellectually and personally, and to provide the necessary storehouse of expertise in science and technology, and the arts and humanities which defines our civilizations and culture.**
>
> Source: *The Future of Higher Education*. London: HMSO, 2003

---

[38] Douglas, *et al.* (2020).

Collini goes on to deconstruct this paragraph by saying: 'There are two sentences in the paragraph . . . The first . . . says that the main aim of the universities is to turn out people and ideas capable of making money. The second . . . says there are a lot of other points that it's traditional to mention in this connection, and that they're all good things too, in their way, and that the official with the glue-pot has been having a busy day, and that we've lost track of the subject of the verb in the last line, and that it may be time for another full stop.'[39]

Setting aside his cutting – and appropriate – sarcasm, Collini is making an important point about the neoliberal marketisation of the higher education sector which he characterises as 'turning out people and ideas capable of making money'. His concern could be seen as a modern take on the disdain for any educational outcome 'which can be weighted and measured', as Newman puts it in his 1852 book *The Idea of a University*.[40]

The era of HiEdBiz predates the 2003 White Paper and is not confined to the UK. Its roots can be traced to the 1980s with the emergence of new public management (NPM) which was an attempt to make public services more business-like, bringing in corporate practices focused on efficiency, incentives and the markets. In many ways, the application of NPM to the higher education sector has been a necessary modernising step as part of ensuring that universities are run in an economically sustainable and well-governed way, and to end what economists call 'producer capture' where the goals of an institution are self-serving rather than focused on serving citizens or 'customers', such as students. The trouble comes when these ideas and values collide with the notion that some part of a university's purpose is about service and being socially responsible. Could it be that, as they have learnt to navigate this new market economy, universities have lost sight of a critical part of their core purpose? For many, the answer is yes. In short, they have put process before people, money before values and management before leadership.

As a consequence, the HiEdBiz university is defined by a number of unsustainable internal contradictions in the way it operates. Take, as an example, the role of security staff and cleaners. Many universities globally have outsourced these functions to service providers such as the (now bust) Carillion, Interserve and Serco. The rationale for such outsourcing was two-fold: first, it would prove cheaper and, second, it devolved management responsibility. Both may be true, but, in delivering on such goals, the universities were

---

[39] Collini (2012), p. 154.
[40] Newman (1852/2008), p. 182.

indirectly engaging people – who are some of their lowest paid staff – on, frankly, unacceptable terms and conditions. In many cases, they were not paid the living wage, had salaries deducted if they were ill and received little in terms of training.

In South Africa, for example, the #OutsourcingMustFall movement became intertwined with the #FeesMustFall[41] movement (which is discussed in Chapter 3). In a post-Apartheid context, the exploitation of lower-paid cleaning staff was a touchstone issue that added to student protests around tuition fee increases and demands that university places should be free.[42] All of this came to a head in 2015 with widespread student strikes leading to a government commitment not to increase fees and a number of universities agreeing to end all outsourcing contracts.

Non-violent civil resistance campaigns in the UK on the same issue, under the banner of 'Justice for Cleaners', have led to a number of universities abandoning their outsourcing policy. Ironically, when these changes are made, universities have found that, at times, they save money – as they are not having to pay value added tax – and often improve the quality of service.

The global plight of low-paid cleaners, security staff and caretakers in universities illustrates how the HiEdBiz university has altered the 'nature, purpose and values of higher education'.[43] This is not the only example I could have used. Other examples are explored later in the book and include the casualisation of academic staff. The point with these practices is that they are motivated by new public management values of driving efficiencies by reducing costs and, as such, by design, are exploitative and are the antithesis of being socially responsible. But, as discussed in Chapter 7, the introduction of new types of flexible working practices in itself is not necessarily a bad thing and could, in fact, be one of the defining characteristics of the New Power University. As we will see, critical to this debate will be understanding the motivations for the new power employment and psychological contracts. In the meantime, and not surprisingly, the new power student, whether in South Africa or the UK, saw through the motivation of outsourcing cleaners and called it out for what it was. More than that, they organised themselves and ran successful campaigns to redress the issue, something that is being increasingly copied by students (and staff, too) on this and other causes around the world.

[41] Habib (2019).

[42] https://brooklynrail.org/2016/03/field-notes/outsourcing-must-fall. [Accessed 11 November 2019.]

[43] Naidoo and Williams (2014), p. 1.

The point here is not that universities need to be run in a fiscally responsible way – they do, otherwise they are simply wasting the money of their major customers, the students and the taxpayer. But it has to be stressed, in the loudest voice, that the primary purpose of the university is not and cannot be commercial. The primary purpose is inevitably multifaceted, but has accumulated over time focusing on learning, on research and on social responsibility. As we look to the future, we need to move away from seeing the HiEdBiz as the end, and see it more as the means – albeit a moderated means – to enable the university to focus on that purpose of learning, research and social responsibility.

The future will see the next evolution of the university embracing new power

In this chapter, I have raced through 2,500 years of university history, skipping centuries, amplifying anecdote and, quite possibly, doing great injustices to the complexities and nuances of that story.

My aim, nonetheless, is to make the point that the public purpose of the university has evolved necessarily over time in response to changing contexts, beliefs and motivations. Universities must grapple with how they accommodate the different parts of that purpose: learning, research and social responsibility. How they should do that in a way that harnesses the dynamics of new power is the subject of the next section.

Part Two

The missions of a New Power University

A university is, first and foremost, a social undertaking to create a social good.

Amy Gutmann, president, University of Pennsylvania (2017)

Universities have lots of power – new and old – and how they choose to use it, or not use it, will have profound impacts. The new power of a university lies in empowering the students it educates, enhancing the lives of the beneficiaries of the research it undertakes and working together with the communities in which it resides.

This deliberately and consciously inverts the relationship away from the old power concept of the academy – a self-referential, entitled and fundamentally elitist notion that is no longer fit for purpose in the 21st century.

Making such a comment will upset many of my friends and colleagues but I will justify this when I examine the role of the new power academic. In the meantime, I review the three missions of the university – learning, research and social responsibility – and illustrate how a different public purpose for universities will emerge through the application of new power values and thinking to these missions.

Chapter 3

New power learning and world-ready students

New power learning will graduate world-ready students with increased participation in higher education globally

In the previous chapter, I briefly told the story of how universities were exploiting low-paid cleaners. This is a story of power that Matthew Bolton, the director of Citizens UK, elaborates on in his book, *How to Resist*. Citizens UK is a charity that helps deliver social change through community organising. One of Bolton's first campaigns was on the living wage. In his book, he talks about how he helped persuade a UK university to take back cleaning staff into their direct employment, rather than outsource these services to a third party, and to pay them a living wage. This was the beginning of a very successful movement that led to the establishment of the Living Wage Foundation.[44] As of August 2019, in the UK, 38 of around 130 universities have signed up to the living wage (although, shamefully, many others have still to do so)[45] along with over 6,000 other companies, charities and employers.

---

[44] https://www.livingwage.org.uk.

[45] https://twitter.com/LivingWageUK/status/1161910398305656832.

In reviewing the experience of this campaign, Bolton identifies two critical aspects that made it successful – the first was power and the second was self-interest. His argument is that to deliver any social change you need to either have power or, more likely, persuade those who have power to use it. To do that, you have to appeal to the self-interest of those that hold power.

In my own university, in the spring of 2018, we had a student occupation at the same time as the academic strikes on pension reform. For this reason, it was assumed that the students were occupying in support of their academic colleagues. After about a week, I and a colleague were asked to go and speak to the students to see if we could come to some form of resolution. It was a strange and transformative moment for me. I remember the first meeting when we listened to the students – sitting on the floor in a corridor outside the principal's office, filled with sleeping bags, duvets and litter with an unpleasant odour of sweat (the students had not showered for a week). This was the first of a number of meetings where I learnt so much. It turned out that, while the students were sympathetic to the striking academics, their main focus was on insourcing the cleaners at King's. About half of the occupying students were members of 'Justice for Cleaners' and the other half were interested in the pension issue. The second realisation was how deep their knowledge and understanding was of both the cleaning industry and the challenges with the regulation and valuation of pensions that had led to the problems with the academics. It was that knowledge that provided the final lesson, that these students were largely right in their analysis and that the cleaners were being unfairly treated and the pension valuation – which was the root cause of the industrial dispute – was contestable.

I took these lessons back to my boss, the president and principal of King's, and told him that the students had a point and we needed to bring our cleaners back inhouse and challenge the current pension valuation. To his credit, when he heard the evidence, like me, he was persuaded by it and we began the process of insourcing and proposing a panel to review the methodology used to value the pension deficit.[46] In short, the students used their power to persuade me to use my limited power to persuade the principal to use his significant power to deliver change. They did this by appealing to our self-interest in showing us that insourcing would strengthen the culture at King's at no extra, or limited, cost and that engaging in the pension valuation

---

[46] This led to the establishment of the Joint Expert Panel (JEP) – see https://ussjep.org.uk/joint-expert-panel-members/ for more information.

methodology would rebuild some trust with our disaffected academic colleagues.

The reason for describing these events is to emphasise that students have power. We saw that in the founding of the University of Bologna in the 11th century and, more recently, with the #FeesMustFall movement in South Africa and the 'Water Movement'[47] in Hong Kong. In the rest of this chapter, we will see how this power will shape what is learned in the New Power University, how that learning happens and what this means for who the learners of the future are. I'm deliberately using the word 'learn' rather than 'teach', as the power dynamic is shifting, away from academic faculty and administrators and into the hands of students. This is a key governing principle for the New Power University.

The future 'decolonised' curriculum will better represent the diversity of knowledge

One of the most extraordinary books I have read in recent times is Adam Habib's 2019 account of the #FeesMustFall movement in South Africa, *Rebels and Rage*. As vice-chancellor at University of Witwatersrand (or 'Wits', as it is known), where the movement began in October 2015, Habib provides a deeply personal narrative that is laced with emotion and empathy. He is also adept at evaluating what happened, something that is not surprising given Habib is a political scientist and professor of political geography. #FeesMustFall was primarily about the impact on students and universities of an unsustainable increase in tuition fees across South Africa before spawning a number of other movements in the country, including #OutsourcingMustFall and #RhodesMustFall.

All of these Global South student-led movements have impacted on higher education agendas in the Global North but it is #RhodesMustFall that has had the most impact on the content of learning, specifically in its call for the (so-called) 'decolonisation' of universities and decolonising of the curriculum. I cautiously use the parentheses as there are understandable and appropriate sensitivities about the right language to use in commenting on

---

[47] As a side note, the term 'water movement' pays tribute to one of Hong Kong's most renowned celebrities, Bruce Lee the kung fu movie star from the 1970s. In a TV interview in 1971, he said, 'Be formless, shapeless, like water . . . Water can flow, or it can crash — be water, my friend.' For more detail, see: https://www.ft.com/content/d1f60a3a-cd58-11e9-b018-ca4456540ea6.

these issues. Indeed, Habib himself has a chapter in his book titled 'What's in a name?' noting:

> **Rather than entertain the debate about terminology, we adopted the term [decolonisation] in hope that it would enable a real conversation about the substance of the issue. But instead, all it did was locate the debate at the highest level of generality, on the level of the polemic and the rhetoric, rather than in specificity of the subject matter and the pedagogy – which is where the conversation needs to be located if we are to make real progress on curriculum reform.[48]**

My colleague 'Funmi Olonisakin, vice-president and vice-principal (International) at King's and founder of the African Leadership Centre,[49] prefers to use the language 'internationalisation'. This forces us to focus on the cultural competencies ('able to view the world through the lens of others', as she likes to say) of our all our students ('home and abroad') as opposed to a managerial focus on recruiting profitable high-fee international students.

In a recent paper, Olonisakin and colleagues comment:[50]

> **The demand/campaign for decolonisation of the university curriculum presents a challenge for the university. Yet it also presents a major opportunity to transform the university in ways that make it fit for the 21st century . . . The decolonisation of education agenda addresses structural racism . . . [meaning that] the status quo cannot be justified . . . Inordinate attention is focused on the reading list as a key method of decolonisation. However, simply populating the reading list with names of authors that are non-Western only superficially addresses the problem. Rather, what is needed is an approach which tackles the structural roots of the challenge of exclusion in higher education in its multi-dimensional forms, while transforming the student experience, creating global citizens able to contribute to global problem solving.**

What Habib and Olonisakin are getting at is the fundamental question of whose knowledge is it and, in the context of higher education, what knowledge is shared through the curriculum that a university offers? The issues to

---

[48] Habib (2019), p. 109.

[49] https://www.kcl.ac.uk/alc.

[50] Olonisakin (2021).

be thought through in answering these questions are deeply complex and take us into the realm of epistemology and philosophy, areas in which I am definitely not qualified to comment. But what they do highlight is that the content of the curriculum made available for learning by students – what is 'taught' using old-power language – and how that content is shared is a key and defining issue for the New Power University.

Of course, as with any challenge to the status quo, there is a nervousness within the academic community – at least in the UK – about what decolonising the curriculum entails. For example, Doug Stokes, from Exeter University, wrote a piece for *Quillette* arguing that 'the desire among the progressive *professoriat* to neuter the West, to reduce its power, to deconstruct its narratives, to challenge its philosophy and overthrow its institutional order, is an impulse rooted in an earlier and more geopolitically stable time when less was at stake'.[51] However, many academics do see the need for change. Stokes' article prompted James Muldoon, a colleague at the University of Exeter, to write a piece in *The Guardian* countering that 'this narrow view has become a common complaint of those who feel threatened by recent challenges, yet what these critics miss is that decolonising universities is not about completely eliminating white men from the curriculum. It's about challenging longstanding biases and omissions that limit how we understand politics and society.'[52]

Most critically, this desire for change is not coming from the academy or the 'executive' but is being driven by students and the ideas that gained momentum under the #RhodesMustFall banner are increasingly echoed worldwide. I support these views. The university curriculum needs to be 'internationalised' and made more representative of the diversity of human history, cultures and ideas. Rather than excluding courses on Western knowledge, the new power academic will listen to and engage with the student activism and locate that knowledge on a broader and more critical canvas. This is a recurrent theme in a collection of essays edited by Jonathan Jansen in *Decolonisation in Universities: The Politics of Knowledge*. Writing in its introduction, he states, 'Rather than assume passivity and dependence on hegemonic knowledge from the West, the book examines ways in which African leadership in

---

[51] https://quillette.com/2019/03/03/forget-about-decolonizing-the-curriculum-we-need-to-restore-the-wests-telos-before-its-too-late/.

[52] https://www.theguardian.com/education/2019/mar/20/academics-its-time-to-get-behind-decolonising-the-curriculum.

knowledge production emerges inside these historical constraints so that the question of "whose knowledge matters" is made complex by the flattening of relationships in knowledge partnerships between rich countries in the North and poor nations in the South.'[53]

The future curriculum will better help students to be 'world ready'

Most students are focused on acquiring the knowledge and skills that will support their future careers. This is something that universities are consistently letting them down on. The 2019 'Global Learner Survey'[54] of over 11,000 students across 8 countries and 3 regions (carried out by Pearson, the multinational education company and publisher of this book) found that almost two-thirds of respondents considered that 'colleges and universities aren't teaching the right skills for today's job market' (ranging from 57% in Canada to 79% in China). The same survey reported that 78% of respondents agreed with the statement that 'I need to develop my soft skills, for example critical thinking, problem solving and creativity' (ranging from 66% in the USA and UK to 95% in China).

This view is shared by employers. The *Harvard Business Review* recounts, 'We often hear employers and business leaders lament the unfortunate gap between what students learn in college and what they are actually expected to know in order to be job ready'.[55] The same article goes on to say that 'universities could substantially increase the value of the college degree if they spent more time teaching their students critical soft skills'. However, I prefer to use the phrase 'world ready' rather than 'job ready' to emphasise a more rounded approach in the spirt of the New Power University. This seems to me a subtle but important distinction as the 'right skills' (to use the language in the question from the 'Global Learner Survey', above) are unknowable for a future job market. In some fields, it may be the case that taught knowledge is actually out of date by graduation, so focusing on analytical tools and ways of learning may be a sensible strategy for universities to pursue despite the critique from students and employers.

---

[53] Jansen (2019), p. 3.

[54] Pearson (2019).

[55] https://hbr.org/2019/01/does-higher-education-still-prepare-people-for-jobs.

Some may see this as further support for Collini's critique of the HiEdBiz university (as discussed in Chapter 2), but I take a different view. Not so much to contradict the notion 'that the main aim of the [HiEdBiz] universities is to turn out people and ideas capable of making money'.[56] Rather, to emphasise that a main mission of the New Power University should be to turn out people and ideas that can contribute to the social good, including being able to contribute to whatever line of work they pursue. Consequently, universities have a responsibility to ensure that graduates are employable, are 'world ready', and being perceived to be failing at this is a significant challenge for the New Power University to embrace. The reason I prefer the phrase 'world ready' is it de-instrumentalises the argument and emphasises the social good nature of new power learning.

One approach to deliver on this type of education is through 'service learning', which is a form of credit-bearing experiential learning where students participate in organised community activity. Very common in North American universities, in my view, service learning has three critical ingredients – an academic basis developed in the classroom, community work that meets local need and a reflective element that allows students to draw out the lessons from the educational experience. 'In addition to enhancing academic and real-world learning, the overall purpose of service learning is to instil in students a sense of civic engagement and responsibility and work towards positive social change within society,' as a recent Europe Engage report puts it.[57]

To illustrate this point, at King's, third-year undergraduate students taking a module on 'The political economy of the City of London' are working with Westminster City Council to help design efforts to improve the socio-economic wellbeing of the Church Street Ward. The Church Street Ward is one of the poorest in all of the UK. The students are working with the head of economy and regeneration at Westminster City Council to understand what is happening in Church Street, and to work on social and policy solutions. For the class, students have to prepare a 2,000-word report. They will receive a grade for it, but, crucially, they are going beyond the university campus and walls, and writing the report by speaking with members of the local community, working with local government, and using their academic training to propose real policy solutions.

---

[56] Collini (2012), p. 154.
[57] Europe Engage (2017), p. 99.

New power learning will be increasingly digital

I am an 'analogue'. I remember taking books out of local libraries, buying music on (6 inch) vinyl singles, and using cassettes to load computer games onto our ZX Spectrum. I have lived through an era when these and other relatively recent technologies became quickly redundant and were replaced by new forms of digital media. We use the internet to access a global library of knowledge, we download and stream music to our phones and carry a memory stick on our keyrings, which holds over 500,000-times as much data as the cassette.

Fast forward, and we arrive at today's Generation Z students (whose values, attitudes and behaviour we explore more in Chapter 6). Generation Z were those born between 1995 and 2012 (therefore, aged between 8 and 25 years old in 2020) and they are a unique cohort of digital natives that have a fundamentally different lived experience than their forebears who were either brought up in a wholly analogue world or, like me, have experienced both analogue and digital.

If the aim of the New Power University is to co-create with these students a curriculum that is representative of the diversity of knowledge and relevant to future graduates and society, the next question is how can that education best be delivered? These new power students, the first 'digitals', are already familiar with consuming knowledge independently and online. The change in technology and, as importantly, the attitudes to technology, provide a further opportunity for new-power learning.

Indeed, it is easy when living through such a transformation to become blasé about its revolutionary impact. As Paul Mason points out, the ubiquitous nature of data defines the next 'Kondratieff Wave', with us living through the inflection point between the end of the analogue era and the beginning of the digital one – or, going back again to the words of John Ralston Saul, living through the 'in-between times'. This is a point that was made by Michael Barber (outgoing chair of the UK Office for Students and founder and first head of the prime minister's Delivery Unit under Tony Blair) and colleagues in his 2013 pamphlet 'An avalanche is coming: Higher Education and the revolution ahead'. In the preface to this paper, Barber comments that, 'Our belief is that deep, radical and urgent transformation is required in higher education . . . Our fear is that, perhaps of complacency, caution or anxiety, or a combination of all three, the pace of change is too slow and the nature of change too incremental.'[58] During my time in higher education, I have heard a number of senior leaders dismiss this thesis, but I have to say – and indeed this is one of the central provocations of this book – the avalanche *is* coming, the question is not if but more when.

This creates a massive challenge for universities and their staff, made all the more complex by the shift in power that this involves. The impact of this sharp inter-generational boundary – between those who knew an analogue world and those who have known and will only ever know a digital one – is yet to be fully understood or realised. One obvious conclusion is that future university education will be delivered online with similarly disruptive effects as has been seen in music (think Spotify), books (think Amazon) and taxis (think Uber).

Not everyone anticipates such an impact. *The New York Times* commentator David Brooks has explored the impact of online education on universities in a number of his columns. In one, he makes the distinction between technical knowledge (that can be imparted through online education) and practical knowledge which,[59] as he puts it, 'is not about what you do, but how you do it. It is the wisdom a great chef possesses that cannot be found in recipe books. Practical knowledge is not the sort of knowledge that can be taught and memorized; it can only be imparted and absorbed.'[60] In a later column, he goes on to suggest that 'the future of the university will be found in its original moral and spiritual mission, but secularized, and in an open and aspiring way'.[61] Other commentators reflect Newman's argument that university education is as much about how 'to respect, to consult, to aid each other'[62] as it is about the acquisition of skills and knowledge.

In contrast, and, as the technology commentator Clay Shirky noted in 2012 in an excellent blog titled *Napster, Udacity and the Academy*,[63] the rejection of a digital future is complacent. Shirky points out that, although the (old power) music industry managed to shut down one of the original music streaming services, Napster, for copyright infringement, it effectively 'won the

---

[58] Barber (2013), p. 3.

[59] As Brooks notes, this distinction comes from philosopher Michael Oakeshott.

[60] https://www.nytimes.com/2013/04/05/opinion/Brooks-The-Practical-University.html.

[61] https://www.nytimes.com/2015/10/06/opinion/david-brooks-the-big-university.html.

[62] Newman (1852/2008), p. 126.

[63] https://internet.psych.wisc.edu/wp-content/uploads/532-Master/532-UnitPages/Unit-02/Shirky_Napster-Udacity_2012.pdf.

battle, but lost the war', as it had to change its business model by allowing the consumer to 'rent' a single track, rather than having to buy a full album where three-fifths of the tracks were mediocre, at best.

In 2012, Clay argued the same was starting to happen in higher education through the introduction of massive online courses, or MOOCs. He noted a pattern repeating itself:

> **First, the people running the old system don't notice the change. When they do, they assume it's minor. Then that it's a niche. Then a fad. And by the time they understand that the world has actually changed, they've squandered most of the time they had to adapt.**

To back up his argument, he cites the story of Udacity,[64] an early mover in the online education world and valued at around $1 billion (although, like many technology start-ups, yet to make a profit). One of its founders – Sebastian Thrun – has become an evangelist for digital education, predicting, in an article in *Wired Magazine*, that 'in 50 years, there will be only 10 institutions in the world delivering higher education.'[65]

Can New Power Universities adapt and survive? How much will they have to change their mode of delivery and the business models that they rely on? Glyn Davis, the former president and vice-chancellor of The University of Melbourne, and author of *The Australian Idea of a University* (referred to in Chapter 2), used a 2017 speech to provide encouragement that 'universities have embraced new learning technologies, flipped classrooms, offered massive open online courses, nurtured online degrees, created new accommodation and amenities so students can interact virtually yet still spend time on campus'.[66] Nonetheless, the challenge for the New Power University will be to continue to embrace this innovation so that it actually wins both the battle and the war (as Shirky puts it) and to fully embrace and adopt a new online pedagogy that is aligned with the expectations of the new power student and their lived experience of the digital world.

In practice, and, as Davis noted, this need not mean the end of physical campuses but a more flexible use of space that not only fits with the preferences of students but is also effective in delivering the learning that is

---

[64] https://www.udacity.com.

[65] https://www.wired.com/2012/03/ff_aiclass/.

[66] https://upp-foundation.org/professor-glyn-davis-full-speech-irredeemable-time-rising-tide-hostility-toward-universities/.

needed. We can start to glimpse into the future with the National University of Singapore with its flipped classroom model. Undergraduate students acquire their knowledge online and have to pass a test before moving into a classroom where around 20 students work together in appraising their new knowledge and applying it in practical assessment. Another illustration comes from David Kellerman, at the University of New South Wales, in Australia, who has used Microsoft Teams and OneNote to create an intimate classroom experience with lectures of over 400 students, using cutting-edge techniques both to support learners in real time and to allow him to be guided by AI bots to engage with specific students.[67]

Of course, much of the innovation is happening beyond the boundaries of the higher education world. Exclusively, online learning is already available on the internet, especially for what might be termed 'technical knowledge'. Web-based communities, such as www.scottsbasslessons.com and www.woodworkingmasterclasses.com, illustrate how learning can be delivered online. Both began by offering free videos on YouTube aimed at a very closely defined audience who 'self-identify'. Once their following started to build, they could quickly expand the volume of free content and encourage a community to form by commenting on the videos and getting in touch directly. The next phase was to monetise this by creating their own websites and introducing memberships and premium-level content (for example specific mini-courses) that people pay for. This includes written learning materials as well as videos. Putting aside Newman's requirement 'to respect, to consult, to aid each other', there is no reason that the New Power University could not offer some or all of its curriculum using this business model.

These examples show education providers (in the broadest sense) delivering learning directly to the student, whether younger or older. The other major model that a digital world brings is the role of the intermediary who sits between the provider and the consumer. It is the emergence of such intermediaries in higher education that has the potential for compounding the rate of change in how and where people learn. By packaging and selling learning in radically different ways to the current 'direct marketing' model of universities, 'Amazon-type' platforms could emerge that enable students to access packages of learning that are not currently available (for example made up of simultaneous inputs from multiple universities).

---

[67] See this short 10-minute video for more detail: https://educationblog.microsoft.com/en-au/2019/07/unsws-teams-project-brings-artificial-intelligence-to-student-engagement/.

This, so-called 'stackable micro credits' model is being edged forwards by a number of innovators worldwide. For example, Coursera[68] is an online platform, a bit like Udacity in providing online education, but focuses on aggregating courses from providers across the globe, both universities and private organisations. If you want to, you could study a module on 'Pricing Strategy Optimization Specialization' supplied by the global professional services firm Boston Consulting Group or a module on 'The Science of the Solar System' delivered by academics from Caltech, one of the best universities in the world, according to various rankings. Another example of this approach is Kiron,[69] an NGO based in Berlin, that brings together MOOCS and other 'open educational resources' (OER) from universities around the world and repackages them as modules aimed at refugee students. Kiron is more practically focused so you could 'Learn programming with Python' or take a course titled 'Prepare for a Jordanian university'.

The biggest challenge these types of platforms currently face is that their courses are not accredited or, if they are, they cannot be 'stacked' in a way that allows students to accumulate credits across a number of providers towards a degree. Why? The right to accredit modules lies with universities – often supported by national regulatory frameworks – and this form of old power enables them to maintain a privileged and protectionist position in the market for higher education. This position is not sustainable. New power learning will have profound impacts on how accreditation happens and where value resides in the higher education system. In this way, the new and evolving forms of learning will not only impact on the public purpose of universities as the 'holders of knowledge' but also impact the very nature of the academy.

New power learning should expand access and lead to greater participation in higher education globally

In addition to overseeing a radical shift in what is learned and how it is learned, the New Power University will engage with a broader range of learners from a diverse variety of backgrounds and experiences. Put another way,

---

[68] https://www.coursera.org.

[69] https://kiron.ngo/en/about-us/.

the New Power University will have an unrelenting commitment to provide higher education for everyone, irrespective of race, class, geography, gender or age.

Let's be clear – this is not an argument to 'dumb down' degrees, but to acknowledge two fundamental facts. The first is that our knowledge and understanding of the world around us is self-evidently greater today than it was 100 years ago, meaning there is more to learn. Second, over the past 100 years, there has been a massive expansion in education, meaning there are more learners. A century ago, only 12% of the world's population could read, today it is 88%; school enrolment rates are increasing across the world; globally, the number of children out of school has fallen from an estimated 381 million children in 1998 to 263 million in 2014 (and that is despite an increase in the global young population); and, finally, the number of years of school has also increased across the world.[70] In other words, the world is more educated than ever before.

These two facts should put to bed any argument that not everyone should be given the opportunity go to university, a view often put forward by politicians and commentators, many of whom have been to elite old power institutions themselves. As Nick Hillman, the director of the UK think tank Higher Education Policy Institute (HEPI), pointed out in a tweet in 2019: 'Whenever I say we should prepare for increased participation in higher education, to match the levels in other countries, some people respond by arguing there's too many students and too many universities. It's funny how many of them think 100% of their own children should go.'[71] This followed a number of articles where Hillman made the case that 70–80% of young people should go to university in the UK by the 2030s.[72] In one of these articles, he quoted the 1963 Robbins Report on higher education in England, which stated that 'courses of higher education should be available for all those who are qualified by ability and attainment to pursue them and who wish to do so'.[73] That fundamental principle is as relevant today as it was over 50 years ago. Despite the

[70] See: https://ourworldindata.org/global-rise-of-education for more detail and source data.

[71] https://twitter.com/nickhillman/status/1105759825898758145.

[72] https://www.theguardian.com/education/2019/mar/12/university-place-for-all-way-to-abolish-tuition-fees; https://www.hepi.ac.uk/2019/04/29/what-if-we-really-wanted-to-diversify-access-to-our-universities/; https://www.conservativehome.com/platform/2017/09/nick-hillman-we-must-continue-to-expand-higher-education.html.

[73] https://www.conservativehome.com/platform/2017/09/nick-hillman-we-must-continue-to-expand-higher-education.html; Robbins (1963), p. 8.

merit-focused approach of Robbins, Gavin Williamson, the UK Secretary of State for Education, made a speech in 2020 where he symbolically abandoned former Prime Minister Tony Blair's target that half of young people should go to university. His argument was 'when Tony Blair uttered that 50% target for university attendance, he cast aside the other 50% . . . As Education Secretary, I will stand for the forgotten 50%.'[74] Underneath the rhetoric was a commitment to strengthen further education, which must, unequivocally, be welcomed. However, to present further education versus higher education as a zero-sum game is, in my view, flawed. A stronger further education sector, combined with an 80% target for higher education which, critically, is 'available to all those who are qualified', can only be a good thing, as it would mean the education attainment of the whole of society is improved and, indeed, would put pressure on primary and secondary education to ensure a pipeline of students who are qualified.

Sadly, however, the data tells us that not everyone with the ability and attainment who wishes to go to university can. In their book, *Social Mobility: And Its Enemies*, Lee Elliot Major, the former CEO of the Sutton Trust, a UK foundation that champions social mobility, and Stephen Machin, a professor of economics at the London School of Economics, show that, while enrolment rates into universities have narrowed between rich and poor families, they have actually widened in the UK's most prestigious universities.[75]

As concerning is the overall 'graduation gap' between rich and poor, which has widened, as illustrated in Figure 3.1. The proportion of young people who graduated from universities by the age of 23 increased by 12 percentage points (from 6% in 1981 to 18% in 2013), for the poorest fifth of households compared to a 35 percentage point increase (from 20% to 55%) for the richest fifth of households. As Elliot Major and Machin conclude, 'Robbins' vision of a university system accessible to all has yet to materialise.'[76]

More encouragingly, Figure 3.2 illustrates there has been an increase in overall participation in higher education. One of the successes of today's universities in the UK is that they recently delivered on Tony Blair's 1999 pledge that half of all 18-year-olds should go to university. That is a radical and welcome change in two generations. When my dad graduated over 50 years ago,

---

[74] https://www.gov.uk/government/speeches/education-secretary-fe-speech-with-social-market-foundation?utm_source=3d8b2e7a-4bc0-47b2-822c-1fc489d8608e&utm_medium=email&utm_campaign=govuk-notifications&utm_content=immediate.

[75] Elliot Major and Machin (2018), p. 97.

[76] *Ibid.*

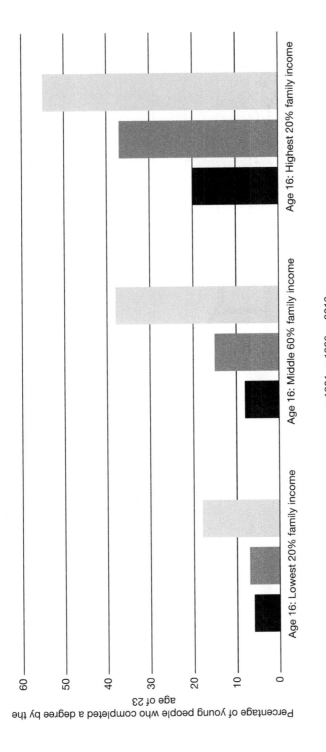

Figure 3.1 Inequalities in the proportion of young people who complete a degree by the age of 23[77]

77 Elliot Major and Machin (2018), Figure 4.4, p. 99.

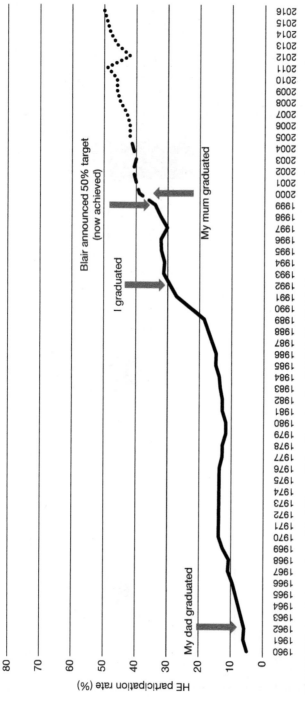

Figure 3.2 Long-term trend in HE participation in the UK (1960–2016)[78]

[78] Lines are drawn from different sources. Solid line is from IFS (2010) Working Paper W10/04 (https://www.ifs.org.uk/wps/wp1004.pdf). Data extracted from Figure 2 using http://www.graphreader.com so may not be entirely accurate. Dashed line is from Figure 1 of House of Commons Public Accounts Committee report on Widening Participation (https://publications.parliament.uk/pa/cm200809/cmselect/cmpubacc/226/22602.htm). Data estimated by reading graph. Dotted line is from Department for Education briefing (https://www.gov.uk/government/statistics/participation-rates-in-higher-education-2006-to-2017) using direct data source.

less than 1 in 10 of young people went to university. When I graduated 30 years later, it was about 1 in 3. Today, it is 1 in 2.

This increase in university participation is neither a UK phenomenon nor a rich country one. The proportion of young people who are in tertiary education has been increasing in every region of the world over the past 20 years, as shown in Figure 3.3.[79] This global 'massification'[80] of higher education indicates that the demand for universities, worldwide, has increased significantly over the past 20 years and is likely to do so at a similar rate over the next 20 years. In 1980, 12% of the world population participated in some form of tertiary education, in 2000 this equivalent figure was 19% and, in 2015, it had reached 36%. Looking forward, the number of enrolments in higher education is expected to increase from 214 million in 2015 to 250 million by 2020 and it is expected it will continue to rise to 377 million by 2030 and 594 million by 2040.[81]

New power learning should support lifelong learning

The projected growth in global demand for education includes estimates for 'lifelong' learning, where older students enrol for a university education throughout their lives. Pursuing learning later in life can result from a whole range of professional and personal motivations. My own mum, for example, decided to do an Open University degree at the age of 52. She did a part-time degree over six years in history of art, graduating with an honours degree in 2000. The focus on the humanities was purely for personal interest and it was a mix of online, correspondence and classroom-based teaching.

Of course, my mother's experience is not unique. *The Economist* reported, in 2017, that more than eight million students in China over the age of 60 had enrolled into 'universities for the elderly'. Evidently, demand outstrips supply

---

[79] This figure plots gross enrolment rates in tertiary education. This is the statistic used by the United Nations as it allows comparison between countries. Technically, it is measuring the number of students who have enrolled in tertiary education, regardless of age, against the size of the population cohort for the five years starting from the official secondary school graduation age. The focus on tertiary means that it will include other non-university education providers such as further education colleges.

[80] A term coined by Trow (1973).

[81] Calderon (2018).

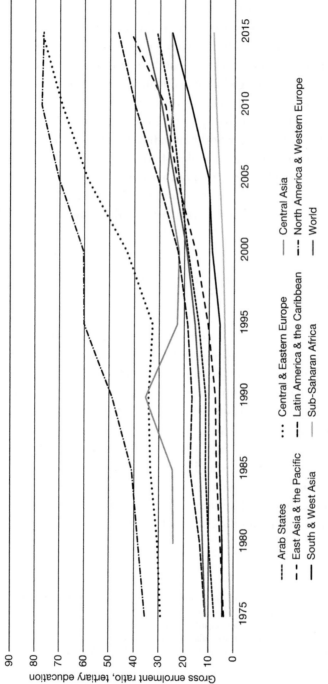

Figure 3.3 Gross enrolment ratio, tertiary education by world region, 1970–2015[82]

82 Calderon (2018), Table 2.

with only one in six students able to enrol at Shanghai's University.[83] As in China, global demand for lifelong learning will only increase in time as people live longer, healthier and wealthier lives and as the digital native Gen Z-ers begin to move into adult life and middle age. This creates an amazing opportunity for the New Power University to engage with an expanding market but, in doing so, to ensure that the new power values are fully embedded into its curriculum and delivery.

A concluding thought on the systemic impact of new power learning on accreditation and place

The New Power University will reimagine the curriculum, redefine the ways that learning is delivered, and reconnect with a diverse and broader range of learners. In short, we have looked at the how, what and who of new power learning. As these ideas come together, they could have quite profound impacts on both the governance of universities and education systems more broadly. We will pick up these implications in the final part of this book, but, as an aperitif, briefly cover two here: the impact on accreditation and the impact on place.

As already noted, it is likely that new power learning will challenge universities' monopolistic power to award degrees through current models of accreditation. Today, universities have a unique power in being able to award degrees. Historically, this power emanated from the Church or Monarchy but, in modern times, has been overseen by a state regulator. Universities register with the regulator who confirms the *bona fides* of the higher education institution and provides assurance to a potential student, or an employer of a graduate, by granting them degree award powers. However, as with all regulated markets, this assurance favours those who are 'inside the club' and excludes those who seek to challenge their position.

A useful thought experiment would be to consider what a university would look like if it consciously decided not to take part in this self-referential model and to avoid participating in the regulatory framework. At the extreme, the value of a university degree is defined by its brand. A degree from Harvard has more perceived value than one from London Metropolitan. If I can persuade a student – and their future employers – that my unregulated degree is of more

[83] https://www.economist.com/the-economist-explains/2018/08/16/why-universities-for-the-elderly-are-booming-in-china.

value than my regulated degree, then the old power concept of degree-awarding power may evaporate. Imagine, if you will, that a global brand, such as BMW, Apple or Huawei, decided to establish a New Power University and used their brand value to assure students and employers of the quality of the educational offering. If there was demand for such an education, then the old power accreditation model comes under threat. Indeed, in the UK, this model is beginning to emerge through modern-day apprenticeship. For example, competition for a Jaguar Land Rover apprenticeship is more competitive than getting into Oxford or Cambridge universities, according to a recent article in the *Financial Times*.[84]

The second systemic consequence of new power learning is the impact on those places where universities choose to reach out beyond their current organisational boundaries. In these locations, universities might take on broader place-based systems leadership for education. This could follow a 'T' model, with the sponsorship or ownership of vertically aligned education providers, such as high schools, becoming more common along with potential post-16 horizontal linkage with further education colleges and other providers of apprenticeships such as Jaguar Land Rover, mentioned above. In some places, you are likely to see the emergence of education health systems analogous to the academic health science centres found in a number of health economies around the world. This systems approach to education will see the New Power University become more ambitious in fulfilling its core social responsibility to enhance social mobility.

While that may sound a bit audacious, as my former colleague, and now chief executive of the Brilliant Club,[85] Anne-Marie Canning pointed out in a blog in 2017,[86] such ideas are floating around in the policy tea leaves. As Canning notes, there is a very important passage in Theresa May's ill-fated 2017 Conservative Party Manifesto in the UK that stated: 'We will make it a condition for universities hoping to charge maximum tuition fees to become involved in academy sponsorship or the founding of free schools.' When this idea was floated, the University of Oxford vice-chancellor, Louise Richardson, reacted by saying, 'We're very good at running a university. But we have no experience of running schools, so I think it would be a distraction.' This is, surely, an old power retort to a new power idea.

---

[84] https://www.ft.com/content/c15891d1-065d-3aea-b8e6-83bbec97c423.

[85] The Brilliant Club is a UK non-profit organisation that aims to widen access to university for students from under-represented groups. See: https://thebrilliantclub.org.

[86] https://wonkhe.com/blogs/comment-universities-raise-school-attainment-yes/.

Chapter 4

The impact of new power research

New power research will address the most pressing challenges people face today, in an open, transparent and involved way, improving the lives of communities everywhere

At the end of the Second World War, US President Roosevelt asked the director of the Office of Scientific Research, Vannevar Bush, to make recommendations for how the scientific and technological progress during the conflict could be applied in peace time. The Office of Scientific Research and Development was seen as a major contributor to winning the war effort, having overseen the Manhattan project and supported the development of the mass production of penicillin.

Bush published his report – *Science: The Endless Frontier* – in July 1945, presenting it to President Truman, who succeeded Roosevelt following his death in office earlier that year. The report set out a blueprint for how the US Government could support and fund research and, in particular, scientific research, which led to the establishment of the National Science Foundation in 1950. Bush believed that universities should be places where research occurs for research's sake and, because of this, researchers should decide on what to research:

> **The publicly and privately supported colleges, universities, and research institutes are the centers of basic research. They are the wellsprings of knowledge and understanding. As long as they are vigorous and healthy and their scientists are free to pursue the truth wherever it may lead, there will be a flow of new scientific knowledge to those who can apply it to practical problems in Government, in industry, or elsewhere.[87]**

It is easy to underestimate the impact that this recommendation has had on science and research policy worldwide. I have been fortunate enough to be involved in a number of projects for research funders from different regions of the world and there is a widely held view that the US National Science Foundation, designed by Bush, is the gold standard when it comes to government funding and support for science.

The trouble is, this 'gold-standard' model is now failing. If I told you that over 85% of the estimated US$120 billion[88] a year that is invested by governments and foundations on biomedical and health research around the world is wasted, you would rightly be shocked. Well, this was the finding that *The Lancet* published in an important 2009 paper by Iain Chalmers and Paul Glasziou. Their compelling data showed that about half of public investments in research are wasted at each of four sequential stages during the research process (see Figure 4.1): whether the research question is relevant; whether the design and methods are appropriate; whether the research papers are accessible; and, whether the report of the research is complete and done in a way that makes it possible to replicate the study. The accumulated waste over these four stages adds up to 85%.

This analysis focused on biomedical research but there is no convincing reason to assume the same is not the case for other disciplines. Scholars from the humanities and social sciences are less likely to publish in open access

---

[87] Bush (1945), Chapter 1.

[88] Røttingen, *et al.* (2013) estimated that, in 2009, total investment in biomedical and health research globally was US$214 billion, 60% from the private sector and 40%, or US$100 billion, from the governments and not-for-profit foundations. If the US$100 billion is adjusted for inflation, the figure would be about US$120 million in today's money.

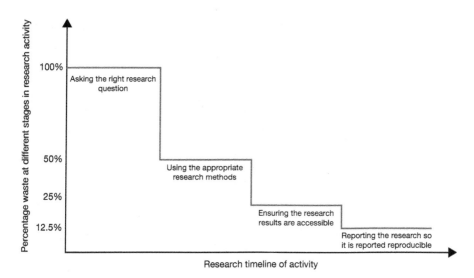

Figure 4.1 Stages of research waste[89]

journals and books[90] (stage 3) and there is evidence of a reproducibility crisis in a range of disciplines, including economics[91] (stage 4).

This level of waste is unsustainable in a world where the competition for public funding grows ever more intense as governments strive to invest in modern infrastructure, pay for the effects of ageing populations and fund initiatives to fight the climate crisis. If seen to be wasteful, the pressure to cut research funding will grow and, with it, the threat to much of the mission and income of the modern university.

When you look at it, the current approach to research funding has come to be an archetype of an old power institution. Who holds the power? The research funding agencies modelled on the National Science Foundation are run by academic researchers for academic researchers. The chief executives of such agencies are usually drawn from the academic community, the strategies of such agencies are often determined by the academic community, the decision as what to fund and what not to fund is decided by the academic community, the research is done by the academic community, and the results

---

[89] Adapted from the figure in Chalmers and Glasziou (2009).

[90] In the UK's Research Excellence Framework in 2014, only 46 out of a total 12,701 titles submitted to panel C (social sciences) and panel D (arts and humanities) were available as open access – see Fund, *et al.* (2019) for details.

[91] Camerer, *et al.* (2016).

of that research are presented in a way that is accessible only by the academic community. It is an old power model and it is no longer fit for purpose.

The defenders of this system will retort with a number of counter arguments. They would say that you need experts to run these agencies as they are the only ones who have the deep knowledge to formulate appropriate scientific strategies and to judge what is suitable to fund. They would also go on to say that they have appropriately prosecuted a strategy that has supported basic or discovery research or 'knowledge for knowledge's sake'. They would argue that, at the time of commissioning the research, it's not possible to know what benefits will arise from scientific discoveries and that you can't predict the outcomes of scientific research due to serendipity.

These longstanding beliefs in the value of basic research partly stem from assertions made many years ago by two scientists, Julius Comroe and Robert Dripps, who claimed that 62% of all reports judged to be essential for subsequent clinical advances were the result of basic research.[92] However, the rigour and objectivity of their analysis was questioned[93] and, when I and others attempted to replicate the analysis, we concluded that it was 'not repeatable, reliable or valid', as well as demonstrating that only 2–21% of research underpinning clinical advances could be described as basic.[94] This confirmed an earlier study where we demonstrated that less than 10% of research underpinning clinical guidelines was basic,[95] while Contopoulos-Ioannidis showed that less than 1% of papers in basic science journals resulted in a clinical intervention some 20 years later.[96]

This is not just a problem for biomedical and health research. Ed Byrne and Charles Clarke, in their recent book, *The University Challenge* (which is published as part of this Pearson series), emphasise that a range of other disciplines can be critiqued for their over-focus on theory and discovery research. As they say, 'Impact on society is not yet at a sufficient level to meet national and global needs.' They go on to note: 'When Queen Elizabeth, in November 2008, asked economists at the London School of Economics, "Why did nobody notice it [the financial crisis]?" she was speaking with the grain of public sentiment. She got an answer when she visited the Bank of England in December 2012, which some might say is typical of the speed of response in the academic world.'[97]

---

[92] Comroe and Dripps (1976).

[93] Smith (1987).

[94] Grant, *et al.* (2003).

[95] Grant, *et al.* (2000).

[96] Contopoulos-Ioannidis, *et al.* (2003).

[97] Byrne and Clarke (2020), p. 14.

Thankfully, this old power, somewhat arrogant, and fundamentally incestuous, model of research funding is beginning to be challenged. To be fair, some of this change is coming from these old power institutions. For example, universities are slowly embracing the need to demonstrate the impact of their research and, along with research funders, beginning to engage with ideas such as the 'grand challenges' that research should address, with talk of 'moon shots' and an increased focus on mission-oriented research. A few universities are also embracing new approaches to how research is carried out and exploring new power approaches like 'open innovation'. Finally, the need to make sure research is not wasted means there is a growing movement to make research outputs more widely available through open access publication and similar initiatives. That said, many of the more transformative changes are being driven from outside the higher education sector, by imaginative new power leaders, entrepreneurial scientists and fresh thinking publishers exploring new platforms for disseminating research. The challenge for the New Power University is to move to the forefront of a transformation in the way that research is designed, delivered and disseminated.

New power research will demonstrably contribute to improving lives and growing prosperity

In the face of so much wasted money on research, why continue to fund it? The answer is because it does pay back. Research gives us many of the advances needed to grapple with the big challenges in today's world and its impacts are directly traceable and quantifiable. Having been involved for more than 15 years in projects that try and assess both the value and impact of research, I have seen how the economic return from biomedical and health research is consistently estimated at around 25%. This is made up of a monetised value of living longer and better lives (c.10%) and the contribution to the gross domestic product (GDP) that is stimulated by undertaking research in a country – what economists call the 'spillover effect' (15%).[98] In layperson terms, that means that, for every £1 you invest, you will get 25p a year in perpetuity.

It is also possible to demonstrate the impact of other disciplines – ranging from theology to zoology – using narrative-based approaches. In the UK, the government runs an assessment of research excellence in universities every five to six years. In the most recent exercise undertaken in 2014, it asked every

---

[98] Grant and Buxton (2018).

discipline in every university to provide case studies of where research has had on impact in improving people's lives. Given the time it takes for some types of research to translate into demonstrable benefits to people, the original work could be up to 20 years old (although, in practice, it typically was 10 years). The 6,679 non-redacted case studies that were written for this exercise are publicly available and, for anyone who is sceptical about the value of research, they should spend some time reading them.[99] A couple of my favourite examples are provided in the following box and illustrate the diversity of both the underlying research and the nature of the impact that it has had.

Examples of research making a difference

Jesus was married[100]

On 18 September 2012, a newly discovered Coptic gospel fragment, purportedly dating from the 4th century, was announced in Rome. It generated worldwide publicity: for, in it, Jesus refers to 'my wife'. Three days later, Professor Francis Watson posted a short paper online, in which he used a form of compositional analysis which he had pioneered to argue that the fragment was, most probably, a recent forgery. Watson's paper was extensively read and reported, and widely regarded as conclusive. An imminent TV documentary on the fragment was promptly postponed indefinitely. Watson's research transformed the way that this fragment was perceived by an international public. As such, it prevented a serious scholarly error from becoming lodged in the public consciousness. It is an example of the power of a timely web-enabled intervention by a scholar in a fast-moving news story.

---

[99] https://impact.ref.ac.uk/casestudies/.

[100] 'The case of the forged gospel fragment', REF 2014 impact case study, see: http://impact.ref.ac.uk/CaseStudies/CaseStudy.aspx?Id=11837.

Elephants and bees[101]

While increasing African elephant numbers in the last 20 years has been a success for conservation efforts, it creates problems for farmers when the elephants raid their crops. Building on local anecdotal evidence, zoologists from the University of Oxford published a study in 2002 reporting that elephants avoided feeding on acacia trees hung with beehives. Partnering with a bioacoustician from Disney's Animal Kingdom, the team went on to show that the buzz of aggressive bees caused elephants to emit a low frequency rumble, causing other nearby elephants to retreat. They went on to develop and test a novel elephant-deterring beehive fence, built using low-tech, easy-to-maintain materials. The fences reduced raids on farmers' crops, improving their food security. In tandem, sales of 'elephant friendly' honey from the beehives offset the costs of building the fence. UNESCO and the World Bank have since backed the use of beehive fences as a means to reduce human–elephant conflict. Projects are now running in farms across Kenya, Botswana, Tanzania, Mozambique and Uganda.

If such substantial impacts can be achieved even when 85% of research dollars are wasted, what more could be possible with a new power model? The application of new power values to research is already encouraging and, perhaps, results in a more positive immediate outlook than for the prospect of new power learning. Over the past decade, a range of exciting new approaches to research have been tried out, including crowdsourcing research questions from the general public, rolling out open innovation platforms and prizes to incentivise researchers to address questions that are relevant to companies and governments, and involving communities and individuals to help source and analyse data. Inevitability, this revolution in research is leading to its own jargon, with words like 'crowdsourcing', 'citizen science', 'open innovation' and 'open access' populating the lexicon (see the following box for some definitions).

---

[101] 'Using honey bees as an effective deterrent for crop-raiding elephants', REF 2014 impact case study, see: http://impact.ref.ac.uk/CaseStudies/CaseStudy.aspx?Id=17588.

> # Definitions of some new power research terms
>
> *Citizen science* Scientific work undertaken by members of the general public, often in collaboration with, or under the direction of, professional scientists and scientific institutions.
>
> *Crowdsourcing* The practice of obtaining information or services by soliciting input from a large number of people, typically via the internet and often without offering compensation.
>
> *Open access* Direct and unrestricted access for readers to the shelves on which publications are kept; the system or policy of such access.
>
> *Open innovation* The use of purposive inflows and outflows of knowledge to accelerate internal innovation, and expand the markets for external use of innovation, respectively. (This paradigm) assumes that firms can and should use external ideas as well as internal ideas, and internal and external paths to market, as they look to advance their technology.[102]

In the rest of this chapter, we will explore each of these concepts, explaining how they are beginning to define the new power research of the future.

New power research will use crowdsourcing and open innovation platforms to identify research questions

The term 'crowdsourcing' first appeared in an article in 2006 in *Wired* magazine by technology journalist Jeff Howe.[103] Entitled 'The rise of crowdsourcing', the article describes a number of new internet start-ups that were using a new organisational model to combine the connectivity of the internet with the creativity and knowledge of the 'crowd'.

---

[102] Chesbrough, *et al.* (2003).

[103] https://www.wired.com/2006/06/crowds/.

One of these start-ups, InnoCentive,[104] was founded in 2001 by Alph Bingham and Aaron Schacht while working for the pharmaceutical company Eli Lilly and Company. The idea is simple: businesses post very specific problems on their website and anyone worldwide will be paid if they can solve them successfully. The people or companies posting a problem are called 'seekers' and those responding are 'solvers'. Spend an hour playing around on the website and you will quickly find a range of different problems posted, including: 'Technologies to Absorb Vibrations'; 'Improving Thermal Stability of Proteins'; and 'Comfortable Protective Summer Clothing for Electrical Work Activities'. Some of the problems that have been solved include: 'Improving Fish Exclusion from Water Diversions and Intakes'; 'Powering Electronic Instruments on a Rotating Shaft'; and 'Novel Method to Treat Biofouling on Vessels in Port'. The problems and solutions are all very well specified and need expert knowledge to address. Crucially, some of the expertise to do this will reside in universities but, critically, not all of it.

It is this type of open innovation platform that Timms and Heimans (2018) refer to in their book *New Power*, citing NASA's approach to open innovation, which has a number of different programmes, including challenges, prizes and an internal problem-solving platform called NASA@work.[105] In fact, when piloting this approach, NASA used InnoCentive to post a number of challenges and one of these has become a poster-child to illustrate the success of open innovation.[106] Solar flares matter to NASA as they create spikes in radiation that can damage equipment. NASA had been using an algorithm which could anticipate such events eight hours in the future with a 50% chance of being right. They decided to post a challenge on InnoCentive to see if the time window and accuracy of such predictions could be improved. They had a number of successful solutions, but the winner was a weather forecaster who developed an approach that could predict 24 hours ahead of time with 85% accuracy.[107]

Can you guess the reaction among some NASA staff? That's right, the internal resistance to introducing this type of innovation at NASA was documented in a Harvard Business School case study.[108] It is another classic old power

---

[104] https://www.innocentive.com.

[105] https://www.nasa.gov/offices/oct/openinnovation/.

[106] https://www.innocentive.com.

[107] Chesbrough (2020), p. 68.

[108] Tushman, *et al.* (2014a); Tushman, *et al.* (2014b).

versus new power struggle playing out within the organisation where scientists and engineers saw the open method as a 'fundamental challenge to their personal identifies. They defined themselves as "problem solvers", but open innovation crowdsourcing didn't let them play that role; instead they had to frame problems for someone else to solve.'[109] To a degree, there is some legitimacy in this concern. The 'solutions' focus of InnoCentive could undermine long-term iterative research that needs an institutional base, such as that being argued for by NASA staff. But I am not sure this is an 'either or' argument. The New Power University can be focused on providing solutions like those cited above, as well as providing a platform for long-term incremental research.

Despite this resistance, these open innovation platforms are impressive and embody the spirit of new power research very effectively. While some of them are based on intermediaries (such as the InnoCentive example), it is possible to cut out this role and go directly to the people that you want to involve in the research. This is most evident in the health arena where 'patient and public involvement' (PPI) in biomedical and health research has become increasingly important over the past 40 years. As Wilson, *et al.* (2015) point out in reviewing the historical roots of PPI, 'Further impetus for the challenge against biomedical authority was provided by a series of high-profile medical scandals, including the retention of deceased children's body parts for research without the knowledge or consent of parents and unexpectedly high mortality rates for children undergoing heart surgery.'[110]

I've also experienced the approach directly with Fight for Sight, a small biomedical research charity in the UK that focuses on eye research, where I was an unpaid trustee. A few years ago, in partnership with other funders of eye research, we commissioned the James Lind Alliance to consult with blind and partially blind people and their carers on the top priorities for eye research in the UK. By asking the potential beneficiaries of research what were the problems they wanted solved, we identified a set of projects that we and others could potentially fund as part of a novel and impactful research agenda. One of the priorities for glaucoma was a simple question, 'How can eye drops be made easier to administer?'[111] Interestingly, this is a question that had not come up in any of the research grants we had funded and, indeed, is more likely to be answered by someone with an engineering, rather than biomedical, background.

[109] Lifshitz-Assaf, *et al.* (2013).

[110] Wilson, *et al.* (2015).

[111] Sight Loss and Vision Priority Setting Partnership (2013), p. 26.

New power research will use citizen science to support the collection and analysis of data

If open innovation uses crowdsourcing to solicit research questions and solutions from anyone willing to provide them, citizen science is a collaborative approach to engaging people to participate in the actual research process itself. There are two forms of citizen science – those projects that use people to collect data and those that are focused on the analysis of data.

The natural sciences have led the way with this innovation, especially in the field of ecology and environmental sciences. eBird[112] uses the knowledge and enthusiasm of birdwatchers worldwide to record the birds they see, contributing to research on conservation, the environment, migration patterns and population levels. As its website says, 'eBird began with a simple idea – that every birdwatcher has unique knowledge and experience. Our goal is to gather this information in the form of checklists of birds, archive it, and freely share it to power new data-driven approaches to science, conservation and education.' If you register on their website, or download the app, you can record the birds you have seen by submitting their names and uploading photos and sound recordings. By the end of 2019, 737 million bird observations had been made by half a million 'eBirders' (as they are called).[113] The website is run by the Cornell Lab of Ornithology, which was founded over 100 years ago and is part of Cornell University in the USA. The publications that have resulted from the data collected by this global community of bird watchers is impressive.[114] One study focuses on 'The expanding distribution of the Indian Peafowl (Pavo cristatus) as an indicator of changing climate in Kerala, southern India: A modelling study using MaxEnt'.[115]

Timms and Heimans also give another example of citizen science in the form of PatientsLikeMe. This is a social network of over 650,000 people living with 2,900 conditions, who have generated more than 43 million data points, creating an unprecedented source of real-world evidence that has led to over 100 research publications.[116] As well as pushing forward knowledge creation, the web platform

---

[112]   https://ebird.org/home.

[113]   https://ebird.org/news/ebird-2019-year-in-review.

[114]   https://ebird.org/science/publications.

[115]   Jose and Nameer (2020).

[116]   https://www.patientslikeme.com/about.

brings huge benefits to its users by connecting patients with similar conditions, so enabling them to provide one another with peer-to-peer advice and support and build global communities of practice around different diseases.

These examples generally use the crowd to collect data that is then analysed by researchers. Beyond this, citizen science can also use the power and knowledge of the crowd to do the analysis itself. In a review of citizen science projects, The Healthcare Improvement Studies (THIS) Institute in Cambridge, UK, highlighted four case studies. One of these was a series of projects sponsored by Cancer Research UK. In the first, Cell Slider, participants were asked to analyse images of breast tissue samples by categorising whether cells were cancerous or non-cancerous and estimating the levels of oestrogen receptors present in the cells. About 100,000 citizen scientists were involved in assessing 180,000 images. While the individual contributors proved accurate in the oestrogen receptor data, it turned out that they struggled with differentiating and accurately counting the cancerous cells. This led to a second project, Trailblazer, where training was provided to participants and the user interface was iteratively refined to ease classification. By the end of this project, the citizen scientists matched the professional scientists 90% of the time.

There can be legitimate concerns about the quality of data[117] that is collected through crowdsourcing and the population representativeness[118] of the citizen scientists themselves (and the biases their lived experience may bring to both data collection and analysis). As with all of these new power innovations, we have to exercise caution as time is needed to evaluate their effectiveness and learn what works and what does not work. Cancer Research UK did just such an evaluation, learning the importance of training and providing feedback to the volunteer citizen scientists. Given the waste we are seeing within professionalised, old-power science, this should not be used as a reason for not engaging people in the scientific process.

The results from new power research will be freely and openly available

Once research has been produced, maximising its impact requires it to be made widely available. Open access is an approach that ensures research results are made freely accessible to a wide audience, including citizen

---

[117] Lichten, *et al.* (2018).

[118] National Academies of Sciences, Engineering, and Medicine (2018).

scientists. The short history of the open access movement is nicely summarised by Glyn Moody in an online essay in 2016.[119] He opens with a quote from 1836, when Anthony Panizzi was giving evidence before a parliamentary committee in the UK. Panizzi was then an assistant librarian but went on to be the principal librarian at the British Museum. At the parliamentary committee, he said:

> **I want a poor student to have the same means of indulging his learned curiosity, of following his rational pursuits, of consulting the same authorities, of fathoming the most intricate inquiry as the richest man in the kingdom, as far as books go, and I contend that the government is bound to give him the most liberal and unlimited assistance in this respect.**

It took some 155 years before this vision began to be realised with the creation of the first 'pre-print' server, arXiv[120] (pronounced archive) by Paul Ginsparg, a professor of physics, computing and information science at Cornell University (interestingly, the same university where eBird was founded). arXiv is simply a server where physicists, mathematicians and researchers from other related fields can upload their papers without needing to pay or seek permission.

Ginsparg's idea was revolutionary as, not only did it initiate the move for the democratisation of research, making it available in digital formats and online, but it also began to challenge some of the roles and functions that scholarly publishers have traditionally provided. Furthermore, this would start to call into question the high profit margins being yielded by several dominant players in the scholarly publishing industry in their pursuit of the publication of research.[121] The emergence of the pre-print server by Ginsparg was, therefore, the spark that ignited the transformation of scholarly publishing.

Traditionally, the scholarly publishing industry provided a service that involved the certification, curation and quality assurance (including peer review), indexing and preservation of scholarly research coming from authors based in academia. Alongside the expanding opportunities presented by online and digital technology to share research, funders, led by the US National Institutes of Health (NIH) and the Wellcome Trust, started to make demands

---

[119] https://arstechnica.com/science/2016/06/what-is-open-access-free-sharing-of-all-human-knowledge/.

[120] https://arxiv.org.

[121] Larivière, *et al.* (2015).

upon their researchers and, in turn, scholarly publishers, that research funded through the public purse should be rapidly and openly accessible to all.[122] And so began the emergence of open access (OA) publishing, starting with the introduction of BioMed Central by Vitek Tracz in 2000,[123] and followed by the emergence of 'born OA' publishers, such as the Public Library of Science (PLOS). The OA policies of the NIH and Wellcome were swiftly followed by those of other public funders so that, by the late 2000s, the volume of research being published OA was growing significantly.

Nevertheless, achieving full OA to research output remains a challenge for several practical, cultural and political reasons.[124] Despite funding agency requirements for OA, and an increase in the number of publishing outlets offering authors a route to publish OA, while increasing year on year, the proportion of research articles being made OA globally each year is still only around 45%.[125] This is, in part, the result of the predominant model used by publishers to make research output OA – though an 'author' (or funder) pays article processing charges (APCs). The APC model can work well if, for example, research is grant-funded (where a research agency has committed to support OA) or the costs for publishing are included in a grant but work less well where research is done outside of a specific research grant (a common approach in the arts and humanities), or in a resource-poor environment. Thus, traditional journal publishing subscription models – where authors do not pay to publish but instead access and readership of the content is paid for through a subscription – remain commonplace and serve as a break on achieving OA for all. Additionally, many publishing companies have been accused of resisting the shift to OA models of funding as this may erode the significant revenues assured through a multitude of subscriptions to research institutions and organisations across the world.

However, in the last five years in particular, new players and partnerships continue to evolve the scholarly publishing landscape, changing the dynamic and presenting new opportunities for the delivery of OA and, more significantly, the ability and speed with which to access, use and reuse research.

---

[122] Fyfe, *et al.* (2017).

[123] https://www.biomedcentral.com/about/open-access.

[124] https://www.fosteropenscience.eu/content/challenges-and-strategies-success-open-science; https://www.universitiesuk.ac.uk/policy-and-analysis/reports/Documents/2017/monitoring-transition-open-access-2017.pdf.

[125] Piwowar, *et al.* (2018).

There has been an expansion in the number and use of pre-print servers created for different disciplinary areas, following arXiv – for example, for biology (bioRxiv[126]), for the earth sciences (EarthArXiv[127]) and for the health sciences (MedRxiv[128]).

Alternative approaches to paying for article OA, for example through library consortia instead of via research grants and APCs, have also been tried and tested, demonstrated by the Open Library of Humanities,[129] which was designed to deliver a cost-effective OA solution for arts and humanities research. There has been the emergence of OA book publishers, such as UCL Press which, in 2016, launched an OA book series. For authors who are not employed by University College London, you have to pay a book publishing charge of £5,000 for a book up to 100,000 words (which compares with article processing charges of around £1,500 for journal papers of around 5,000 words in length). So, while the concerns from the arts and humanities disciplines are legitimate, it is also likely that, with time, they will be addressed.

An increasing number of publishers and service providers are using technology to provide 'platform-based' publication venues as an alternative to journals. In 2013, F1000Research[130] launched what was 'the first open research publishing platform', which used a post-publication peer review model ('publish first, curate second'), effectively combining benefits of Ginsparg's vision of 'pre-printing' (providing rapid publication), with the quality assurance services traditionally provided by a journal (invited peer review), and all in near 'real time' and using fully open and transparent peer review. Furthermore, in a digital age, across many (if not all) disciplines, research output is increasingly not 'article shaped' and can be published in a variety of sizes, shapes and formats (for example data, software, images, videos), and uses digital object identifiers (DOIs) and other identifiers to support its discoverability, citation and persistence. Added to this, the recent trend towards enabling more open and collaborative ways of working, with its aim of accelerating knowledge production and impact, means that some of the established ways of 'doing', sharing and engaging with research are ripe for reinvention.

---

[126] https://www.biorxiv.org/.

[127] https://eartharxiv.org/.

[128] https://www.medrxiv.org/.

[129] https://www.openlibhums.org/.

[130] https://f1000research.com/.

Against the rise in alternative outlets for research output, many publicly funded research agencies have also become more strident in their requirements and provision for OA, most recently demonstrated by the formation of a funder alliance to drive OA through cOAlition S in 2018 and the creation of Plan S to set out the requirements and targets for OA research.[131] This places all research communication and scholarly publishing at a significant juncture. But, as the F1000 website states, 'Our vision is to create a world where scientific discoveries are shared quickly, openly and without barriers' – an excellent articulation of new power research.

New power research will be increasingly multidisciplinary

I am very aware that, so far in this chapter, I have drawn from my experience in biomedical and health research policy and have quietly ignored the arts and humanities and, to a lesser extent, the social sciences. This partly reflects my experience, but it is also the case that there is more data to interrogate when assessing the effectiveness and efficiency of biomedical and health research. This is partly because the outcome should be improved health, which is comparatively easier to measure than, say, the value of visiting a museum. That said, it is important to stress that the focus on open innovation, crowd sourcing, citizen science and open access should apply to all disciplines. Indeed, as we saw with the eye drops, and the boxed examples given earlier, benefits largely arise from research when disciplines come together.

Combined with the complex and often very 'human' nature of the challenges we face globally, now is surely the time for the humanities and social sciences to play a greater part in effecting change across the world. Although often presented as technological and scientific in nature, the challenges societies currently face can be addressed only through informed, inclusive and impactful humanities and social science research and scholarship. This is the case for the rise of anti-microbial resistance, adaptation to climate change,

---

[131] https://www.coalition-s.org/.

the changing nature of politics and political discourse, the opportunities of robotics and artificial intelligence, to name but a few.

In fact, this supposition is supported by the data. The complex array of lines in Figure 4.2 comes from a study I was involved in on the Research Excellence Framework (REF) and attempts to synthesise the main findings on impact from the 6,679 case studies referred to earlier.[132,133] We used text mining approaches to tag each case study as deriving from up to three, out of around 150, research fields. These disciplines are shown on the left-hand side of the figure. We then identified the impacts from each case study using an approach known as topic modelling, looking for clusters of similar words and word patterns in the text. We identified 60 types of social impact that are on the right-hand side of the figure. Each case study was again tagged with up to three social impacts. The lines are 'pinched' in the middle so you can see how the different fields flow into different social impacts. The top cluster of lines is the biomedical and health research, the next cluster the physical and engineering sciences, followed by the social sciences and the arts and humanities in the bottom grouping.

What do we see? First, there are 3,709 unique lines linking the left-hand research fields with the right-hand social impacts. This means that each 'pathway' to impact is hugely variable, indeed, almost bespoke, case by case. Second, 87% of the case studies are based on more than one research field, meaning that the benefits of research arise when it is multidisciplinary. This latter lesson is a critically important observation. It means that, if universities are to solve the sort of problems that crowdsourced research questions identify, they will need to organise themselves in new ways that are not driven by internal 'supply side' disciplinary structures but are, instead, aligned with external 'demand side' solutions. Ensuring that the beneficiaries of research are involved in shaping the research agenda could well mean that publicly funded research is increasingly invested in universities that are not only focused on impact but are also open to new ways of harnessing the power of individuals, communities and businesses to deliver this impact.

---

[132] King's College London and Digital Science (2015).

[133] I am using this data as it is the only dataset of its kind in the world but, in doing so, I am reasonably confident the lessons from it are transferable.

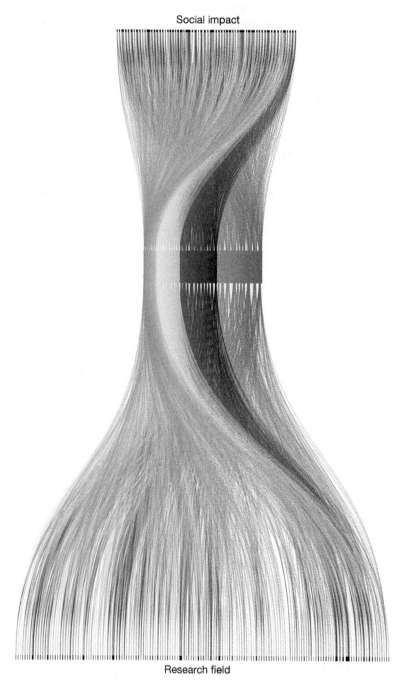

Social impact

Research field

Figure 4.2 Alluvial diagram linking underpinning research with impact topics[134]

[134] King's College London and Digital Science (2015), p. 39.

Chapter 5

The social responsibility of the New Power University

The New Power University will include social responsibility as a core and equal part of its academic mission

A few years ago, a friend told me the story of an aluminium smelter located in Mozal, Mozambique. The smelter was owned by BHP Billiton and was losing money. The company wanted to understand why this was the case, especially as they had made a significant investment of over US$2 billion in the plant. On investigation, it turned out that the low levels of productivity resulted from high rates of absenteeism in the workforce caused by the endemic levels of malaria in Mozal. In response, BHP Billiton implemented an anti-malaria programme. With education, spraying and the provision of bed nets, adult malaria infection rates fell significantly and community health improved. In turn, absenteeism in the work force dropped and productivity rose, such that the improved profitability from this initiative outweighed the costs.[135,136] In other words, the anti-malaria programme generated a positive return: the community and the company both gained measurable benefit as well as immeasurable ones.

---

[135] https://hbr.org/2013/12/the-big-trends-changing-community-development; https://hbr.org/2012/06/why-go-it-alone-in-community-d.

[136] For more detail, see: https://www.bhp.com/media/bhp/documents/investors/reports/2004/norvatis-presentation.pdf; https://hbr.org/2012/06/why-go-it-alone-in-community-d; https://hbr.org/2013/12/the-big-trends-changing-community-development.

The idea that the corporate sector can deliver social good is a topic that has gained increasing attention of late. The *Financial Times* noted in 2019 that, 'There is a growing acceptance among business leaders of the need to broaden the pursuit of shareholder value to one that is based on inclusivity, sustainability and purpose.'[137] As my King's colleague Robyn Klingler-Vidra put it in a recent piece for *The Economist*, 'Businesses around the world . . . increasingly assert their intention to deliver positive environmental and social impact. We are bombarded with headlines about companies wanting to "do good by doing well" and to achieve "profit with purpose". In particular, business leaders speak of, and report on, their organisation's 'social impact'. It seems everyone wants to make a (positive) social impact.'[138] She goes on to note that, 'The wider business community (particularly with the advent of Michael Porter's "Shared Value" approach) spoke of the social good that comes from corporate activities, be it for local communities, for employees or the environment.'

Mark Kramer and Michael Porter's 2011 article 'Creating shared value, how to reinvent capitalism and unleash a wave of innovation and growth',[139] challenged the prevailing notion of corporate social responsibility (CSR). Historically, businesses used CSR as the vehicle to achieve 'social impact', but this was generally marginalised, often appearing, at best, a form of corporate philanthropy where pre-tax profits are given back to social causes with little or no expectation of a return or, at worst, an exercise in enhanced public relations, to detract attention from genuine issues of social or environmental abuse or neglect.

Kramer and Porter instead put forward the idea of creating 'shared value' as a way for businesses to enhance their profitability while, at the same time, communities benefit from the corporate activity. BHP Billiton's anti-malaria programme in Mozal is such an example. Core to their argument is the proposition that businesses were in danger of losing their licence to operate (their 'social contract', in the language of universities) and that the purpose of corporations had to include social as well as economic good. This, they argued, is different from CSR, which is 'a reaction to external pressures [which] have largely emerged to improve firms' reputations and are treated as a necessary expense'. By contrast, shared value is a set of 'policies and operating practices that enhance the competitiveness of a company while simultaneously advancing the economic and social conditions in the communities in which it operates'.

---

[137] https://www.ft.com/content/8a719968-f666-11e9-a79c-bc9acae3b654.

[138] https://eiuperspectives.economist.com/sustainability/social-impact-what-does-it-mean-and-how-should-we-measure-it.

[139] Kramer and Porter (2011).

In making this argument, it is important not to over-emphasise the impact shared value has had on the private sector; critics will argue that a lot of this is still window dressing, using new business jargon, and that genuine shared value is rare. Nevertheless, this shift from CSR to shared value in the private sector mirrors the shift that universities need to make from 'public engagement' to 'social responsibility'.[140] For too long, public engagement (or just simply engagement) has been seen as an 'add-on' or 'nice to have' for universities. Put more negatively, it is not thought of as 'core business'. But social responsibility should be central to the mission of a New Power University and deserves to be on an equal footing to education and research. To repeat the previously quoted assertion by Amy Gutmann in updating the Penn Compact, 'A university is, first and foremost, a social undertaking to create a social good.'[141]

As I'll explore, this centrality of social responsibility, first apparent in the founding of the land grant and redbrick universities of the 19th century, is being rediscovered among the 'civic' and 'permeable' universities of the 21st century. These institutions, as well as in places like King's, my own university, are now seeking to adapt internal policies and practices to be aligned to this ethos and for social responsibility to be at the heart of the New Power University's academic mission.

Social responsibility is emerging as a central mission for universities, rediscovered by some and new to others

On suggesting recently that social responsibility was a new mission for universities, a colleague pointed out that the majority of universities were founded on such a mission. This prompted me to explore whether this was the case and I hired a King's student to help me with the data collection and analysis. We took the top 71 universities in the *THE* World University Rankings 2018 (as Boston University and Ohio State University were tied for 70th place) and looked at whether their founding or current mission statements made a broad reference to social responsibility.[142] From this, we identified founding statements for 42 of the 71 universities and, of these, 7 (17%) made an unconditional commitment to social responsibility, 14 (33%) a conditional commitment and 21 (50%) no commitment (see Figure 5.1).

---

[140] This is an argument that I originally made with my colleague, Deborah Bull, on Wonkhe, a higher education blog, in 2019. See: https://wonkhe.com/blogs/whats-wrong-with-public-engagement/.

[141] https://president.upenn.edu/penn-compact/impact.

[142] https://wonkhe.com/blogs/mission-possible-in-search-of-service/.

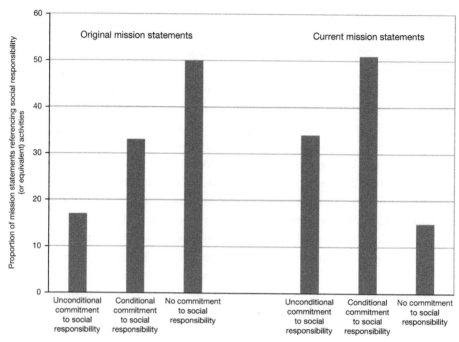

Figure 5.1 Leading universities' commitment to social responsibility (as mentioned in mission statements)

We defined a conditional commitment as occurring when social responsibility was delivered through education or research, and an unconditional commitment as occurring in its own right, that is in addition to education and research. For today's mission statements, we managed to collect data for 67 out of 71 universities. Of these, 23 (34%) made an unconditional commitment, 44 (51%) a conditional commitment and 10 (15%) no commitment at all.

From these data come three observations. First, the proportion of top-ranking universities that have an unconditional commitment to social responsibility is low, both historically (17%) and today (34%). So, for this group, the hypothesis that most are reaffirming their public purpose does not stack up. Second, the increase in unconditional commitments combined with the decline in those with no commitment suggests that social responsibility as a mission is increasingly being acknowledged and adopted by top-ranking universities (albeit from a low base). Finally, and perhaps worryingly, half of the top-ranking universities consider that their social responsibility mission is not a mission in its own right but is, instead, delivered through what they do with respect to education and research.

Despite these findings – which, it should be stressed, are based on the top 71[143] out the c. 25,000 universities globally, of which just over 1,000 are ranked by *THE* and only look at stated rather than actual intentions – there are numerous cases of universities taking an institutional-wide commitment to social responsibility. In David Watson and colleagues' excellent 2011 edited volume *The Engaged University*, over 20 such examples are examined ('profiles', as he calls them) drawn from Asia, Latin America, Africa, Europe, Middle East, Australia and the USA. One example is from the University of Haifa in Israel where social responsibility was incorporated into the university's mission in 2005 by its then president, Aaron Ben-Ze'ev, 'who decided to place additional strategic emphasis on the broad theme of social responsibility'.[144] Today, the university describes itself as 'one of Israel's leading research universities, and it is dedicated not only to academic excellence but to social responsibility as well'.[145]

On the other side of the world, the Tecnológico de Monterrey in Mexico (also known as Monterrey Institute of Technology) is a private non-profit institute founded in 1943 by a group of Mexican businessmen with a commitment to social development and innovation.[146] This commitment is alive and kicking today, providing fabulous examples of social responsibility such as Prepanet, an online high school established by the university in 2004.[147] In a society where many students do not have access to formal high school because of economic, social or geographic disadvantage, Prepanet aims to provide accessible and flexible education to young people across Mexico. It costs less than 5% of the total cost of the traditional high school system and is run mainly by Tecnológico de Monterrey students, who serve as tutors.[148]

Both the universities of Haifa and Tecnológico de Monterrey are members of the Talloires Network, which brings together universities globally that are committed to their civic roles and social responsibility.[149] A browse of their website reaffirms the impression that you get from reading *The Engaged University* – universities around the world are doing amazing things to support local communities and to deliver on their social responsibilities.

---

[143] 71, as 2 were tied and we originally wanted to look at the top 70.

[144] Watson, *et al.* (2011), p. 75.

[145] https://www.haifainternational.com.

[146] Watson, *et al.* (2011), p. 102.

[147] http://sitios.itesm.mx/prepanet/.

[148] Douglas, *et al.* (2020).

[149] https://talloiresnetwork.tufts.edu/who-we-are/.

The challenge, though, is that these universities are still a minority in placing social responsibility at the heart of their mission, with parity to education and research. Moreover, where there are good examples, the university sector as a whole fails to communicate the impact of these social goods in ways that combat the often-negative perception of the contributions that universities make to society today.

This soul searching has prompted a number of recent reports exploring and advocating universities' social responsibility. In the UK, key among these would be 'Truly Civic' (2019), from the Civic University Commission, and 'The Permeable University' (2019). For example, in 'The Permeable University', Mary Stuart and Liz Shutt of the University of Lincoln argue 'That institutions in the 21st century will need to embrace a more fluid, more contingent and more permeable relationship to wider society than ever before, precisely because of the complexity, interrelationships and unpredictability of our times . . . The permeable university seeks to remove barriers and blocks to interaction, both within the institution and all around it.'[150] Meanwhile, Lord Kerslake, in the foreword of 'Truly Civic', noted that, 'While universities are vital to their places, they also need the active support of their communities in these turbulent and challenging times.'[151] However, as noted in Chapter 2, these ideas are not new – John Goddard, while at the University of Newcastle, UK, was a passionate advocate of the civic university, as captured in his 2009 Nesta pamphlet, 'Re-inventing the civic university'.[152]

King's College London adopted 'Service' as its way of delivering social responsibility within its academic mission

The global movement towards greater social responsibility of universities impacted on King's College London when, in 2016, I was asked by Ed Byrne – the president and principal of King's – to 'hold the pen' in developing a new strategy for the institution. As already noted, King's is an archetype of an old power university. Sitting on the banks of the Thames, in grand buildings, it was founded nearly 200 years ago by King George IV and the Duke of Wellington in the tradition of the Church of England.

---

[150] Stuart and Shutt (2019), p. 16.

[151] Civic University Commission (2019), p. 4.

[152] Goddard (2009).

However, King's is also a surprisingly progressive university. In the mid-19th century, it led the UK in widening access to higher education by providing degree-level study through evening classes at heavily subsidised rates. As Charles Dickens commented in 1858:

It was an opening not only of college doors, but of doors into higher life for hundreds of men who have since shown how prompt and how able they were to pass over the threshold when the bolts were once drawn.[153]

It is this ethos that resonated throughout the strategy workshops we hosted in the first half of 2016, seeking the views of students, staff and alumni on the future direction of King's. In developing a new strategy for King's, we adopted a new power approach – a meaningful, innovative and creative listening exercise – building on the old power of an established and venerable institution that can be traced back to Dickens' time and beyond. A standout from this process was how the phrase 'in service of society' was mentioned in all of the 25 workshops we ran as part of a consultation exercise. The line itself was inspired by the 'College Prayer'[154] and emerged in the 1990s during an earlier visioning exercise. Since then, it has been widely adopted as an informal motto. Given the passion and unanimity with which this sentiment was raised, we proposed that 'Service' be placed alongside education and research as part of King's academic mission. This was quite a radical proposition but one that was welcomed and adopted by colleagues.

I subsequently went on to be responsible for developing and implementing this element of King's mission. I mention this as it marks the beginning of my engagement with a number of the ideas explored in this book and, in particular, the need for universities to see social responsibility as a core and equal part of their academic mission – to repeat again Amy Gutmann's words, 'a social undertaking to create a social good'.

At King's, Service is how we describe this commitment to creating social good. We operationalise Service using the acronym SERVE, where S stands for social reform, E for educational experience, R for research impact, V for volunteering and the second E for environmental sustainability. Education and research were deliberately included as we wanted the three elements of the academic mission – education, research and service – to interact with each other. In the New Power University, the sweet spot is where these things come together rather than working in silos.

---

[153] Dickens (1858), p. 58, quoted in Hearnshaw (1929), p. 256.

[154] https://www.kcl.ac.uk/aboutkings/principal/dean/chaplaincy/prayeratkings/collegeprayer.

In developing a framework for delivering the Service strategic priority, we explicitly adopted the language and approach used by social movements. There is always a tension between taking a planned, centralised and led approach or, alternatively, using a devolved, localised and empowered way to build engagement. The idea of a movement attempts to resolve that tension by capturing and building on the grass-roots enthusiasm and commitment to Service that has always been so evident at King's. While movements are strategic, they require different framing than top-down, goal-led initiatives and we gave people 'permission to dance' (using Derek Sivers' TED talk metaphor) putting in place policies, procedures and practices that encourage students, staff and alumni to develop and build their own Service ideas. As these ideas began to take root, we saw others copying them – either by joining existing projects or starting up their own. Some of these are shown in Table 5.1. This helped build momentum in the social movement around Service.

Table 5.1 Examples of being socially responsible from King's Service strategy

S *Social reform*	The **King's Maths School** was founded in 2014 as a free sixth form specialising in mathematics and sponsored by King's College London. The King's Maths School is for students with a particular aptitude and enthusiasm for mathematics and aims to widen participation in mathematical degrees and careers at the very best universities and institutions. 40% of the King's Maths School's intake come from financially challenging backgrounds and, in 2018, 47% of the intake were female, thereby challenging the under-representation of women in STEM. For the last few years, the King's Maths School has had the best A-level results in the UK, seeing the majority of its students progressing to some of the best universities in the world.
E *Educational experience*	**Philosophy in Prisons** is a student-led initiative run with the support of the King's Philosophy Department to provide a philosophy course at Belmarsh Prison. In 2016, the King's Department of Philosophy piloted an eight-week philosophy course for prisoners at HMP Belmarsh in southeast London. Participation on the course was voluntary and averaged at 90% with a 0% dropout rate. The course was designed to be accessible to participants with a broad range of educational backgrounds. While 40% of the cohort had undertaken some form of higher education, 30% had either finished formal education at school or had no formal qualifications whatsoever. Since then, three further courses have been delivered with the support of the Faculty of Arts and Humanities, The Evan Cornish Foundation and The Philosophy Foundation. A course has also been developed specifically for learners with English as a second language.

R Research impact	Ambulances aim to get to emergency medical situations quickly to provide care and save lives. Complicated decisions need to be made rapidly about which ambulance should respond to each incident, under dynamic conditions of uncertainty. The **Data Awareness for Sending Help (DASH)** project explores the potential impact of integrating new and emerging data sources on emergency response and wider policy. This new data includes traffic conditions, air pollution and population mobility, which could be considered to better inform decisions about ambulance dispatch, with the long-term goal of reducing response times. Researchers in the DASH project have reported that sharing this data could be crucial for ambulances to respond more quickly in life or death situations. In December 2018, the London Assembly Health Committee recommended that the Mayor should make the DASH project's suggested new data initiatives a focus of renewed efforts to support the London Ambulance Service.
V Volunteering	In November 2019, King's took part in *Wrap Up London*, the annual coat collection created by charity Hands On London, with hundreds of staff and students donating their winter wear. Since the first Wrap Up London in 2011, the campaign has collected and distributed 137,980 warm coats to local community groups which offer direct support to the homeless, refugees, children in poverty, the elderly and people fleeing domestic violence. King's volunteers delivered 25 giant Wrap Up London sacks to the King's Cross Safestore location, ready to be redistributed by Hands on London to local community groups. The volunteers also collected over five large sacks of warm clothes and passed them on to the Chaplaincy's clothes collection for The Manna Centre at London Bridge.
E Environmental sustainability	**King's has made a commitment to be zero carbon by 2025.** King's has successfully decoupled carbon emissions and growth and has cut its emissions by 30% since 2005–6. The university aims to cut its carbon emissions by 43% compared to a 2005–6 baseline by 2020, and to have net zero carbon emissions by 2025. To achieve these ambitious targets, King's continues to invest in onsite renewables, such as solar panels, as well as low-carbon, energy efficiency and behaviour change projects across its estate. Since October 2017, all electricity procured by King's comes from certified clean renewable energy sources. King's has also pledged to divest from all fossil fuels by the end of 2022, and to increase its investments with socially responsible benefits to 40% by 2025.

In all of this, we were heavily influenced by the work of Marshall Ganz, who drew on his experience in organising and documenting the power of social movements to develop a framework for social action based around the *heart* (narrative), the *head* (strategy), and the *hands* (action).[155] We told the stories of what was happening at King's, linking that to our overall strategy and the strategic priority of Service, and provided support to enable people to engage with the movement, if they so wished.

This approach has led to a massive diversity of impactful projects which go beyond what you would traditionally expect of an old power university like King's. In addition to being able to say that we were delivering King's Service mission, we found that the approach helped to shape the culture at King's, contributing to student and staff pride in the institution. An interesting unexpected benefit is that we found this pride and commitment was especially evident with our professional staff. My explanation for this was that Service was a direct way these colleagues could contribute to King's academic mission. In addition to these internal benefits, we received external validation, being ranked fifth in the inaugural THE Impact Ranking and receiving a THE award in 2019.

Looking to the future, the challenge will be to continue to embed Service as part of King's academic mission, ensuring a parity of esteem with education and research. This requires continued changes in processes for reward and recognition of all staff – for example in promotion criteria and personal development plans – and the embedding of a 'service culture' within the curriculum so that King's 'graduates are distinguished not just by their knowledge but by their wisdom, character, service ethic and global mindset'.[156]

The social good of the New Power University is delivered through its institutional being

The principle of 'do no harm' is often associated with medical ethics but has increasingly been used in the humanitarian context and could sensibly be applied to universities. As already discussed, the fact that universities were harming their lowest paid staff through shoddy outsourcing practices and by not paying a living wage is, in itself, shameful. Indeed, at King's, as an early part of our Service strategy, we accredited ourselves with the Living Wage Foundation and insourced our cleaning and security services. But universities

---

[155] Ganz (2010).

[156] King's College London (2018), p. 5.

also do harm indirectly – and, perhaps, unwittingly – through their endowment investments in, say, mining or defence companies and by contributing to the climate crisis through international travel. The first step in incorporating social responsibility into a New Power University's academic mission is to get your own house in order. The second step is to then use your assets – procurement, places and people – to 'do good' through, for example, purchasing policies. In this section, I will explore these two strategic imperatives, which are different sides of the same coin, that can be surmised as the 'institutional being' of the New Power University.

See no evil, hear no evil, speak no evil . . .

In the West, the 17th Japanese proverb 'see no evil, hear no evil, speak no evil' has erroneously come to mean turning a blind eye to something that is legally or morally wrong. The proverb, derived from a carving on a shrine in Japan that depicts three monkeys, covering their eyes, ears and mouth (see Figure 5.2), is actually thought to be inspired by Confucius having said: 'Look not at what is contrary to propriety; listen not to what is contrary to propriety; speak not what is contrary to propriety; make no movement which is contrary to propriety.'[157]

In addition to outsourcing and not paying a living wage, old power universities are guilty of being 'contrary to propriety' in a number of other areas. A really interesting example is the impact of international travel on the climate. Milena Buchs, an associate professor at the University of Leeds in the UK, has estimated that the carbon footprint from academic travel in the UK is over 1 million tonnes of CO_2 emissions per year. Scaled up internationally, that is 184m tonnes of CO_2 globally, nearly half of the UK's total CO_2 emission in 2017.[158] If, like me, you can't really get your head around the numbers, this is equivalent to driving around the world in a (petrol) car 15 million times. To offset the environmental impact would require growing 3 billion trees.[159] Even worse, as Buch points out, this does not include student travel, which for the UK could add another 2 million tonnes per year.

The challenge for the New Power University is that academic travel, often long-distance by air, is core to the current operational model of higher

---

[157] https://grammarist.com/proverb/see-no-evil-hear-no-evil-speak-no-evil/.

[158] https://theconversation.com/university-sector-must-tackle-air-travel-emissions-118929.

[159] See https://www.epa.gov/energy/greenhouse-gas-equivalencies-calculator for an equivalence calculator. The estimate of the number of trips around the world is my calculation based on the circumference of the earth of 29,901 miles.

Figure 5.2 Carving from above the door in Tōshō-gū shrine in Nikkō
Source: Moshe Torgovitsky/Alamy Stock Photo

education. Such travel has been considered important for professional esteem as academic excellence is frequently linked to building a nationally and internationally recognised reputation.[160] The ability to present at, and attend, conferences enables academics to develop connections and build a valuable network for future collaboration. As Buchs notes, 'International recognition forms an important criterion for academic job descriptions and promotions, and universities increasingly benefit from international student fees and international research funding.' Of course, international travel is only one part of the impact that universities are currently having on the climate crisis. Universities – like all of us – are also consumers of energy and food, as well as generating waste through their day-to-day operations. But international travel is a particular totem of the negative impact that universities have on the climate.

A related area where universities have acted 'contrary to propriety' is the way they, historically, have managed their endowment investments. In the UK, the National Union of Students (NUS) has been running a campaign with People & Planet,[161] a student network promoting social and environmental justice, to persuade universities to divest their endowments from fossil fuel companies (and then to reinvest into socially responsible companies).

---

[160] International travel may also be related to an academic discipline, such as international development, where it is important to ensure that unconscious biases are not occurring in assuming how other regions of the world are operating and thinking.

[161] https://peopleandplanet.org/about/about-us.

In January 2020, they had persuaded half of all universities to withdraw their investments from these sorts of businesses.[162] It remains to be seen if other universities will commit to use their wealth in this way, although it is worth acknowledging that the higher education sector is leading the way in divestment compared to large institutional investors in the UK. In Australia, such divestments are not without their critics. For example, in 2014, when the Australian National University decided to divest from a number of fossil fuel companies, the then treasurer of Australia (and now its ambassador to the USA), Joe Hockey, said:

> I would suggest they're removed from the reality of what is helping to drive the Australian economy and create more employment . . . Sometimes the view looks different from the lofty rooms of a university.[163]

'Do well by doing good'

I have highlighted three examples – employment conditions for low-paid workers, international academic travel and investment policies – where universities are wittingly or unwittingly doing harm. It should be stressed, however, that there are also outstanding examples of where universities are 'doing good'. The phrase 'do well by doing good' is often attributed to the founder of the University of Pennsylvania, Benjamin Franklin (which sharp readers will note is the same institution where Amy Gutmann presides). As noted above, some of these examples of 'doing good' are the flip side of the harms that I have already identified. Some universities have pledged to become carbon neutral and have implemented policies, such as taking meat off catering menus, to support that.[164] Others have directed their investment policies to support socially responsible enterprises[165] or reverted their bad practices by insourcing cleaners and paying a living wage.[166] All of these initiatives should be welcome and celebrated.

---

[162] https://www.theguardian.com/environment/2020/jan/13/half-of-uk-universities-have-committed-to-divest-from-fossil-fuel.

[163] https://www.theguardian.com/australia-news/2014/oct/13/coalition-accused-of-bullying-anu-after-criticism-of-fossil-fuel-divestment.

[164] https://www.theguardian.com/environment/2019/aug/12/goldsmiths-bans-beef-from-university-cafes-to-tackle-climate-crisis.

[165] https://www.ed.ac.uk/sustainability/what-we-do/responsible-investment/policy/positive-investment-and-social-finance.

[166] https://twitter.com/LivingWageUK/status/1161910398305656832.

Universities can further use their institutional being to achieve social impact with respect to procurement, places and people. An excellent example of using procurement for doing good comes from The University of Manchester, in the UK. Here, the university incorporated social responsibility as part of its academic mission in 2011 and was recognised by coming top in Europe and third in the world in the THE 2019 Impact Ranking. When visiting in 2019, I was deeply impressed not only by the breadth of activities the university was engaged with but also their depth. One particular programme stood out for me and it was The Works,[167] which has supported more than 4,000 local people into work since its inception in 2011. Beginning in a housing trust building in Moss Side, it later moved to an adjacent ward in a Salvation Army building in Ardwick (a socially and economically disadvantaged inner-city community) situated opposite the university. Run in partnership with Greater Manchester's Growth Company, The Works is a 'one-stop shop' facility based in a local community setting, providing thousands of people with ring-fenced access to training, advice and job opportunities – both at The University of Manchester and with a host of other partner employers such as constructors Balfour Beatty.

I mention Balfour Beatty as, a few years ago, they were awarded a £230 million contract to build a new engineering campus. In the procurement process for this contract, potential companies were asked how they would support The University of Manchester's commitment to social responsibility. Balfour Beatty offered to provide some funding for The Works but, critically, also offered to provide employment opportunities on the construction site. I was given a tour of the site and was so impressed with a photo montage of portraits of about 40 people who had come from The Works, obtained an apprenticeship with Balfour Beatty and were now working on the construction site. The symbolism of walking across Oxford Road, from The Works to the engineering campus, captured the transformative journey these individuals had been on and how that transformation came from an innovative partnership between a university and a company, both parties using the procurement process as an instrument for creating social good.

The Works example also shows how space can be used to 'do well by doing good' and universities can use their estates in a variety of ways to support local communities. The obvious examples are galleries and sporting

---

[167] https://www.manchester.ac.uk/connect/jobs/equality-diversity-inclusion/the-works/.

facilities, which many universities open up to the general public. Other innovations include Widener University, in Chester, Pennsylvania, USA, where, as we saw in Chapter 2, the university had used its assets to create spaces through a new school and a physiotherapy clinic, to name a few. Of course, the nature and characteristics of the estate dictate the sort of good it can do. For campus universities that are located in rural or semi-rural locations, their connectivity is less obvious than for city-based universities – whether based in an urban campus or scattered across the city. The University of Melbourne, Australia, is a good example of a city-based campus university. Located to the north of the central business district, the university has been working hard both to open up its public realm and to integrate within Melbourne Innovation District[168] alongside RMIT University and the City of Melbourne.

The final 'p' is for people. There are over 250 million students worldwide and, with a student staff ratio of 1:25, an estimated 10 million academics and probably another 10 million professional staff. The collective power of people associated with higher education consequently amounts to some 270 million people. Consider the impact if each of those 270 million people committed to 1 or 2 days a year of voluntary activity to further the social purpose of higher education. To make that happen, universities need to consciously put in place policies and procedures to support such activity. For example, the University of Technology Sydney (UTS) has just launched 'Social Justice Leave', which is offered as part of the UTS Community Leave entitlements with staff provided with five days' additional leave to support the delivery of its Social Impact Framework.[169] But this idea is not new. Tom Levitt (a former UK MP) notes in his book, *Welcome to GoodCo: Using the Tools of Business to Create Public Good,* that Boots the Chemist required a 'senior manager to spend 3 days a year working in a shop and allowing every member of staff 3 days leave a year to volunteer for a good cause'. This, he concluded, 'led to high levels of employee satisfaction and retention: one member of staff in three has been with the company for 10 years or more, and the company has a top 25 ranking in the *Sunday Times* "Best Big Company to Work For" list . . . Customer satisfaction is also excellent, explaining Boots' consistently high ranking on UK surveys of brand reputation and consumer trust.'[170]

---

[168] https://mid.org.au.

[169] https://www.uts.edu.au/node/311731/uts-social-impact-framework.

[170] Levitt (2015), p. 195.

Delivering social good directly through the academic mission

Not doing harm and using the assets of the university to do good are the basic requirements for an institution to consider itself to be a New Power University. But this is not enough. The New Power University then needs to positively assert its social purpose through learning, through research and through being socially responsible. In doing so, social responsibility becomes a core element of the New Power University's academic mission, in the same way that shared value is integrated into the business practice of corporations.

New power learning will include curriculum reform both to decolonise content and to ensure that students are 'world ready' through service-learning. New power research is focused on delivering solutions to the problems people face through open and transparent engagement with citizens. Both these pathways help deliver social responsibility but are not sufficient in their own right. In the New Power University, social responsibility needs to be an explicit mission, supporting projects that are above and beyond what you would expect of an (old power) university.

Some examples have already been cited, including Prepanet in Mexico and the King's Maths School in London. A further example is PADILEIA, an online education resource for refugee students in the Middle East. PADILEIA stands for a Partnership for Digital Learning and Increased Access. It is a collaboration between Al al-Bayt University in Jordan, the American University of Beirut in Lebanon and King's College London, as well as Kiron Open Higher Education (a digital-education NGO) and FutureLearn (a leader in online learning). Funded through a UK Department for International Development (DFID) grant, PADILEIA aims to increase access to higher education for refugee and disadvantaged host communities in Jordan and Lebanon. PADILEIA provides online and blended education to displaced individuals living in Jordan and Lebanon. The PADILEIA partnership also runs two eight-month foundation programmes in Jordan and Lebanon for over one hundred students a year, led by the American University of Beirut and Al al-Bayt University, alongside custom-made online study programs using massive open online courses (MOOCs) and blended activities run by Kiron. At the time of writing, just under 100,000 learners had registered to take up short courses worldwide, with nearly 1,000 self-identifying refugees completing courses in English and healthcare. Nearly 200 students had completed the foundation of which 31 students now have either employment or scholarships at local universities, which may sound a low number but, given the context and challenges these refugee students face, I think it is extraordinary. Put simply, 31 young people have had their lives transformed by this programme.

For me, the acid test of whether these extraordinary initiatives can be described as new power is whether they are delivering social goods that would not have been pursued based on the old power articulation of a university. King's did not need to set up a Maths School or partner in the PADILEIA project. Monterey need not have set up Prepanet. Widener did not have to found a school or physiotherapy clinic. But, in all these cases, the institution – and, critically, the individuals that make up the institution – have decided to use their assets (intellectual, financial, physical) to create a social good that goes beyond the traditional old power articulation of a university's mission – that of education and research.

Some people reject this thesis and argue that universities are entering the domain of social services. They warn that this mission creep dilutes the educational and research impact of universities. A more nuanced view comes from Collini in his book *What Are Universities For?* He notes 'The longstanding tension between serving a variety of social needs and being in some way withdrawn from society, even offering a form of resistance to the dominant values and practices of that society.'[171] The challenge for the New Power University is to manage this tension, requiring a degree of political sophistication in how universities operate, a competency that is often lacking in university leadership and which I'll return to later. Nevertheless, successfully navigating these complexities is the defining and differentiating characteristic of the New Power University.

Contemporary ideas on place will need to evolve as the New Power University delivers social good as part of its academic mission

Central to much of the literature on social responsibility of universities is the idea of place. Concepts and phrases such as 'place making' and 'anchor institution' are scattered throughout the many reports and papers I have referred to in this chapter, with the core argument being that universities, as civic institutions, have a unique responsibility to the geographical regions within

---

[171] Collini (2012), p. 25.

which they reside. This is a powerful argument but, based on the ideas discussed so far in this book, it may not be the entire story for the future New Power University. As you engage with the ideas of social movements and social media connectivity, this brings to the forefront a number of alternative ways of understanding the concept of 'place'.

First, the New Power University will need to be 'anchored' simultaneously to both local and international communities and take on both a physical and a virtual form. Consider, if you like, the new power student in Jordan studying English through the PADILEIA programme. The content of that course is provided by colleagues based at King's in London. So, is the 'anchor' in Jordan or in London? Or take the eBird website, with 500,000 eBirders worldwide providing data to a US-based university in New York. Is the 'anchor' where the bird observation is made or in New York? Or the geographical location of the research setting or the location of the actual researchers (such as Kerala, South India, as is the case for the paper on Indian Peafowl cited in Chapter 4).

Deborah Bull of King's recently challenged the idea of an 'anchor', arguing it was an unhelpful concept. She noted, 'Anchor characteristics – immobility and permeance – can also be seen as inflexible and hierarchical, especially in the age when useful knowledge is frequently co-produced with the many stakeholder communities that surround the university.'[172] She goes on to note, 'Anchor institutions are revisiting the idea of the civic university as a better way of articulating their role in ensuring that cities – and the communities that live in them – thrive.' But the challenge for the New Power University is that those communities may not actually reside in the same place as the civic university. They may reside physically elsewhere – potentially tens of thousands of miles away – and they may reside virtually.

---

[172] https://www.kcl.ac.uk/london-needs-a-civic-heart.

Part Three

People, power and voice

When the whole world is silent, even one voice becomes powerful.
Malala Yousafzai, Gen Z student and education campaigner

New power is about people – how they relate, how they connect and how they come together to create social change. The New Power University is made from three constituencies of people: the students, the staff and the community within which it resides, physically and virtually.

It is through understanding these groups of people, their motivations, concerns and ambitions, that their individual and collective power and voice can be mobilised to shape both the social purpose of the New Power University and wider society.

But to deliver on that social purpose, the New Power University will need to listen and think carefully about its relationship with students, staff and communities. It will be transformed through this listening, exploring new ways of organising itself – some radical and controversial – as well as adopting a range of novel practices, including shorter-term conditional affiliations, open and transparent collaboration and participation, and a degree of self-organisation and a 'maker culture': all shaped by the people who make up the New Power University.

Chapter 6

New power Gen Z students

New power Gen Z students are change makers who will help take the world into a less ideological and more humanitarian era

Like every generation, today's students have their own set of values and lived experiences that shape their expectations of a university education. Unlike other generations, though, they are coming to that education at an historically rare 'in-between time', such that their attitudes, behaviours and ways of seeing the world are likely to have an unusually profound effect on the social purpose of the New Power University.

Generation Z – usually shortened to Gen Z – is a term that has been adopted by demographers to denote anyone born between 1995 and 2012, so aged between 8 and 25 years old in 2020. The so-called Millennials were born between 1980 and 1994 (aged 26–40 in 2020), Gen X between 1965 and 1979 (aged 41–55 in 2020) and the Boomers generation between 1946 and 1964 (aged 56–74 in 2020). This makes me and my partner Gen X-ers and our two children Gen Z-ers.[173]

---

[173] Some commentators use the term iGen instead of Gen Z and have slightly different views on the date boundaries but, for the purpose of this chapter, we will use these definitions.

When you examine the data, it is clear that Gen Z, taken as a whole, are better behaved, safer and more socially active than their predecessors but, at the same time, seem more vulnerable than the Millennials with higher rates of depression, self-harm and suicide.[174] Ipsos MORI, the market research company, explores some of these issues in its 2018 report *Beyond Binary*, which is based on survey data synthesised from a number of countries worldwide.[175] This shows a number of clear differences between Gen Z and the immediately preceding Millennials generation (see Figure 6.1).

There are declines in youth crime, smoking, sexual activity and drinking, with half as many Gen Z teenagers trying alcoholic drinks compared with Millennials. There is a clear shift towards higher participation in social

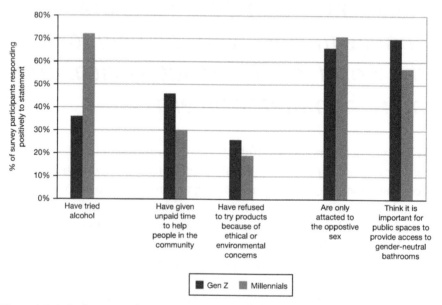

Figure 6.1 Behavioural and attitudinal differences between Gen Z and Millennials[176]

---

[174] Twenge (2017).

[175] Ipsos MORI (2018).

[176] Ipsos MORI (2018). Data on alcohol consumption is taken from p. 37 and is based on a survey of English 13–15-year-olds; data on community citizenship is taken from p. 139 and is based on a survey of UK school children aged 14–16 years; data on sexual identity and gender-neutral bathrooms is taken from pp. 26–9 and is based on UK (sexual identity) and US (gender-neutral bathrooms) surveys of 15+ and 13–20-year-olds respectively.

activism – a central new power behaviour – with nearly half of 14- to 16-year-olds saying they have given their time to help out in the community in the past 2 years, compared to 30% in 2005. This trend is matched on other social issues, including ethical buying, where a quarter of UK school children say they have avoided certain products because of the conditions under which they were produced, up from 19% of Millennials at the same age.

There are also some fascinating data suggesting that Gen Z have less binary views on sexuality, with only two-thirds of Gen Z identifying as exclusively heterosexual (71% of Millennials, 85% of Gen X and 88% of Boomers), and with seven in ten of Gen Z thinking it is important for public spaces to provide access to gender-neutral bathrooms.

Of course, these broad generalisations mask the diversity within any one generational cohort. Every individual is different and, on each dimension, people will have their own place on the distribution curve for any given measure. Nonetheless, from my perspective, these data overall describe a reaffirming shift in attitudes and behaviours.

More worryingly, though, the research also raises concerns about the vulnerability of Gen Z. There is increasing evidence of a mental health crisis among young people and, as we will explore below, this is often associated with the use of social media, smartphones and screen time, all of which are key tools for the new power movement. Consequently, there is an apparent tension between the set of new power values that seem to characterise Gen Z – informality, open-mindedness and a willingness to participate – and the serious mental health crisis that is affecting these young people today.

Some have concluded, whether in the popular press or the open field of social media, that the young people of Gen Z are 'coddled', 'snowflakes', who are not resilient enough to face up to the challenges of the 21st century. Given that many of these individuals will turn into higher education students, universities should understand and respond to this, especially as new data reveals how the attitudes, values and behaviours of Gen Z students compare with non-students in terms of volunteering, civic responsibility, attitudes to climate change and ethical buying. Rather than resisting the ideas and inclinations these young people bring, universities have a duty to gear themselves up to accommodating this new and exciting generation of students at a unique time of change, not least as the social activism that characterises Gen Z will fuel the voice and power of students to shape the social purpose of the New Power University in the 21st century.

A longer transition into adulthood is more likely to explain the mental health crisis among Gen Z-ers than the ubiquitous use of digital technology

There is mounting evidence of a mental health crisis among Gen Z, with rising levels of anxiety and depression among pre-student and student populations and significant increases in depression and self-harm (when compared to the Millennials). A recent UK study published in the *International Journal of Epidemiology* compared a cohort of 11,000 Gen Z individuals born in 2000–1 with 5,600 Millennials born in 1991–2.[177] When surveyed at the age of 14 in 2015 and 2004 respectively, Gen Z-ers showed higher levels of depression (15% up from 9%) and self-harm (14% up from 12%). This went alongside parent-reported emotional difficulty, hyperactivity and problems with peers. As one of the paper's co-authors, Suzanne Gage, said in an accompanying press release: 'It has seemed for a while that mental health difficulties in young people are on the rise, but this study really highlights the scale at which this increase might be occurring.'[178]

The consensus among mental health professionals is that this epidemic is real and not an artefact of improved reporting. Even if the rise relative to previous generations turns out not to be the case, the fact that the scale of the problem is now highlighted by young people being willing and able to discuss an issue that, for my generation, was unspoken, is significant in its own right.

The causes of the Gen Z mental health crisis are widely debated and explored in Jean Twenge's delightfully message-led titled book, *iGen: Why Today's Super-Connected Kids Are Growing Up Less Rebellious, More Tolerant, Less Happy – And Completely Unprepared for Adulthood, And What That Means for the Rest of Us.*[179] She cites two explanations for the rise of adolescent and student anxiety and depression. The first is the pervasive use of smartphones and the second is that Gen Z are growing up more slowly.

Gen Z is the first generation to grow up entirely in an always-on, connected-everywhere digital world. According to Twenge's analysis, the Gen Z mental

---

[177] Patalay and Gage (2019).

[178] https://cls.ucl.ac.uk/depression-is-on-the-rise-among-young-people-but-antisocial-behaviour-is-down-new-research-shows/.

[179] Twenge (2017).

health crisis has coincided with the widespread use of social media platforms accessed via smartphones and other devices. Twenge interrogates (US) data by looking at reported daily activities of young people and shows that 8th graders (that is about 14 years old) who spend more time on screen increase their risk of depression by 27% compared with those who do non-screen activities.[180] But, as we know well, correlation does not prove causation and, for this reason, a number of other academics contest any conclusion that lays the blame for increased levels of mental ill health at the door of digital interactions. For example, Odgers and Jensen (2020), in reviewing the literature, conclude, 'The most recent and rigorous large-scale preregistered studies report small associations between the amount of daily digital technology usage and adolescents' wellbeing that do not offer a way of distinguishing cause from effect and, as estimated, are unlikely to be of clinical or practical significance.' They also go on to explicitly critique findings from Twenge *et al.*, (2018):

It is also worth noting that one of the primary studies that has been frequently cited as a source of panic related to a possible connection between social media and depression is the Monitoring the Future Study in the United States. This paper (Twenge *et al.*, 2018) reported on a correlation that accounted for <1% of the variation in depressive symptoms; that is 99.666% of the variation in adolescents' depressive symptoms was due to other factors, and the small correlation between digital technology usage and depression (0.4%) was cross-sectional and was estimated based on both self-reported depressive symptoms and technology usage.

This is not a lone study, with other literature reviews reaching similar conclusions, namely that the effect of screen time on depression and other indicators of mental illness 'do not deliver concrete results' with calls for further and more robust research into the issue.[181]

The other explanation that Twenge offers for the increase in depression and anxiety among Gen Z is the slowing of the life course. As Figure 6.1 showed, individuals in Gen Z are less likely to have tried alcohol than their Millennial predecessors at the same age, and this is also the case for dating, having sex, driving, working and a range of other behaviours. As Twenge notes, 'These are all things that adults do that children do not. Most people try them for the

---

[180] Twenge (2017), Figure 3.8, p. 82; Twenge, *et al.* (2018).
[181] Orben (2020).

first time as teens – the transitional time between childhood and adulthood.' She goes on to suggest that:

> **Childhood has lengthened, with teens treated more like children, less independent and more protected by parents than they once were. The entire development trajectory – the time when teens begin to do things adults do – now happens later . . . Adolescence is now an extension of childhood rather than the beginning of adulthood.**[182]

In short, Twenge argues that a lot of these trends are life course effects. These young people will have sex, drink, drive and work but they are taking longer to reach those milestones. At the same time, however, the majority of Gen Z students are still entering university at the same age as previous generations (that is 18–19 years old) so, perhaps it is not too surprising that they are less prepared for university life and struggle when they get there.

Labelling Gen Z as 'unprepared, coddled snowflakes' distracts from dealing with the complex set of factors changing the experience of university for this generation

The sociologist Frank Furedi, in his book *What's Happened to the University?*, argues that in responding to the social and demographic trends that Gen Z embodies, universities have overacted in ways that threaten academic freedom and, indeed, the very existence of the university. In a thesis that has the tendency to look backwards to old power structures, he noted, 'One of the most significant and yet rarely analysed developments in campus culture has been its infantilisation'.[183]

This dramatic proposition follows on from a famous essay in *The Atlantic* in 2015 by Greg Lukianoff and Jonathan Haidt (a free speech campaigner and a social psychologist) who argued that the introduction of a new set of policies and practices in US universities were damaging education and dangerous for student mental health. Lukianoff and Haidt were concerned that concepts such as 'trigger warnings' (where students are alerted to content in lectures that they may find emotionally challenging), 'microaggressions' (indirect, subtle or

---

[182] Twenge (2017), p. 41.

[183] Furedi (2018), p. 6.

unintentional discrimination against members of a marginalised group) and 'safe spaces' (where certain words and ideas are prohibited) were 'creating a culture in which everyone must think twice before speaking up, lest they face charges of insensitivity, aggression, or worse'. The consequence of what they called this 'vindictive protectiveness' is to teach 'students to catastrophize and have zero tolerance', thereby inhibiting freedom of expression:

> **If campus culture conveys the idea that visitors must be pure, with resumés that never offend generally left-leaning campus sensibilities, then higher education will have taken a further step toward intellectual homogeneity and the creation of an environment in which students rarely encounter diverse viewpoints . . . If students graduate believing that they can learn nothing from people they dislike or from those with whom they disagree, we will have done them a great intellectual disservice.[184]**

It is this sensitivity and perceived political correctness that led to the adoption of the label 'snowflakes' to describe Gen Z. To be clear, Lukianoff and Haidt do not use this term in their *Atlantic* article.[185] It is widely assumed that the label was adopted in popular culture from a line in Chuck Palahniuk's *Fight Club* in 1996: 'You are not special. You are not a beautiful and unique snowflake. You are the same organic and decaying matter as everyone else.'[186] Irrespective of the etymological origins of the word, it has become widely used as an insult to describe Gen Z. A quick Google search identifies a number of tabloid headlines, including '"Snowflake" Oxford University students ban clapping and replace it with "jazz hands" to stop "anxiety"',[187] 'Snowflake kids get lessons in chilling',[188] and 'Don't call us snowflakes – it damages our mental health, say young people'.[189]

---

[184] Lukianoff and Haidt (2015).

[185] Nor is it indexed in their subsequent 2018 book on the same topic, *The Coddling of the American Mind*.

[186] This is the quote from the book (p. 134). In the 1999 adaptation for film the quote is: 'Listen up, maggots. You are not special. You are not the beautiful or unique snowflake. You are the same decaying organic matter as everything else. We are the all-singing, all-dancing crap of the world. We are all part of the same compost heap.' It is also worth noting that this is disputed, with an alternative origin dating from 1860s Missouri, USA, to describe someone who was opposed to the abolition of slavery. See https://www.merriam-webster.com/words-at-play/the-less-lovely-side-of-snowflake for more detail.

[187] https://www.thesun.co.uk/news/10202049/oxford-uni-students-ban-clapping/.

[188] https://www.pressreader.com/uk/daily-star/20181207/282870846896432.

[189] https://www.telegraph.co.uk/news/2017/12/06/dont-call-us-snowflakes-damages-mental-health-say-young-people/.

What is not clear from this debate is causality. Is it the attitudes and behaviours of Gen Z students that are creating this 'vindictive protectiveness' and 'intellectual homogeneity' in universities? Or is it the practices and cultures of old power universities in the 21st century that are graduating a generation of snowflakes? This is an issue that Lukianoff and Haidt explore in *The Coddling of the American Mind*, a 2018 book that was inspired by the response to their *Atlantic* article and explores the issues they initially identified in more depth.[190] As you would, perhaps, anticipate, the causes of this new university culture of 'safetyism', as it is often called, are multifactorial, with six explanations being offered:

1 Rising political polarisation and associated hate crime.
2 Rising levels of teenage anxiety and depression.
3 Changes in parenting practices.
4 Loss of free and unsupervised play in childhood.
5 The growth of campus bureaucracy.
6 An increasing passion for social justice.

While each of these trends will affect students in different and unequal ways, they are all interacting to shape a new environment that, as Lukianoff and Haidt argue, is potentially damaging both education and the mental health of students. Although some of these factors are hard for universities to change or influence – for example, they cannot be held accountable for changes in parenting practices or the loss of free and unsupervised play – they can organise to mitigate and adapt to this changing context so as to have a positive effect on learning and to support young people in maintaining their mental wellbeing.

One of the trends Lukianoff and Haidt cite that is influencing a new university culture is rising political polarisation. They see the political debate in the USA as increasingly polarised between the right (Republicans) and the left (Democrats), with rising levels of hatred between these two political tribes. At the same time, they contend that the political centre of gravity of both students and staff has shifted leftwards, putting universities on one side of this political divide. This has legitimised the harassment of a number of high-profile academics by members of the right for something they have said. Somewhat paradoxically, at the same time, the right has argued that their voice is being

---

[190] Lukianoff and Haidt (2018).

'chilled' at universities, as academic and student members of their tribe feel inhibited in expressing their opinions.

Is this view of polarisation correct? A recent UK study I was involved with looked at views on free speech among both students and the general public.[191] There is, in fact, considerable agreement between these groups on a range of issues relating to freedom of expression. The research also shows that 81% of students think that freedom of expression is more important than ever, with students more concerned that it was being threatened in the UK overall, than in their own university.

Even on the political views of academics, where students are more likely than the general public to agree with the statement that 'the majority of academics are left wing', the overall evidence points to no significant shifts in political polarisation. A recent paper tried to answer the question 'Are universities left wing bastions?'[192] and, while it concluded that, yes, 'professors are more liberal and left leaning than other professionals, it found that there is no greater homogeneity of political orientation among the professoriate relative to other specific professions'.[193] In other words, academics are only as left leaning as any other professional group.

Ulrich Baer takes this issue head on in his book *What Snowflakes Get Right. Free Speech, Truth and Equality on Campus*. He argues against the absolutist position that all views 'must be heard first to reject them', noting that the 'idea of freedom of speech does not mean a blanket permission to say anything anybody thinks. It means balancing the inherent value of a given view with the obligation to ensure other members of a given community can participate in a discourse as fully recognized members of that community.'[194] He makes a compelling case that the right to free speech is rooted in equality, noting that the 'parameters of public speech must be redrawn to accommodate those who previously had no standing', arguing the rights of transgender people against discrimination are 'a current example in a long history of such redefinitions'. In the concluding section of the book, which he calls 'The courage of the snowflakes', he comments, 'The witticisms produced by writers

---

[191] Grant, *et al.* (2019).

[192] This phraseology is a nod to the right-wing commentator in the UK, Toby Young, who, in a *Mail on Sunday* column, 2018, noted: 'Our colleges have become seminaries of politically correct nonsense – Left-wing madrassas whose purpose is not to disseminate knowledge and promote understanding but to suppress politically incorrect facts and stifle debate.' See: https://www.dailymail.co.uk/debate/article-6075017/TOBY-YOUNG-no-wonder-degrees-going-fashion.html.

[193] van de Werfhorst (2019), based on data from European countries.

[194] Baer (2019), pp. 94 and 95.

and pundits who label students "snowflakes", "coddled", "overly sensitive", "excellent sheep", "entitled" and "not really for the real world" have one underlying note: condescension.' In fact, today's students are 'tremendously courageous in carrying on, in excelling in study and research, and in claiming their right not to be placed in a position to defend their existence, or the existence of their peers'.

One of the reasons why transgender rights has become a touchstone issue for the debate on freedom of expression is the fluid and non-traditional identities of Gen Z. I fully acknowledge that the phrase 'non-traditional' may, in its own right, be offensive to some and betrays my Gen X lived experience. What I mean is that the ideas of gender identity and sexuality have evolved from what most, in previous generations, would have been uncomfortable in accepting or being open about. In this way, the emergence of greater diversity does not mean that these identities did not exist before but that, thankfully and largely because of Gen Z activism, we are beginning to be comfortable with the idea that not everyone fits into a dichotomy of male and female genders.

Figure 6.1 illustrated some of these changing attitudes to gender identity, with the Ipsos MORI 'Beyond Binary' report providing further insights. For example, there is evidence that gender neutrality is more of a norm among Gen Z than Millennials and that, in 2016, 74% of Gen Z respondents in a US survey said they were more accepting of non-traditional gender identities than they were a year previously, compared with 64% of young Millennials.[195] In the same research, 56% of Gen Z respondents said they knew someone who used non-gender binary terms, compared to 47% of young Millennials and 43% of older Millennials. Likewise, the 'State of the Youth Nation' report by YouthSight, a UK market research company that specialises in surveying young people, reported that 56% of young men aged 16–25 do not feel pressure to conform to a masculine stereotype, leading the authors to conclude that 'young people are questioning their identity, reclaiming labels and rejecting the status quo to make the world fair and equal'.[196]

Not only does the Gen Z feel less constrained to fit within stereotypes, it also has a more fluid relationship with all the social constructs that an individual can connect with. As 'Beyond Binary' describes, Gen Z-ers are 'less

---

[195] Ipsos MORI (2018), p. 28.
[196] YouthSight (2019), p. 4.

boxed in' – they are not as wedded to a single political party and show less affiliation to particular consumer brands, pop groups and other aspects of popular culture than their predecessors.[197] In the language of new power values, they show 'short term conditional affiliation', which has potential repercussions for university brand value and, indeed, alumni fundraising in the future.

This fluidity also reaches beyond identity and affiliation to further free up the roles that people can take (again, for example, in ways that from a Gen X viewpoint may be labelled 'non-traditional'). So, for example, Malala Yousafzai and Greta Thunberg are both young women who have become household names for different reasons and have challenged perceptions about their own identities – Yousafzai as a young Muslim woman and Thunberg living with, and celebrating in her own way, Asperger's syndrome.

Gen Z students are change makers who will use their new power activism to navigate the 'in between time' into a 'less ideological and more humanitarian era'

Malala Yousafzai is a member of Gen Z. Born in 1997 in Mingora, Pakistan, she was banned from going to school by the Taliban at the age of 11. Like many of her peers, she did not accept this imposition but, unlike many who find themselves in similar situations, she began to speak out publicly on the right of girls to education. Developing a profile by appearing on TV programmes and writing various articles and blogs, she demanded that she and her friends be allowed back to school. Her global persona increased with nominations for prizes and endorsements from activists worldwide. Archbishop Desmond Tutu nominated her for the International Children's Peace Prize in 2011 and she was awarded Pakistan's first National Youth Peace Prize in December of that year.

A year later, her world was turned upside down when, in October 2012, at the age of 15, she was shot on the left side of her head by a masked Taliban gunman. As her website recounts, she 'woke up 10 days later in a hospital in Birmingham, England'. Following months of surgery and rehabilitation, she was joined by her family in the UK where they have now

---

[197] Ipsos MORI (2018), p. 9.

settled. As she says, 'It was then I knew I had a choice: I could live a quiet life, or I could make the most of this new life I had been given. I determined to continue the fight until every girl could go to school.'[198] And so she did. In 2013, she wrote the best seller *I Am Malala*, highlighting both her story and the plight of girls worldwide in their fight to be educated.[199] In 2014, she became the youngest ever Nobel Laurate. As Yousafzai said on her campaigning, 'When the whole world is silent, even one voice becomes powerful.'[200]

Another inspirational Gen Z-er who has used their voice and power to campaign for change in a silent world is Greta Thunberg, the climate activist and leading light of the school strikes movement. Thunberg is five years younger than Yousafzai, born in Sweden in 2003. In August 2018, she decided not to go to school for one day, starting a 'school strike for the climate' outside the Swedish parliament. This was the beginning of a global movement for action against the climate crisis to get Gen X and the Boomers to take responsibility for the damage done to the planet. As Thunberg said to politicians and civil servants in Brussels:

The political system that you have created is all about competition. You cheat when you can, because all that matters to you is to win, to get power. That must come to an end, we must stop competing with each other, we need to cooperate and work together and to share the resources of the planet in a fair way.[201]

Thunberg has also achieved international recognition for her work, including becoming the *Time* magazine Person of the Year in 2019 and being nominated for the Nobel Peace Prize. Nonetheless, like Yousafzai, she is not courting fame but forcing change. As she said in a post on Facebook in February 2019: 'I agree with you, I'm too young to do this. We children shouldn't have to do this. But since almost no one is doing anything, and our very future is at risk, we feel like we have to continue.'[202]

---

[198] https://www.malala.org/malalas-story?gclid=CjwKCAiA98TxBRBtEiwAVRLqu2jkyomDuDUO9WgBfJDuSAkn55Wd4IS174Oog8mCPh41DP1crXtdgBoCHQoQAvD_BwE.

[199] Yousafzai (2013).

[200] Although this quote is widely attributed to Yousafzai on the internet, I have been unable to find the original source.

[201] Thunberg (2019), p. 38.

[202] Thunberg (2019), p. 33.

These two amazing young women personify many of the core qualities of Gen Z, all of which align with the new power values identified by Timms and Heimans (2018), summarised as follows:[203]

- Informal opt-in decision making.
- Self-organisation.
- Networked governance.
- Open source collaboration.
- Crowd wisdom.
- Sharing.
- Radical transparency.
- Do-it-ourselves 'maker culture'.
- Short-term conditional affiliation.
- More overall participation.

They manage to stay connected, both through technology and through their values – some apparent but others seemingly unwritten, at present. As such, they are becoming catalysts for urgent and accelerated social change, not on the terms of the Gen X and Boomers, but on their own, perhaps characterised by longer-term horizons, a focus on sustainability (in all its meanings) and working in a more collaborative, rather than competitive, way. Above all, Gen Z is not content with the status quo. It wants change and will take ownership for making that change happen. As so impressively demonstrated by Thunberg's activism, sustainability is an issue that has united a generation of young people. The same YouthSight data referred to above has also been tracking how important different political issues are for young people. The issue of climate change as the most important issue has increased from 13% of 16- to 17-year-olds in September 2015 to 51% in June 2019. In turn, this has seen large numbers of Gen Z-ers alter their behaviours including, for example, enduring increases in veganism and vegetarianism.[204]

The climate crisis is an issue for which Gen Z hold my generation and, perhaps, more sharply, Boomers, accountable and so, increasingly, creates inter-generational tension. Interestingly, it is a conflict that the old power universities have helped to generate, as they have educated a generation of

---

[203] Timms and Heimans (2018).

[204] YouthSight (2019), p. 6 (June 2019 data – unpublished and provided via personal communication).

leaders who have let climate change go unchallenged. David Orr, an academic from Oberlin College, Ohio, USA, argues that 'education can equip people to be more effective vandals of the earth',[205] noting the destruction of the planet 'is not the work of ignorant people. It is largely the results of work by people with BAs, BScs, LLBs, MBAs and PhDs.'[206] Putting social responsibility, including the fight against climate change and the search for more sustainable ways of living and working together, is what the new power Gen Z student wants not just as part of the academic mission but at the heart of the social purpose of the New Power University in the 21st century.

Do new power Gen Z students differ from Gen Z-ers who choose not to go to university?

Throughout this chapter, I have drawn from available data that examines the attitudes, values and behaviours of Gen Z, making the case that they are not 'coddled snowflakes' but new power activists who will ensure we emerge into Saul's 'less ideological and more humanitarian era'. In coming to this conclusion, I'm very conscious that the data combines Gen Z students with Gen Z-ers who choose not to go to university and that these two subgroups may, indeed, have different sets of attitudes, values and behaviours. The published data does not make this potentially important distinction, so I decided to engage a King's student to help me explore this key issue further. As explained in more detail in Appendix 1, we looked at a range of survey data to see whether, first, we could separate Gen Z students from Gen Z non-students and, second, whether they collected information that could indicate attitudes, values and behaviours on a range of issues broadly related to social responsibility. As illustrated in Figure 6.2, students were more likely than non-students to: (a) take part in formal volunteering at least once a month; (b) agree that involvement in local community can change the way that an area is run; (c) worry about climate change; and (d) feel that choosing products for political, ethical or environmental reasons is important, even if they cost a bit more. These data seem to confirm the hypothesis that Gen Z students differ from Gen Z-ers who choose not to go to university, although there are three caveats. First, as explained in Appendix 1, the effect size is relatively

---

[205] Orr (1994), p. 1.
[206] Orr (1994), p. 4.

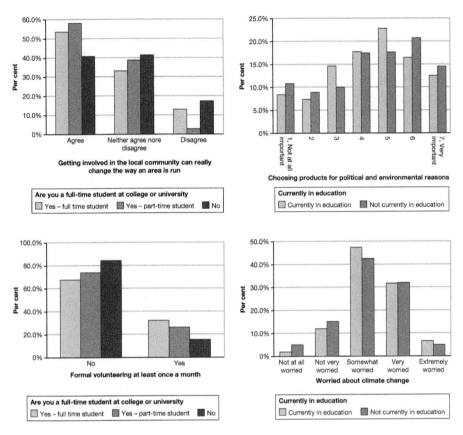

Figure 6.2 Attitudes, values and behaviours of Gen Z students and non-students

small, meaning that being a student (or educational status) does not play an important role in determining those statistically significant differences. Second, these data do not illustrate whether the act of going to university is causing these differences, or whether Gen Z-ers who exhibit these values, attitudes and behaviours are more likely to go to university. Third, it may be that people who go to university have more in common across universities than within their own generation with similar differences being evident in earlier cohorts. Nevertheless, it is important to acknowledge that young people who choose not to go to university may have a different set of values than those who do and this can have impacts on broader social and political cohesion which, in itself, is a challenge that the New Power University needs to be cognisant of.

The New Power University must reappraise its relationship with Gen Z to make sure it supports the learning, freedom of speech and mental wellbeing of these students

The values, attitudes and behaviours of Gen Z students result in some profound implications for the New Power University. First, the New Power University must stand 'shoulder to shoulder' with their Gen Z students, countering the damaging narrative that they are 'snowflakes'. The new and unique set of attitudes, behaviours and values that Gen Z-ers broadly embrace is shaped by their experience of living in a world that has largely been shaped by people like myself, that is Gen X and the Boomers. As the ones who brought them up, rather than complain, we should listen, understand what they want and then help them deliver on that. At its heart, that is what the New Power University is about.

The New Power University also needs to support Gen Z students as they move into university life. The idea of a delayed transition from childhood (or a new life course stage of 'early adulthood') will reshape how a university prepares new students for the experience they are about to embark on. The New Power University has a responsibility to develop, explicitly and consciously, programmes that help students move from a schooling environment into a higher education one.

This links to a third point, the provision of effective mental health support by a university for its students. The rise in depression, self-harm and even suicide among Gen Z students places even more weight on the duty of care that a New Power University has to develop the necessary counselling and other pastoral support (including acute clinical interventions) for all of its students. This has to be appropriately resourced and evaluated as an institutional – and, indeed, sector – priority.

Next, the New Power University has to demonstrate its commitment to the climate emergency. Embedding sustainability and social responsibility into the academic mission and institutional being of a New Power University will be one of its defining characteristics. Through its research for nearly a generation, the sector, as a whole, has been warning about the consequences of climate change but has failed, for many complex reasons (many outside its control) to translate this knowledge into behaviour and policy change. Now that the scientific evidence on climate change is so unequivocal, universities have to be models of leadership in tackling that and in demonstrating how modern organisations can be fully sustainable.

Finally, the New Power University has to support that activism of its Gen Z students. This means educating them in new power values and on how to deliver effective change through social movements. This could involve courses, modules and extra curricular activities that guide students in channelling their activist goals into tangible change. There are lots of studies and academic papers on community organising, social movements and activism that should become core and, arguably, compulsory educational modules for all new power students. Indeed, in all likelihood, it is by helping create a generation of effective social activists that universities will maximise the wider social impact of higher education in the 21st century.

Chapter 7

Staffing the New Power University

The instrumentalised managerialism of today's university will only end through disruptive innovation of how the New Power University is staffed

One of the most surprising aspects of university life I discovered on becoming an academic in 2014 was the divide between administrators and academics. It quickly reminded me of my Naval upbringing where there is also a divide, in that case between 'officers' and 'ratings'. The difference, though, is that the military divide, which is horizontal, is possible to cross. The divide in universities is vertical and is very difficult to cross. I used to term this (somewhat inappropriately) 'academic apartheid' but then discovered there was a body of literature using this phrase but in a slightly different context – drawing a separation between what in US university parlance is the tenured faculty and the adjunct faculty.[207] Tenured meaning those mostly senior academics who have

---

[207] https://www.psychologytoday.com/us/blog/somebodies-and-nobodies/201312/ending-academic-apartheid; https://www.amazon.com/Academic-Apartheid-Waging-Adjunct-War/dp/1443828599.

a job for life while adjunct (also referred to as casual or sessional) academics tend to be more junior and on short-term contracts. However you define the idea of 'academic apartheid', you have to conclude that the use of such emotive language, and the fissures it refers to, mean there is something critically wrong with the way that old power universities are staffed.[208]

At the core of the issue of staffing are the concepts of 'the academy', 'academic freedom' and 'institutional autonomy', which I suggested earlier are self-referential, entitled and fundamentally elitist notions. One of the people who reviewed the proposal for this book inadvertently reinforced this observation by saying, 'I have never met anyone outside of a university who uses the word "academy" to describe academics (policymakers *never* use the term).'

I don't disagree with this but I know the term is widely used within universities, often as a tool to generate identities that separate and, to a degree, protect academics from what they portray as 'the centre' or 'the bureaucrats'. It is often seen as the means to counter the old power instrumentalised managerialism that characterises the way today's institutions are organised and run. In this regard, Chad Wellmon, associate professor of German studies at the University of Virginia, proposes that the university and the academy have different purposes. In a speech he gave in 2017 entitled 'The university is dead, long live the academy', he argued, 'Many of the criticisms levelled against The University are not necessarily criticisms of The Academy.'[209] The purpose of the university, he states, is to 'educate students for particular social and political orders' and this is used to 'routinely justify universities by identifying the external goods they serve. Universities, we rightly argue, satisfy a range of political, economic and social goods.' On the other hand, 'the purpose of The Academy is to cultivate those activities, practices, and virtues whose end is the creation, transmission, and legitimation of knowledge and the education of others to do the same. And that's something worth defending.' As he summarised in a more recent article in *Inside Higher Education* (a US trade magazine for universities): 'I'm no longer in the business of defending the university. I'm here to defend and argue for the academy.'[210]

The concept of the academy is closely related to the idea of academic freedom, something that can be dated back to the founding of Europe's first

---

[208] It also speaks volumes that the alternative meaning was actually all about the academy and nothing to do with the broader university community.

[209] https://chadwellmon.com/2017/10/26/after-the-university-long-live-the-academy/.

[210] https://www.insidehighered.com/news/2020/01/27/discussion-about-future-academy.

university, the University of Bologna in the 11th century. The Emperor of the Holy Roman Empire, Frederick Barbarossa, wanted to guarantee the safety of scholars travelling to and from Bologna. As they were foreigners, they found themselves without legal rights, so Barbarossa issued a decree *Authentica habita* (also known as *Privilegium scholasticum*) granting them imperial protection.[211] For those who have watched the television adaption of Philip Pullman's *His Dark Materials*, this is equivalent to the 'scholastic sanctuary' that is provided to the university by the fictional (and brutal) church the Magisterium. Today, this protection or sanctuary has been re-interpreted as the broader and more amorphous concept of 'academic freedom' which UNESCO defines as being 'freedom of teaching and discussion, freedom in carrying out research and disseminating and publishing results'.[212]

The assumed rights that come from academic freedom are then, in turn, used to support the notion of institutional autonomy for universities. This exhibits itself as 'the necessary degree of independence from external interference that the University requires in respect of its internal organisation and governance, the internal distribution of financial resources and the generation of income from non-public sources, the recruitment of its staff, the setting of the conditions of study and, finally, the freedom to conduct teaching and research.'[213] As with academic freedom, this is a very privileged and self-asserted right coming from the International Association of Universities.

Consequently, the criticisms levelled against the university are justified in also being criticisms of the academy by questioning the over-reach of ideas around academic freedom and the pursuit of institutional autonomy. It's clear that academic freedom is often played as a trump card to say 'no' to something, while institutional autonomy, sustained by the idea of academic freedom, is brandished as a defence by university leaders to push back against government policies. This resistance has held back the changes needed to widen access to education, increase the impact of research and ensure universities organise and run themselves in equitable and sustainable ways.

I prefer to think of the academy as a form of guild, as Kerr (1963) does in explaining the conservatism of universities in his book *The Uses of the University* (where he also introduced the concept of the multiversity, as

---

[211] http://humanstudy.org/tag/privilegium-scholasticum/.

[212] http://portal.unesco.org/en/ev.php-URL_ID=13144&URL_DO=DO_TOPIC&URL_SECTION=201. html, paragraph 27.

[213] https://iau-aiu.net/IMG/pdf/academic_freedom_policy_statement.pdf.

described in Chapter 2).[214] The online dictionary, Merriam-Webster, defines a 'guild' as an association of people with similar interests or pursuits.[215] Indeed, as we also saw in Chapter 2, the University of Bologna was exactly founded on this model, albeit with students not their teachers. The problem arises when the 'guild of the academy' pushes its assumed rights and privileges in ways that disconnect it from the world it exists within and serves.

This disconnect reveals itself most clearly in the contractual relationships between employer and employee, whether academic or professional staff. The 'guild' defends the right of independence and freedom, through concepts such as tenure, from the institutional being of the university which, in turn, is creating both forms of 'academic apartheid'. Central to those assumed rights and privileges are the old power dynamics which embed and protect long-standing employment structures and practices. The rest of this chapter explores how the New Power University of the 21st century will need a very different staffing model based on ideas that are controversial and, perhaps, counter-intuitive but are, nonetheless, logically coherent with new power values. To bring about the proposed radical changes will also require sophisticated and nuanced leadership within universities.

'Third space' professionals, high-value 'gig' working and tenure for junior academics will be the main drivers of future staffing models

The organisation, culture and competencies of the current university workforce are unable to deliver the missions of the New Power University. The combination of a disaffected academic workforce with the emergence of new skills for both academic and professional staff means that radical change is inevitable. The future of work in universities, as with many sectors, is likely to be very different from what it is today.

This is, understandably, making those who work in universities very anxious, as is illustrated by a quick survey of higher education blog sites. For example, in a piece titled 'Our university workforce has become a fragmented, casualised "gig economy"', two Australian academics, Paul

---

[214] Kerr (1963), p. 72.

[215] https://www.merriam-webster.com/dictionary/guild#synonyms

Richardson and Amanda Heffernan, commented, 'The Australian academic workforce is experiencing excessive workload demands, intrusive managerialism and bureaucratic reporting requirements, widespread work dissatisfaction, work related stress and burnout.'[216] They also note that the workforce is 'highly casualised, and reliant on sessional academic staff at the lowest appointment levels to undertake face-to-face and online teaching and marking'. Similarly, *University World News* cited a study published by the University and College Union (UCU)[217] in reporting that, in the UK, the 'casualised academic staff are being denied academic freedom and are treated as invisible, second-class citizens, prevented from choosing what they will research or teach, unable to plan a professional or home life, and vulnerable to exploitation by permanent staff'.[218]

The challenge for everyone in the higher education sector, employees and employers alike, is to recognise that the current system is broken and that we need to use the 'in-between time' to develop a new model for the 21st century. This should not give in to the desire, as is often the tendency, to revert to some sort of idealised model of university staffing from the mid-20th century. Instead, a completely different, more radical, new power model is proposed.

The 'third space' professional is an emerging force in the New Power University

Whether it be designing online material, curating citizen science networks or ensuring carbon neutrality, delivering the three missions of the New Power University in learning, research and social responsibility will require new skills and competencies among the workforce. While the necessary skills do exist in universities today, they are not widespread enough nor suitably recognised in recruitment or within the incentive systems around personal development, promotion and pay.

Part of the challenge for the New Power University is that these competencies are best found in roles that are neither academic nor professional. It is for this reason that Celia Whitchurch, a researcher from the Institute of Education in London, coined the phrase 'third space professions': 'The concept is used as

---

[216] https://www.aare.edu.au/blog/?p=4087.

[217] https://www.ucu.org.uk/media/10336/Counting-the-costs-of-casualisation-in-higher-education-Jun-19/pdf/ucu_casualisation_in_HE_survey_report_Jun19.pdf.

[218] https://www.universityworldnews.com/post.php?story=20200121072332456.

a way of exploring groups of staff in higher education who do not fit conventional binary descriptors such as those enshrined in "academic" or "non-academic" employment categories.'[219] Whitchurch borrows the idea of 'third spaces' from social theory where it has been employed in a number of contexts such as looking at the dualisms between, for example, east and west cultures. Critically, for the framing of this book, she notes, 'The significance of *in-between* spaces, which are likely to be invisible in that they are not written into organisation charts or job descriptions, and may not have dedicated physical space associated with them, is recognised in a wider literature including on community of practices, actor-network theory and social capital' (my italics).[220] These are all ideas that have intellectual antecedents to the practical concepts of new power and new power values that Timms and Heimans advocate. In the context of universities, these third space professionals are 'blurring . . . the perceived binary division between academic and non-academic roles'.[221]

Take instructional designers of online content as an example. From Chapter 3, it is clear that new power learning will be delivered online (either in its totality or as part of a blended classroom experience) and that the content of these courses will be co-created with students to ensure they are representative of human knowledge. The development of such online modules will require a collaboration between content and design experts informed by student expectations. This is very different from conventional course and module development. As White (2018) notes in a PhD thesis on the topic: 'Academic staff (sometimes as individual educators) take responsibility for conventional course development in a process which can be "solitary" and without significant consultation with others. In contrast, studies of online course development show that for educators, "autonomy yields to collaboration" with a variety of stakeholders, amongst which the "role of the learning designer is crucial" to achieve quality in courses produced.'[222] In the future, the development of new learning content will not only be team-based but it will be a team that, by necessity, will require equal participation in terms of time and power of the learning or instructional designer.

---

[219] Whitchurch (2015).

[220] Whitchurch (2013), p. 21.

[221] Whitchurch (2013), p. 24.

[222] White (2018), p. 29.

Similar arguments can be made for the research and social responsibility missions of the New Power University. Having experts engaged inside universities who know how to create and curate networks is a critical skill in ensuring that research makes a societal impact as well as mobilising the support for citizen science. Likewise, having experts who understand the complexities and interdependences of carbon neutrality and how that not only impacts on university estates but also on traditional academic practices such as international travel is essential for delivering the social purpose of universities in the 21st century.

Indeed, when you consider Whitchurch's definition of third space, you quickly realise that this group of people will become the dominant workforce in terms of numbers in the future university. Yes, you will have a professional staff who are focused on core functions such as finance, HR, student and research services and, yes, you will still have academics, but both groups are likely to be smaller in size with the third space professional being the largest group of staff. This takes us towards a future model of the university workforce, as shown in Figure 7.1.

The upper panel provides a conceptualisation of the current old power model where we can see both definitions of 'academic apartheid' at play: the one dividing academic and professional staff, and the one dividing tenured and casual/adjunct staff. In the middle, you find a small group of 'third space professionals' running down the spine of the university.[223] The lower panel in Figure 7.1 sets out the proposed alternative. Here we have the third space professional as numerically the largest part of the university workforce.

It is important to note that the idea of third space professionals is not simply a re-labelling of either academic or professional staff. These individuals are bringing in a new set of skills, values and ways of working into universities that align with the demands of the future. Whitchurch explores this

---

[223] The shape of this population pyramid is broadly representative of UK universities: in 2018/19, there were 440,000 staff working in universities, roughly half of them were academics and the other half professional staff; about 12% of academics were professors or other senior staff; 34% of academic staff were employed on fixed-term contracts (25% for full-time employees and 50% for part-time); and, of those academics on part-time contracts, 38% were hourly paid; 4,240, or 2%, of academics were employed on a zero hours contract (see: https://www.hesa.ac.uk/news/23-01-2020/sb256-higher-education-staff-statistics).

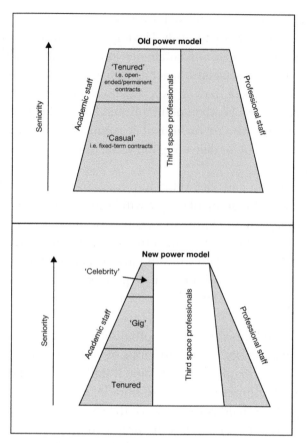

Figure 7.1 Conceptual change in the university workforce

in synthesising the results of a number of interviews of existing third space professionals and notes:

> The narratives [in interviewing people] also revealed ambivalence about the concept of being a professional in the traditional sense of belonging to an exclusive group, defined by the possession of core skills, knowledges and attitudes. Key characteristics, rather, included being able to handle shifting bundles of activity, working to both long and short deadlines, with multiple partners and collaborators, in a mutable environment. Those working in *Third Space* were able to cope with ambiguity and to accommodate, and even use productively, the tensions that they encountered.[224]

---

[224] Whitchurch (2015).

In concluding her book, *Reconstructing Identities in Higher Education: The Rise of 'Third Space' Professionals*, Whitchurch observes how the third space professional may positively change the dynamic of 'intrusive managerialism' and 'casualised academic staff' that critics of the old power system are raging against in the aforementioned blogs: 'Third space professionals are contributing to new definitions of management, leadership and professionalism that focus more on development, facilitation and collaboration than on control. They are likely to invest in colleagues in the broadest sense, leading by example, acting as an advocate for specific causes, tapping into networks, sharing information and acting on feedback.'[225] As such, 'Third space activity may contribute to . . . ways of moving beyond "dialectical managerialism" to develop "creative management thinking" and "make external ambiguity manageable for governors, staff and students" . . . In all these ways, third space might be described as representing "discursive space that is neither "managerially" nor "ideologically constrained".'[226] In other words, third space professionals are applying and acting out many of the values that are critical to the success of the New Power University.

At the same time, it is important to acknowledge that not everyone will migrate to the third space and there will remain a cohort of professionals, albeit a smaller one than exists now. These staff will occupy a range of roles including finance, HR, security and such like and it will be important, through recruitment and appraisals, to ensure that these individuals align with the values of the New Power University. In my time in academia, I have seen examples where this has not occurred, partly as the behaviours of some professional staff were simply not aligned with the values of university life but also because there are times when operational objectives drive academic objectives – or, as one colleague put it to me once, 'the HR tail wagging the organisational dog'. While such behaviours and practices cannot be justified, it also seems to me that they arise partly because of the 'academic apartheid' and sense of being undervalued. The challenge for the New Power University will be to take a holistic, institute-wide approach to some of the reforms I am advocating in this chapter that ensures all staff – irrespective of their role or contractual status – feel aligned to the social purpose and values of the New Power University.

---

[225] Whitchurch (2013), p. 143.
[226] Whitchurch (2013), p. 144.

Encouraging and supporting the 'gig academic' will renew the psychological contract with the New Power University workforce

If the third space provides an opportunity to blur the dualism of academic and professional staff, then re-energising the psychological contract is a way of improving the strained employment relationships within old power universities, especially with academic staff.

The psychological contract is an idea that emerged in the 1960s and is used to describe the unwritten expectations – 'the deal' – between employer and employee. It has become more relevant as a concept at a time when employers have been unable to offer the life-long career and job security of the past and is seen as a useful lens when considering the future and nature of work across a number of sectors. Tech companies, for example, have a near mythical reputation of providing free food, pool tables and on-tap beer as an integral part of the work environment. It is a well-earnt reputation. Google has topped *Fortune*'s 'The 100 Best Companies to Work For' list for six years running, between 2012 and 2017.[227] As noted in one blog on workplace culture: 'Google's culture is flexible (employees are encouraged to work when they like and how they like), fun (offices have nap pods, video games and ping pong) and founded on trust. Collaboration is key – so much so that employees are encouraged to coach each other in the "Googler to Googler" programme. This includes key business skills such as public speaking, management and orientation as well as extra-curricular activities like kickboxing.'[228]

In considering how best to re-energise (or create) this psychological contract in a university setting, you immediately run into the challenge of having to do this with a workforce that is 'highly casualised, and reliant on sessional academic staff at the lowest appointment levels'.[229] In Australia, it is estimated that between 20% and 25% of the academic workforce are employed on 'sessional contracts' (that is staff who are engaged and paid on an hourly basis),[230] while, in the UK, 13% of academic staff are paid by the hour (and for part-time staff that is 38%).[231]

---

[227] https://fortune.com/best-companies/2017/search/; although, in 2018, Google decided to no longer participate in the ranking.

[228] https://peakon.com/blog/workplace-culture/google-company-culture/.

[229] https://www.aare.edu.au/blog/?p=4087.

[230] Crawford and Germov (2015).

[231] https://www.hesa.ac.uk/news/23-01-2020/sb256-higher-education-staff-statistics.

In the USA, 75% of academic staff are off tenure track, with about half of these (or 40% of all academic staff) on part-time adjunct contracts.[232]

Fortunately, the research suggests that it is not the form of employment (tenure versus off tenure, full-time versus part-time) per se that is the critical aspect of the psychological contract, but rather the ability to choose which form of contractual relationship employees wish to have. David Guest is a researcher who has explored the psychological contract and its relationship with flexible working conditions. It might be assumed that fixed-term and temporary contracts are associated with job insecurity, but the reality is more nuanced and Guest's counter position is that the 'growth of the knowledge worker has created a new opportunity for freedom and autonomy from the controls exercised by organisations. The concept of the "free worker" who thrives on independence and high levels of employability has been presented as an opportunity to turn the tables and assert power of the knowledge worker over the knowledge-hungry organisation.'[233] He goes on to note that 'the evidence suggests that the state of the psychological contract of workers on flexible employment contracts is at least as positive and sometimes more positive than that reported by workers on permanent contracts' and when that flexibility is the 'contract of choice' then this has an 'important bearing on attitudes and behaviours'.[234]

Guest's ideas were confirmed in an EU-funded study that explored the wellbeing of temporary workers compared with permanent staff across six European countries. This found that temporary workers, irrespective of the type of temporary work, reported higher levels of wellbeing than permanent staff. Although the data for that study were collected between 2005 and 2007, before the global financial crash of 2008, subsequent analysis suggests that the findings still hold true in Northern Europe (in Southern Europe there is a more pervasive sense of job insecurity).[235]

These lessons should encourage the New Power University to consciously (and proudly) embrace sessional working as a way of actively providing more senior and/or experienced academic staff with flexible contract terms. I appreciate that this is counter to the prevailing debate in academia but it is the coherent position when you apply the concepts of new power to the university

---

[232] http://www.newfacultymajority.info/facts-about-adjuncts/.

[233] Guest (2004).

[234] Guest (2004).

[235] Guest and Isaksson (2019).

workforce. Encouraging and rewarding the growing breed of 'gig academic' is in line with the new power values of opt-in decision making, networked governance, open source collaboration and short-term conditional
affiliation.

Making this work will need universities to create the necessary means to
contract for and support these flexible working arrangements. One such institution is the University of Newcastle (UON) in Australia. In 2011, the UON
commissioned a review of its casual workforce that led to the development
of a strategy to engage, support and effectively manage casual and sessional
academic staff.[236] Following the review, and after lengthy consultation, the
UON Academy was established in 2013. The strategy was established to
recognise the importance of the contribution of sessional and casual staff
(who are engaged and paid on an hourly basis) by providing systematic support for their engagement, development and performance. Of University of
Newcastle's approximately 1,000 academic staff, about a fifth are employed
on this basis, amounting to about 200 individuals. For many of its students,
the sessional staff are the 'face' of the institution and are critical in shaping
its reputation. As its Academy website states, 'The UON Academy recognises
the key role that sessional academic staff play in the delivery of a world-class
education.'[237] Here you will find teaching and learning resources, professional development opportunities, library access, customised induction,
commitments to support pension payments and a LinkedIn group. The
important point is that the UON Academy is being honest with its sessional
staff in acknowledging their role in the university and then celebrating and
supporting it. This is backed up in the data where the UON has seen an
increase in staff satisfaction from its annual survey for these people. Staff
engagement results saw a significant shift from 2014 (70%) to 2016 (79%)
after the implementation of various initiatives and support mechanisms,
including access to professional development and more rigorous recruitment and selection processes for hiring. The latest survey, in 2019, indicates
a positive sessional academic culture with 97% of respondents saying, 'I like
the kind of work I do' and 88% of respondents saying the main reason for
working as a sessional academic is 'a way of giving something back to my

---

[236] Crawford and Germov (2015).

[237] https://www.newcastle.edu.au/current-staff/teaching-and-research/uon-academy.

profession'. Other positive results from the 2019 survey include 85% of respondents feel they have adequate resources, 82% feel 'people in their work area treat others with respect' and 82% 'would like to continue to work as a sessional academic'. In other words, the UON is consciously and successfully redefining 'the deal', the psychological contract, between the university and its staff.

Newly qualified academics will be given job security through tenure to establish themselves before moving to a 'gig' system when they are more experienced

One of the ironies of the current casualised, adjunct or sessional employment of academics is that it disproportionately impacts on those at the early stage of their careers who have yet to build up the skills and track records of their more experienced colleagues. Perversely, then, the system offers employment security to those who need it least when they are more advanced in their academic careers. In the USA, that is when you achieve tenure. For other countries, which do not have as rigid a system as in the USA, more senior academics get de-facto tenure through open-ended contracts, which can only be terminated through some form of gross misconduct or via a redundancy process that has regulated compensation payments. By contrast, the generally more junior colleagues on short-term, zero-hour, contracts have no security nor compensation if their services are no longer required.

The idea of tenure is that it protects academic freedom – that fact that you cannot fire me means I am at liberty to say what I want. This became an issue in 1900 when Edward Ross was not reappointed at Stanford University because Jane Stanford, the widow of Leland Stanford, the university's founder, didn't like his views. At the time, this provoked outrage with a number of academics resigning their positions from Stanford in protest.[238] Prompted by this and other scandals, some 15 years later, the American Association of University Professors (AAUP) was founded to ensure the academic freedom of its members, an enduring mission that still holds today.[239]

---

[238] Ludlum (1950).

[239] https://www.aaup.org/about/mission-1.

At the time, the notion of academic freedom was still a novel concept, so the AAUP convened a *Committee on Academic Freedom and Academic Tenure*. In 1915, it reported that:

> **To the degree that professional scholars, in the formation and promulgation of their opinions, are, or by the character of their tenure appear to be, subject to any motive other than their own scientific conscience and a desire for the respect of their fellow-experts, to that degree the university teaching profession is corrupted.**[240]

The Committee went on to offer some 'practical proposals' that included:

> **In every institution there should be an unequivocal understanding as to the term of each appointment; and the tenure of professorships and associate professorships, and of all positions above the grade of instructor after ten years of service, should be permanent (subject to the provisions hereinafter given for removal upon charges).**

The aim of such a proposal was 'to render the profession more attractive to men [sic] of high ability and strong personality by insuring the dignity, the independence, and the reasonable security of tenure, of the professorial office'.

A hundred years on from then, Steven Levitt, the economist and co-author of the book *Freakonomics*, now argues that tenure has passed its sell-by date. 'It distorts people's effort so that they face strong incentives early in their career (and, presumably, work very hard early on as a consequence) and very weak incentives forever after (and presumably work much less hard on average as a consequence).'[241] This only makes sense 'if one needs to learn a lot of information to become competent, but once one has the knowledge it does not fade and effort is not very important. That model may be a good description of learning to ride a bike, but it is a terrible model of academics.' Levitt goes on to note that 'the idea that tenure protects scholars who are doing politically unpopular work strikes me as ludicrous . . . Tenure does an outstanding job of protecting scholars who do *no* work or *terrible* work, but is there anything in economics which is high quality but so controversial it would lead to a scholar being fired? Anyway, that is what markets are for. If one institution fires an academic primarily because they don't like his or her politics or approach, there will be other schools happy to make the hire.'

---

[240] https://www.aaup.org/NR/rdonlyres/A6520A9D-0A9A-47B3-B550-C006B5B224E7/0/1915Declaration.pdf.

[241] http://freakonomics.com/2007/03/03/lets-just-get-rid-of-tenure/.

Accepting this, one radical idea for the New Power University would be to turn the use of tenure on its head, instead offering it to those early career academics who are disproportionately casualised at present. This will give them the time and job security they need to develop their skills ('to learn a lot of information to become competent') and establish a reputation in their discipline. Every entry-level academic could be offered 10–15-year contracts, albeit with the ability to dismiss someone for underperformance or gross misconduct as is the norm in other sectors. Once they have successfully completed this tenure, they have to then compete in the open market as a 'gig academic'. Alternatively, they could move into third space roles where they are procuring and managing the subcontracts for the outsourced senior academics. This will remove the uncertainty of fixed-term post-doctoral and short-term teaching contracts for early career academics, while ensuring competition continues for senior academics.

In part, this model already exists for those research groups that are funded externally. It is not that unusual for a research team to move from one university to another, taking with it the competitive research grants that it has been awarded. In this new power world, the research team would explicitly compete for external funds but do it directly, not through its host institution. Similarly, teams of academics could form consortia to teach certain modules or courses and contract with a range of universities worldwide to deliver these. Such consortia could include young tenured academics who are affiliated with an institution, as well as unaffiliated senior academics. The consortia could be formed as a network of self-employed individuals, although, in time, you could envisage small start-ups offering specialised packages or major suppliers such as Udacity, Coursera or Pearson entering the market. At the extreme, there could be a small number of 'celebrity' academics who are managed through agencies in the same way that occurs for footballers and actors. These academics would be contracted to deliver a number of keynote lectures, classes and seminars in a given university before moving on to the next one.

Now, you might think that this sort of model which, in effect, 'outsources' more experienced academics is inconsistent with the arguments for insourcing cleaners and security staff that I passionately argued for in Chapter 5. The difference is the issue of motivation. As discussed above, it is not necessarily having a particular form of work contract that determines the strength of the psychological contract, rather the ability to choose flexible working, if that is an option. The choice of the cleaners and security staff at King's was, indeed, to be insourced as employees of the institution. They rightly assumed that would give them better job security and improved pay and working conditions. In the same way, the new power model of academic work offers the preferred choice for staff at different stages in their careers. Tackling the fractious, casualised and frankly exploitative model of today, it also addresses the inequity of tenure, abolishes the academic–professional staff dualism and strengthens the psychological contact across the workforce.

The current staffing crisis in Anglo-Saxon universities is occurring elsewhere, suggesting the new power model can be applied in other countries

In the preceding section, I largely draw on data and experience from the UK, Australia and USA to make the case that the current model of staffing universities is no longer defensible and should be replaced with a new power model for the future. To counter any Anglo-Saxon bias, I tested these ideas with colleagues in Spain, Romania, Cameroon and Nigeria, checking how they resonated in the context of their institutions and countries. I asked seven specific questions:

1 Is there a divide between academic and professional staff and, if so, does that divide impact on the function and culture of the university?

2 Do you have issues of casualisation (where academic staff are employed on short-term contracts with little job security) and, if so, how are you addressing this, if at all?

3 Does tenure – or something equivalent – exist in your jurisdiction and, if so, is it creating the type of perverse behaviour described in the draft text?

4 Would the introduction of an expanded and dominant cohort of third space professionals break down the academic–professional staff dualism in your jurisdiction?

5 Would the introduction of UON Academy type function/department help to address the issues around the casualisation of academic staff and to reset the psychological contact?

6 Would the ending of tenure for senior academics – and the introduction of tenure for junior academics – be a viable solution for the management of academic careers?

7   Would the explicit acceptance of a 'gig academic' model address some of the challenges currently faced by universities in your jurisdiction?

The detailed responses are captured in Appendix 2. Overall, there was a strong consensus around the first three questions on the challenges of old power university staffing models. There is a 'frozen culture' (as one respondent put it) between academic and professional staff, the use of short-term contracts is common, and tenure blocks the progression of more junior academics.[242] There was less support for my ideas around ending tenure and the introduction of the 'gig academic', mainly as these proposals were considered to be less feasible. In the countries where these colleagues work, both academics and professional staff are employed as civil servants. This makes reform more challenging to achieve as it would require primary legislation. On the UON Academy model, the feedback was more mixed, with some thinking it would not work or was not relevant to their jurisdiction while others liked the focus on renewing the psychological contract. There was, though, widespread support for the expansion of third space professionals. Perhaps the most striking observation from this limited survey was how colleagues from a very diverse range of jurisdictions shared the view that the current old power model is not working. There is a demand and a need for reform globally, and it seems that the new power values and principles are central to those reforms.

Creating the changes to bring about a new power workforce will require sophisticated and nuanced leadership within universities

The transition from an old power to a new power staffing model will take exceptional leadership and, it should be stressed, followership. This is the case across the many clefts that currently exist within universities – whether between the vice-chancellor/president and their senior management team, and the most junior lecturer or accountant; whether between academic staff and professional staff; whether between those on permanent or tenured contracts and those on short-term or casualised contracts. All will have to embrace

---

[242] One of the Spanish respondents referred me to an article in *El País* that recounts an academic's experience of being on repeated short-term contracts on a very low income. In the article, he describes the competition for pre-doctoral research contracts as being like the *Hunger Games*. See: https://elpais.com/ideas/2020-03-13/el-despilfarro-universitario.html?prm=enviar_email.

a new power model of working and leave behind some of the old power tropes that have their roots in notions of the academy, tenure and academic apartheid.

This will not be easy. Much has been written about university leadership and the role of the vice-chancellor/president, not least following a number of scandals associated with vice-chancellor pay and expenses, personal conduct, and such like. A recent UK article in *The Guardian* contained interviews with a number of headhunters on what they thought the key attributes of incoming vice-chancellors should be. One responded that 'the ability to engage with all stakeholders and to want to work in partnership with them and to do so in a low ego way' was critical. She went on to describe this as 'the servant model of leadership rather than the heroic alpha leader of the past'.[243] In other words, the application of new power values, albeit with an old pedigree, as Clark Kerr (1963) noted that the university president is:

> **a many-faced character . . . The university president in the United States is expected to be a friend of the students, a colleague of the faculty, a good fellow with the alumni, a sound administrator with the trustees, a good speaker with the public, an astute bargainer with the foundations and the federal agencies, a politician with the state legislature, a friend of industry, labor, and agriculture, a persuasive diplomat with donors, a champion of education generally, a supporter of the professions (particularly law and medicine), a spokesman to the press, a scholar in his own right, a public servant at the state and national levels, a devotee of opera and football equally, a decent human being, a good husband and father, an active member of a church. Above all he must enjoy traveling in airplanes, eating his meals in public, and attending public ceremonies. No one can be all of these things. Some succeed at being none.[244,245]**

The issue of leadership and the transition facing leaders as they progress towards and inhabit the role as a head of university (that is as a vice-chancellor, president, etc.) is explored in depth by Tom Kennie and Robin Middlehurst (2021) in *Leadership Transitions in Universities: Arriving, Surviving and Thriving at the Top*.[246] The subtitle *Arriving, Surviving and Thriving at the Top* also

---

[243] https://www.theguardian.com/education/2018/nov/01/have-university-leaders-changed-after-the-vice-chancellor-pay-scandal.

[244] Kerr (1963), p. 22.

[245] Cited by Amy Gutmann in a 2008 lecture, available at: https://president.upenn.edu/sites/default/files/pullias-lecture.pdf, and bought to my attention, with thanks, by Glyn Davis.

[246] Kennie and Middlehurst (2021).

captures some of the headline challenges. Using their own work as leadership developers (including with new heads of university), combined with insights from numerous interviews with experienced, new and former heads, they make the case to move towards a new model for identifying, assessing, appointing, transitioning and supporting new heads of university. They also recognise the shifts taking place in the expectations which, as Kerr (1963) points out, the many different stakeholders have of those inhabiting these roles. How should appointing panels (often the great and the good – perhaps with an 'old power' preference?) assess a new generation of candidates for the right balance of 'old' and 'new' power experience and characteristics?

As Timms and Heimans (2018) point out in *New Power*, both Obama and Trump employed elements of new power in their respective campaigns to be elected president of the USA. Trump's approach, however, was to use new power skills and tactics in the service of old power as he concentrated the power for himself. By contrast, Obama used new power skills and tactics to start a social movement to support his candidature, and thus was dispersing power.

It is, perhaps, not surprising that Obama used this approach as one of his advisors was the Harvard academic Marshall Ganz. Ganz has written extensively on social movements and the role of leadership in those. He was involved in organising the grass roots social activism that supported Obama's 2008 presidential campaign. Ganz – like the work Matthew Bolton describes in Chapter 3 on campaigning for a living wage for cleaners in a London university[247] – is influenced by the ideas of community organising. This is based on building relationships, creating a shared story or narrative, thinking strategically and identifying a set of key actions or results that you are trying to achieve.[248] Indeed, Ganz argues that 'leadership is learned experientially, combining "heart, head, hands"', briefly introduced in Chapter 5.[249] This framework provides a useful way to think about leadership in the New Power University. The new power leader has to have a strong social purpose with a supporting narrative, has to be deeply analytical, supported by data and a strategic outlook and, critically, has to get their 'hands dirty' – that is demonstrate the ability to deliver on the missions of the New Power University, through directly supporting learning, through their research and through being personally socially responsible.

---

[247] Bolton (2017).

[248] Ganz (2010).

[249] Ganz and Lin (2011).

In modelling these leadership qualities, it is also necessary that the many communities in the New Power University demonstrate active followership. As introduced in Chapter 1, Derek Sivers' TED talk, 'How to start a movement', makes this point with clarity. You will recall that the three-minute clip has a young man dancing on his own on a grassy hill. Shortly, he is joined by one and then two co-dancers and then, as the film rolls on, the whole hill is covered with dancers. As Sivers says:

> **The biggest lesson . . . is that leadership is over-glorified. Yes, it was the shirtless guy who was first, and he'll get all the credit, but it was really the first follower that transformed the lone nut into a leader . . . If you really care about starting a movement, have the courage to follow and show others how to follow.**[250]

In the New Power University, everyone has a responsibility to apply new power values and skills. Any abdication from that – whether by a leader or a follower – is, in itself, a reversion to the instrumentalised managerialism that we are trying to move away from.

---

[250] https://www.ted.com/talks/derek_sivers_how_to_start_a_movement/transcript?language=en.

Chapter 8

The university integrated with its community

The New Power University must shift from the idea of place making towards community organising

The relationship between a university and the people who live around it has often been a tense one. As we saw in Chapter 1, the 11th century founding of the *nationes* in Bologna, Italy, occurred because the soon-to-be-students felt persecuted by the locals. This community activism was the grit that grew into the University of Bologna, Europe's oldest university. In a similar vein, after two Oxford scholars were hanged in 1209 by some locals for a murder that they did not commit, a number of their colleagues fled to Cambridge, leading to the foundation of the university there. Tensions in Oxford continued for the next 100 years, with the university exerting more and more power over the town, so that, on St Scholastica's Day (10 February 1355), riots broke out, leading to the ransacking of university property and the killing of a number of academics.[251]

Sadly, the scholars who fled from Oxford to Cambridge didn't learn their lesson and the same 'town and gown' friction is evident in the University of

---

[251] http://news.bbc.co.uk/local/oxford/hi/people_and_places/history/newsid_9158000/9158705.stm.

Cambridge's medieval history. In the 1300s, Edward II used royal charters to give academics legal authority over local people while, in 1440, Henry VI evicted townspeople from their homes and shops to build the iconic King's College.[252] This favouring of the 'gown' over the 'town' was reinforced in 1561 when Queen Elizabeth I gave authority to the university to arrest and imprison women who were 'suspect of evil'. These powers extended to control over licences for ale houses and an exemption for the university in paying land tax. As Oswald (2012) describes in her fascinating history of the policing of prostitution in Cambridge, these powers were deeply resented by the locals, leading to violent confrontations:

> **Sometimes, the area became a battle-ground for the young students and the town youths. In 1846, Josiah Chater, a local draper, noted in his diary that there was a demonstration in the Market Square against the borough police by crowds of undergraduates. He recorded: 'The Proctors and Masters were all out, but to no purpose . . . gownsmen threw glass bottles on to the townsmen's heads, and water and stones, which so enraged the townsmen that they went to all the colleges and smashed the windows to pieces.' It seems that neither the borough police nor the proctors could control mobs of town youths or of university students.[253]**

Tensions could be found in other countries, too. The universities of Sydney (founded 1850) and Melbourne (founded 1853) were established on indigenous ground taken by the colonial powers. Today, when you visit any university in Australia (and indeed any public institution), there is an 'acknowledgement of country' which is an opportunity to pay respect to the traditional owners and ongoing custodians of the land. So, for example, the host for a public meeting at The University of Melbourne will often begin by saying, 'I also would like to begin by acknowledging the traditional owners of the land we meet on, the Wurundjeri people of the Kulin nations. I pay my respects to their Elders, past, present and emerging.' While this acknowledgement is clearly well-meaning, it seems, to me, at risk of becoming transactional, with the university retaining its (old) power through a performative act, rather than sharing that power on equal terms. This is a point supported by

---

[252] Oswald (2012).

[253] Oswald (2012), p. 457.

Megan Davis, an Aboriginal Cobble Cobble woman from Queensland and Balnaves Chair in Constitutional Law at the University of New South Wales, in an article in *The Monthly* magazine, where she argues that such acknowledgements are 'perfunctory . . . only for empty symbolism as opposed to substantive rights'.[254] To be fair, Australian universities would respond by arguing that they have put in place substantive 'Reconciliation Action Plans', which commit them to taking tangible actions that support the words by offering more places and academic support to indigenous students, more employment for indigenous scholars and administrators, more engagement with communities.

Examples of tensions between communities and universities continue into the 20th century. The University of Chicago was involved in racist housing policies that 'kept black families confined to the so-called South Side "Black Belt", a crowded neighbourhood of low-income housing', as an article in *The Chicago Maroon*, the university's student newspaper, recounts. The article goes on to recall, 'In 1954, professor Julian Levi . . . articulated his vision of University self-interest. "We're not a public improvement association. We're not supposed to be a developer. We're not interested as a good government association. The only standard you ought to apply to this is whether The University of Chicago as an academic entity requires a compatible community," he argued to university president Lawrence Kimpton.'[255]

In her book, *The University & Urban Revival: Out of the Ivory Tower and into the Streets*, Judith Rodin, president of the University of Pennsylvania between 1994 and 2004, opens with a moving account of how biochemist Vladimir Sled and his fiancée were robbed one Halloween evening, when walking home from his lab at the university. Sled was stabbed multiple times and died shortly afterwards at the medical centre. This tragic event occurred in 1996, 18 months into her tenure, and followed a number of other violent incidents and murders that had occurred around the university campus in West Philadelphia. Sadly, Penn itself had helped create the social deprivation that fuelled this crime wave. Like many universities, it has used its power to further its own self-interest, including driving out local residents, either directly by buying up cheap housing and land for redevelopment or indirectly

---

[254] https://www.themonthly.com.au/issue/2020/july/1593525600/megan-davis/reconciliation-and-promise-australian-homecoming#mtr.

[255] https://www.chicagomaroon.com/article/2017/9/15/university-south-side/.

by pushing up the prices of housing and land, making it unaffordable. As Rodin describes:

> **The reality for urban universities, whose infrastructures root them in densely populated areas, has been that growth could be achieved only through encroachment on, and often destruction of, surrounding neighbourhoods.**[256]

This thousand-year conflict still continues today. Although less often characterised by violence, the resentment among local people to their university neighbours continues to simmer. A recent article in *The Guardian* describes how 'Britain's burgeoning universities are anything but a blessing, as the thousands of students they attract transform the neighbourhoods they move into, raising property prices, disrupting locals' lives with their exuberant lifestyles, transforming areas that rush to cater for the tastes of their new young clientele. The process has even spawned its own, ugly term – studentification.'[257]

New Power Universities must renew the social contract with their affiliated communities

Given this rift between 'town and gown', which spans time and place, it is not entirely surprising that universities attract so many of the negative headlines mentioned in Chapter 1. As already noted, this has prompted an ongoing debate in universities about 'place', their responsibilities as 'anchor' institutions and what it means to be a 'civic' university. Often, this debate centres on the social contract between a university and the local community, which provides the institution with a 'licence to operate' in that place. Many now contend that this contract is broken because universities have become too 'remote from life' (referring back to Amy Buller).[258] So, for example, the recruitment of as many international students as possible in pursuit of revenues in a global higher education market has often been at the expense of local communities.

In response, universities are encouraged to implement a range of new strategies, policies and agreements that express their commitment to the geography within which they reside, backing that with a range of laudable initiatives,

---

[256] Rodin (2007), p. 24.

[257] https://www.theguardian.com/education/2018/sep/23/town-v-gown-is-the-student-boom-wrecking-communities.

[258] Buller (1943), p. 136.

some of which we have already advocated in this book. While not against this, I do find it an uncomfortable approach. It has a tinge of self-interested paternalism: 'we need to engage the locals so we can sustain our licence to operate' as opposed to the idea that 'we are part of a community that can help shape what we do and maximise our social impact'. Yet, while this debate is happening now, it also feels dated, based as it is on the assumption that any given university is rooted in a place. We already saw in Chapters 3 and 7 that the same university may be delivering educational content online to students tens of thousands of miles away through the engagement of gig academics who will have a temporary relationship with the institution.

Timms and Heimans (2018) address this intellectual itch in *New Power*, when they draw out the difference between historic indicators of 'civic health' and the 'transient affiliation' of new power. They cite Robert Putnam's book *Bowling Alone*, which argues that there has been a long-term decline in the 'social capital' of US communities. The OECD defines social capital as 'networks together with shared norms, values and understandings that facilitate co-operation within or among groups',[259] although I prefer David Halpern's simple explanation that 'it's about how people are connected with one another'.[260] *Bowling Alone* is data-rich and pervasive and is summarised in its two-word title: since the 1960s, there has been a dramatic and sustained decline in the number of Americans participating in 10 pin bowling leagues and a corresponding rise in those who bowl by themselves. As Putnam points out, 'The broader social significance [of this trend] . . . lies in the social interaction and even occasionally civic conversations over beer and pizza that solo bowlers forgo. Whether or not bowling beats balloting in the eyes of most Americans, bowling teams illustrate yet another vanishing form of social capital.'[261] However, Timms and Heimans (2018) argue that this is an old power framing, getting to my itch about the current debate concerning the position of universities as 'civic' 'anchor' institutions. New power thinking implies that, rather than committing to a lifelong relationship with a university, people are more likely to opt in and out at different times. Indeed, this was an argument that I made in a blog with my colleague Deborah Bull where we shared our 'dislike

---

[259] https://stats.oecd.org/glossary/detail.asp?ID=3560.

[260] Halpern (2005), p. 1.

[261] Putnam (2000), p. 113; Putnam also caveats this comment by noting, 'Strictly speaking, only poetic licence authorises my description of non-league bowling as "bowling alone". Any observant visitor to her local bowling alley can confirm that informal groups outnumber solo bowlers.'

for the term "public engagement" as it disregards, at least semantically, what we were trying to achieve. We have observed . . . that, in its form as a noun, it too easily becomes a responsibility that can be passed to others and something that can be considered, at some point, concluded or "done". We see engaging with the world beyond the university as a holistic, active and ongoing process – a cycle of iteration and reiteration improved and enhanced by interaction with broader and diverse communities.'[262]

Figure 8.1 attempts to conceptualise the subtleties of how these relationships should work in a new power world. On the horizontal axis, you have the local community (town) and the university (gown) while, on the vertical axis, you are either physically 'rooted' in a particular place or you are 'affiliated' through either a transient relationship or virtually through online education. For the latter, the dichotomy between town and gown does not work and thus this cell is a single box. The arrows detail different types of relationship that can exist. Arrow A is, in effect, the classic 'old power' relationship but one, I should stress, that is of value as we will see in the way the University of Pennsylvania responded to the murder of Vladimir Sled. Arrow B is consciously less institutional, based on the principles of community organising and is illustrative of the future town and gown relationship that the New Power University should aspire to. The example I will use is Parent Power from the UK. The final set of arrows labelled C represent the diverse set of relationships that could exist for those affiliated communities who are not rooted in the geographical place of the New Power University. The next sections explore each of these arrows in more detail.

The University of Pennsylvania reinvented the traditional old power town and gown relationship to demonstrate sustained commitment in reviving West Philadelphia

The murder of Vladimir Sled was, in Rodin's words, 'a decisive moment – one seminal incident – that leaves no choice but to seek an entirely new paradigm'.[263] For Rodin, this new paradigm was about building on the ethos of the University of Pennsylvania's founder, Benjamin Franklin, in 'doing well by doing good' (as discussed in Chapter 5), creating a proactive partnership between the universities and their local communities that would unite town and gown. This is the type of relationship illustrated by arrow A in Figure 8.1.

---

[262] https://wonkhe.com/blogs/whats-wrong-with-public-engagement/.

[263] Rodin (2007), p. x.

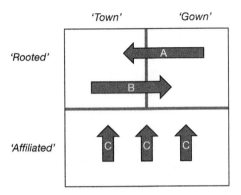

Figure 8.1 Conceptual model of new power relationships between universities and their communities

At the heart of the 'Penn Model', as it has become known, is the recognition that university–community partnerships must involve mutual respect which, going back to Matthew Bolton's analysis of social change, is based on an understanding of power and self-interest. Critically, as Rodin notes, 'The economic and social changes that Penn sought to achieve [occurred] by operating holistically and with long-term commitment to the redevelopment of its local community.'[264] This long-term commitment was shared by the trustees of Penn so that, when they came to appoint Rodin's successor, Amy Gutmann, they required a commitment to this strategy. As we saw in Chapter 5, Gutmann captures this nicely in her observation that 'a university is, first and foremost, a social undertaking to create a social good'.

In practical terms, in 1996, Rodin oversaw a deliberative process that resulted in the West Philadelphia Initiative. She made this the top institutional priority for Penn, backed up by a public commitment that the university would not expand its campus into residential areas and, instead, focus future growth on brownfield sites and commercial land. The West Philadelphia Initiative had five integrated aims. First was to ensure that local neighbourhoods were safe and clean. Second was to stabilise the housing market, making it affordable for locals and attractive for university staff. Third was to stimulate economic activity by buying locally. Fourth was to encourage shops, restaurants and such like to establish a presence in the area. Finally, there was a focus on improving local schools.

---

[264] Rodin (2007), p. 17.

Although the Penn Model is an example of an old power intervention from a leading civic institution, as I saw when I visited in 2015, it succeeded in ensuring the university was *for* the city, not *of* it. Perhaps, more exactly, it can be viewed as a mixed model of old and new power in the way that it was both formulated and implemented. The approach adopted by Rodin and colleagues resonated with community organising techniques through listening campaigns, power analysis and an understanding of the university's self-interest. But the interventions themselves – especially the more physical and infrastructural ones – were classically old power.

It is important to realise that the West Philadelphia Initiative was not Penn's first foray into community organising. For some time, Ira Harkavy, one of the pioneers of service learning in the USA (as discussed in Chapter 3), had been running the 'Penn Program for Public Service' with students delivering courses at local public schools. In 1992, Harkavy was appointed director of the Center for Community Partnerships (CCP) at Penn, mobilising students, staff and faculty to work on social, economic and health problems of West Philadelphia. The CCP was the predecessor organisation to the Netter Center mentioned in Chapter 2, and today is the way that civic and community engagement is advanced at Penn, bringing together the assets of the university and local community to address problems such as poverty, sustainability and health inequality.[265]

The West Philadelphia Initiative, though, was the most significant institutional commitment at scale that the university has made and, critically, the values of initiative were both authentic and empathic, with Rodin noting that 'leadership has to be gentle'.[266] In the context of the New Power University, Rodin was ahead of her time in commenting on the centrality of community:

> **I am convinced that sustained community partnerships will help define successful universities in the twenty-first century; without a continuous civic dialogue, such partnerships will fail, and both the universities and their neighbourhood will suffer.[267]**

[265]   https://www.nettercenter.upenn.edu/about-center/our-mission.

[266]   Rodin (2007), p. 22.

[267]   Rodin (2007), p. 20.

How listening to the local community resulted in an award-winning movement to empower parents in supporting their children's educational choices

Moving on to arrow B in Figure 8.1, Parent Power is an excellent example of the new power approach to town and gown. Parent Power is a community-led project that resulted from a partnership between Citizens UK and King's College London's Widening Participation (WP) department. Citizens UK, a charity that Matthew Bolton heads up, 'organises communities to act together for power, social justice and the common good'.[268] At the time, King's WP department was led by my former colleague Anne-Marie Canning (now chief executive of the Brilliant Club), working with young people from under-represented groups to help them access higher education.

As we saw in Chapter 3, there are still deep inequalities in those who get to go to university. In the UK, the proportion of young people who graduated from universities increased by just 12 percentage points for the poorest fifth of households compared to a 35 percentage point increase for the richest fifth of households (see Figure 3.1). As part of its role in addressing this gap, King's WP department provides specific support to pupils with academic potential who come from families with no history of university participation. One idea Canning's team wanted to develop was parental engagement – the literature was rather promising in showing that a good way of closing educational inequality was through engaging parents. However, when they tried this, in her words, 'it was bit of a damp squib'.

So, in 2017, Canning and colleagues teamed up with James Asfa, one of the community organisers at Citizens UK, and ran a 'listening campaign' with local schools in South London. They and their teams invited parents of children aged 11–14 to attend meetings and asked them to share their thoughts about education. Participants were then offered a 'one-to-one' meeting with a community organiser who would listen in more detail – and in a safer space – to the challenges their children were facing in accessing a university education.

This type of listening campaign is a key part of the community organiser's toolkit and differs from standard public consultations in the way it is built on developing relationships and trust. At the core of a listening campaign is the

---

[268] https://www.citizensuk.org.

'one-to-one', where an organiser has a very deep and, at times, personal conversation with a member of the community where both participants share their stories ('lived experience' in the jargon) and develop mutual understanding of shared issues which, in time, can lead to ideas and action.

During the campaign, Canning, Asfa and their colleagues engaged with over 50 parents in two South London boroughs (Lambeth and Southwark). They heard about a range of difficulties in gaining university admission and decided to hold a 'town hall' meeting where parents were asked to pick three issues on which they would campaign. The chosen themes were the cost of academic summer schools, the difficulty of visiting universities outside London and the cost of British citizenship applications (which prevented access to student loans).[269] This was the beginning of the social movement that adopted the name Parent Power.

Critically, Parent Power followed the 'iron rule' of community organising: 'Never do for others what they can do for themselves.' Instead, staff from King's and Citizen's trained parents to become both experts in university access and campaigners on educational equality within their communities. Since the project's inception in July 2017, the project has involved over 200 under-represented parents, recruiting 35 as local parent power leaders. The parents meet every six weeks to discuss issues concerning educational inequality and receive training and advice from King's staff members on related topics, such as the unaffordability of private tutoring, social and cultural capital, competitive university applications and youth violence. Daniel Bennet, a heating engineer from Brixton, was one of the first to join Parent Power to help his son Darntá get into university. 'I didn't hear the word "university" until I had left school,' he said in an interview for King's website.[270] 'I was quite smart but I didn't know it. I was very quiet and sat in the background. No issues, no trouble but I got no encouragement from teachers. That's not going to happen to Darntá.' It is tapping into this self-interest that has enabled Parent Power to run a series of successful campaigns, most notably securing bespoke, fully funded open days at universities across the UK and winning bursary places at private summer schools. The movement has expanded, with groups of parents forming in Oldham, in the UK and, most recently, in

---

[269] https://www.theguardian.com/education/2019/apr/10/social-and-community-impact-award-winner-and-runners-up.

[270] https://www.kcl.ac.uk/parent-power-2018.

Sydney, Australia, with the support of University of Technology Sydney (UTS). As Paul Webb, one of the widening participation officers at King's, said in a blog on Wonkhe:

The success of Parent Power lies in listening – really listening – to those whom it intends to help. Providing information, advice and guidance to help parents understand the UK higher education system is important. Arguably more important, though, is getting to know parents as human beings and opening up about your own experiences.[271]

This was a point stressed by Canning when I recently asked her for some reflections on Parent Power. She wanted to 'talk about the emotions of what we did'. As she went on to say, 'there is a lot of love and support in Parent Power. To know the children and families who were once 'numbers on a spreadsheet' was transformational and deeply satisfying. I am still in contact with the parents. I often text them and see them in other organising spaces and we are equals. I know their babies and do their passport applications even though I've left King's.'

One of the other lessons I take from Parent Power that can be applied to the New Power University is the patience that Canning and her colleagues showed in putting together the programme. As one reviewer of a draft of this book put it, 'The need sometimes to prioritise the "slow" over the "fast" . . . You have to build trust, show willingness to enter someone else's world, return favours. Parent Power . . . is a wonderful example of that.' But all of that takes time, potentially giving the New Power University a unique advantage over the private sector and government in allowing slow, reflective spaces to emerge to enable this type of deep and meaningful community building.

Deep two-way learning will be a core characteristic of the relationships between the New Power University and its affiliated communities

It took me some time to fully comprehend the nature of arrow C in Figure 8.1 and I am very grateful to Shaun Ewen for some insightful conversations exploring the issue. Shaun is pro-vice-chancellor (Indigenous) at The University of Melbourne and is himself an Aboriginal person. In 2019, he wrote a

---

[271] https://wonkhe.com/blogs/power-of-parents/.

piece with his Melbourne colleague Daniel Hanrahan that explored the 'civic' framing of universities and their relationship with indigenous people in Australia.[272] In this piece, they introduce the concept of *Bala lili*, which means 'to give and take, listening and understanding'. The concept comes from the Yolngu Matha in Arnhem land, northern Australia, and 'refers to the phenomenon where saltwater and freshwater rivers meet, mix, and flow on together. Where these waters combine, they bubble up together to create something exciting, something new.' In short, *Bala lili* is humanity's original take on community organising.

Ewen and Hanrahan challenge the framing of the 'civic university' in the context of indigenous Australia and, in doing so, unpack the concern I raised earlier. They note that the term 'civic' is in itself exclusionary and reinforces a western civilisation approach to knowledge and learning, ignoring as it does that other paradigms exist – whether within indigenous communities in Australia or through the lived experience of parents in South London. Their second critique is the notion that, in the words of the UK Civic University Commission, 'A civic university cannot serve everywhere, and that means someone must fall on the wrong side of the boundary'.[273] As Ewen and Hanrahan note, 'Indigenous people have traditionally been placed the wrong side of the university boundaries.' Their final concern is the emphasis placed on a university's duty to benefit local students, employers and communities when, they argue, 'The opposite is needed for engagement with Indigenous knowledge. Australian universities can internationalise local Indigenous knowledge by connecting it with established global knowledge systems, including the dynamic global dialogue surrounding Indigenous knowledge systems.'

These issues of knowledge, boundaries and connectiveness speak to the new power values articulated by Timms and Heimans (2018):

- Informal opt-in decision making.
- Self-organisation.
- Networked governance.
- Open source collaboration.
- Crowd wisdom.

---

[272] https://pursuit.unimelb.edu.au/articles/the-unique-value-of-indigenous-knowledge.
[273] Civic University Commission (2019).

- Sharing.
- Radical transparency.
- Do-it-ourselves 'maker culture'.
- Short-term conditional affiliation.
- More overall participation.

For the New Power University, the relationships with its communities – both physical and virtual – will be beyond any boundaries defined either by geographical place (as with the University of Pennsylvania) or the 'taking part' of particular groups (as in the example of Parent Power). Many relationships will be short-term and those moments of connection will need to be meaningful. This could be in the form of accessing open source educational material, participating in citizen science or, as a gig academic, delivering a weeklong module on a one-off contract. If the New Power University gets it right, such 'transient affiliations' will lead to greater participation where the boundaries around a university increasingly blur into a single affiliated community where the distinctions between students and staff, between physical and virtual, and between town and gown are less and less marked. As part of this, spaces – whether physical and virtual – will need to be shared and collaboration based on the principles of *Bala lili* to give, take, listen and understand. Power becomes distributed and shared equitably.

It is hard to describe exactly how all this will look in practice, though, in part, this is because the exact forms of these relationships have the potential to vary hugely depending on the situation and approach of each university. Perhaps one comparison can be found in the world and culture of online video gaming. *Fortnite*, which launched in 2017, now has 250 million people registered worldwide, with nearly 80 million active players recorded in August 2018:[274] that is a community equivalent in size to the 20th largest country in the world. For those of you who have not come across this phenomenon (I only know it as my 13-year-old son is a gamer!), perhaps the most interesting thing is how the community has grown around the game and how it behaves – for good and for bad. My son, for example, will be playing with friends he has never physically met but has got to know online. You can overhear them looking out for each other as well as, sadly, bullying one another at times. All of this is in a virtual space with a set of values and behaviours being created

---

[274] https://www.gamesradar.com/uk/how-many-people-play-fortnite/.

and moderated within a network. This virtual world spills over into physical gatherings at gamer conferences and events organised around LANs,[275] where people compete on their computers but in close proximity to one another. You can watch games on YouTube and Twitch, which provide commentaries on the game and also act as a gateway to a range of other topics – from mental health through to whether it is worth going to university or not.[276] Again, from my Gen X perspective, some aspects of this are more positive than others.

The point is that all this has happened in a similar way to that described in Chapter 3 with other web-based communities such as www.scottsbasslessons. com and www.woodworkingmasterclasses.com. These communities create their own values, norms and acceptable behaviours. So, the lesson for the New Power University is that it has to embed the notions of *Bala lili* – 'to give and take, listening and understanding' – into its value system in ways that shape the interactions with the affiliated communities that form up around it. Or, as Ewen and Hanrahan conclude:

> **The differing context, geography and history of other nations will mean this form of civic relationship with Indigenous peoples may not be relevant to other universities. The responsibilities of a university in London, Johannesburg or Shanghai will depend on the needs, deeds and histories of their *place*. However, the concept of *bala lili* is applicable to all.**

The New Power University should secure and enhance the economic impact on its affiliated communities

The preceding section examined the relationship between a university and its affiliated communities through the lens of social cohesion. But, as we have already noted a number of times in this book, universities also have major economic impacts. For example, they employ people – including low-paid cleaners and security staff – and they generate value through the research they undertake and the students they graduate. There is a long history of

---

[275] Local area networks.

[276] https://www.youtube.com/watch?v=Xi9meLsJGOg.

universities assessing and reporting on their economic impact. Some of this is effectively lobbying as part of that desire to strengthen the social contract and licence to operate. Nonetheless, such studies are interesting as they do illustrate the impact universities have in their local communities, be that through jobs, the creation of new businesses or their activity as an enterprise.

One of the first studies that explored the economic impact of a university was a 1997 report by BankBoston's economics department, focusing on the Massachusetts Institute of Technology (MIT) in the USA.[277] Using a database of companies founded by MIT graduates, BankBoston examined the scale of national job creation by a single research university. As the report concluded:

> **If the companies founded by MIT graduates and faculty formed an independent nation, the revenues produced by the companies would make that nation the 24th largest economy in the world. The 4,000 MIT-related companies employ 1.1 million people and have annual world sales of $232 billion [$374 billion in today's money].[278] That is roughly equal to a gross domestic product of $116 billion [$187 billion in today's money], which is a little less than the GDP of South Africa and more than the GDP of Thailand.**

The largest number of MIT-related companies were in the Greater Boston area (where MIT is located), with over 1,000 firms headquartered in Massachusetts. Generating worldwide sales of $53 billion ($85 billion in today's money), these businesses employed over 350,000 people worldwide and 125,000 people in the state (5% of total state employment). MIT has continued to keep an eye on the entrepreneurial activity of its alumni, reporting in 2014 that they have launched over 30,000 active companies, employing roughly 4.6 million people, and generating roughly $1.9 trillion in annual revenues. That revenue total now falls between the world's 9th largest GDP, Russia ($2.097 trillion), and the 10th largest, India ($1.877 trillion).[279]

In the UK, Nottingham Trent University and the University of Nottingham recently published a report suggesting their annual combined regional economic contribution was £3.8 billion, equivalent to around 14% of the local economy, and that 25,000 extra jobs were supported by the economic activity of the two universities, which meant that, together, they would be

---

[277] http://www.saveourheritage.com/Library_Docs/Bank%20Boston%20Impact%20of%20Innovation.pdf.

[278] Inflated using CPI inflation calculator, available at: https://www.in2013dollars.com/us/inflation/.

[279] http://web.mit.edu/innovate/entrepreneurship2015.pdf.

the third largest direct employer in the county.[280] This type of analysis is reinforced in a 2017 report by Universities UK (a trade body), which states that the higher education sector supported almost one million jobs in the UK economy and contributed £21.5 billion to the country's gross domestic product.[281]

While such big numbers can be hard to get your head around (and can sometimes seem too large to be believable), more robust academic analysis does confirm the positive economic impact of universities. For example, Valero and Van Reenen (2019) have developed a dataset on the location of nearly 15,000 universities in about 1,500 regions and across 78 countries dating back to the 11th century.[282] Using this, they model the relationship between the number of universities and future regional GDP growth between 1950 and 2010, controlling for a range of other factors that could explain this relationship. Their analysis shows that a 10% increase in the number of universities per capita is associated with 0.4% higher GDP per capita and that 'the relationship between GDP per capita and universities is not simply driven by the direct expenditures of the university, its staff and students. Part of the effect of universities on growth is mediated through an increased supply of human capital and greater innovation.'[283]

So, what can the New Power University do to secure and enhance this indisputable economic impact on local communities? As discussed in Chapter 5, the first response is to do no harm by ensuring it is paying living wages, is being cognisant of local environmental impacts, and is using socially responsible procurement policies to support local and social enterprises. Beyond that, 'innovation districts', around which there is a growing literature, align nicely with some of the concepts and values of new power and, arguably, are to new power what science parks are to old power. Julie Wagner and colleagues set up The Global Institute on Innovation Districts and, in one of their reports, they argue that 'innovation districts embrace the attributes of density and proximity to facilitate collaborative, "open" innovation and strong social networks'.[284] In other words, innovation districts rely, to a certain extent, on hyper local networks between universities, local enterprises and city administrators, with

---

[280] https://www.universitiesfornottingham.ac.uk.

[281] https://www.universitiesuk.ac.uk/policy-and-analysis/reports/Pages/economic-impact-universities-2014-15.aspx.

[282] Valero and Van Reenen (2019).

[283] Part of this is the spillover effects that arise from research, as described in Chapter 4.

[284] Wagner, et al. (2019).

the aim to build an innovative and entrepreneurial community, not – as is the case with science parks – a collection of buildings for rent.

It is important to caveat that while 'place' is a critical element of an innovation district it is not, as we have discussed, a central principle of new power. Nonetheless, the ideas are important when considering how to maximise economic impacts and are further explored in van Agtmael and Bakker's (2018) book, *The Smartest Places on Earth. Why Rustbelts Are the Emerging Hotspots of Global Innovation*. They argue that there has been a transformation to some of the traditional heavy manufacturing cities, such as Pittsburgh in the USA or Eindhoven in the Netherlands. In recent generations, these types of city have suffered economic decline and deprivation as old industries have closed down (hence 'rustbelt') but have begun to reposition themselves, often in partnership with local universities, as high-tech centres relying on a set of new power values. 'The brain belt phenomenon involved connecting people in a process (brain sharing) as well as connecting the digital world of IT, data analytics, and wireless communications with new and old ways of "making things" to create new technologies and products.'[285] As with innovation districts, van Agtmael and Bakker argue a university 'should not be an ivory tower but rather an open source of knowledge and a connector among the public and private entities'. In other words, there is a role for the New Power University in this form of place making where the emphasis has to be on new power values such as open source collaboration, radical transparency, networked governance, and such like.

A concluding thought on how a university education is dividing our communities

Rodin finishes the opening chapter of *The University and Urban Revival* with a quote from *The New York Times* columnist David Brooks, in writing about the devastating impact of Hurricane Katrina on New Orleans:

Especially in these days after Katrina, everybody laments poverty and inequality. But what are you doing about it? For example, let's say you work at a university or a college. You are a cog in one of the greatest

---

[285] van Agtmael and Bakker (2018), p. 253.

inequality producing machines this country has known. What are you doing to change that?[286]

I read Brooks on a regular basis, as he provides a challenging but often fair critique of 21st century (old power) universities. As noted in Chapter 3, he believes that 'the future of the university will be found in its original moral and spiritual mission, but secularized, and in an open and aspiring way'.[287] His overall thesis, it seems to me, is not far removed from the arguments I make in this book about the New Power University. At its heart is the recognition that universities have lost sight of their purpose, which should include the 'social good' that Amy Gutmann talks about.[288]

It is, therefore, worrying that Brooks believes that old power universities are 'inequality producing machines' but, sadly, the data supports this view. As higher education participation rates have increased, this divide has become easier to see. As Robert Ford, a professor of political science at The University of Manchester, put it in a *New Statesman* article, 'The past three decades have been terrific for university graduates and terrible for unskilled school-leavers.'[289] This, in part, results from the shifting nature of work towards higher skilled graduate jobs, at the expense of traditional blue-collared manufacturing jobs. (Although, this argument can be challenged on the grounds of causation. Do universities cause the inequality or is the inequality caused by an economy that requires high-level technical skills supplied by universities?)

The split between graduates and non-graduates also extends beyond considerations of work. We know from a number of recent elections – in the UK, in Europe and in the USA – that one of the defining characteristics of how people vote is whether they went to university or not. Graduates tend to share more liberal views on a range of topics, including interest and involvement in politics, environmental awareness and concern, perceptions of gender roles, attitudes to immigration and immigrants, perceptions of welfare benefits and benefit recipients, national identity and entrepreneurship.[290]

---

[286] https://www.nytimes.com/2005/09/25/opinion/the-education-gap.html.

[287] https://www.nytimes.com/2015/10/06/opinion/david-brooks-the-big-university.html.

[288] Although not directly related to universities, Brooks' book *The Road to Character* gives you an excellent insight on his thinking. This book provides the stories of a number of men and women through history who have wanted to 'serve the world' (p. *x*).

[289] https://www.newstatesman.com/politics/2017/01/want-know-how-someone-votes-start-asking-if-they-went-university.

[290] BIS (2015).

This combination of economic prosperity and a progressive set of social values has created a 'graduate class', as Ford calls it, that lined up behind 'Miliband, Clinton, Van der Bellen and the European Union. Those with few or no formal educational credentials lined up behind Farage, Trump, Hofer and Brexit.'

There is a chicken and egg question at the heart of this debate which is very difficult to disentangle. Are those young people who go to university more likely to already have liberal and progressive values or is it the case that the experience of going to university inculcates these? The literature on this is not clear, not least as it is empirically difficult to answer.[291] However, from the perspective of community cohesion, it must be of concern to old and new power universities alike that education itself is creating some of the economic and political fissures that are characterising democracies in the early part of the 21st century. While, historically, the relationship between a university and its local community might be seen through the lens of 'town and gown', a more dispersed and less anchored world risks having this divide magnified at a national level, infiltrating politics and inevitably putting universities on one side of a political debate. This is a topic we will return to in Chapter 10, which considers how the New Power University should engage with, inform and shape political and policy debates.

---

[291] Brennan, *et al.* (2013).

Part Four

The conduct of the New Power University

Any reform movement which is limited to correcting slovenly or slipshod abuses in our university will lead inevitably to a reform which is equally slovenly . . . An institution is a machine in that its whole structure and functioning must be devised in view of the service it is expected to perform. In other words, the root of university reform is a complete formulation of its purpose. Any alteration, or touching up, or adjustment about this house of ours, unless it starts by reviewing the problem of its mission – clearly, decisively, truthfully – will be love's labour lost.

José Ortega y Gasset (1946)

Having considered how the New Power University must evolve in terms of its purposes and its relationships with students, staff and affiliated communities, the final question is how should it conduct itself, both internally, in terms of the structures and governance, and externally, in the way it engages with the wider world of policy and politics.

The existing and long-practised organisational structure of the university into cognate disciplines may no longer be fit for purpose, and a new approach should be adopted, focused on the wide range of difficult-to-solve challenges that face the world today. This will free the New Power University to participate in the different types of ecosystems that are necessary to tackle these complex problems, some located in nearby geographies, others connected through transient affiliations globally. This, in turn, requires a more pluralistic and informal approach that eliminates the separation of academic from operational oversight, with a more networked, 'opt-in' governance, that has the delivery of the social good of the university as its main priority.

When looking outwards, the New Power University must engage with the policy and political debates of the day. The 'sitting on the fence' position that many old power universities adopt on issues of contemporary importance is untenable. Instead, the New Power University must become an advocate on issues that matter. To pretend that universities are apolitical is a hypocrisy that undermines their social purpose and makes them remote from life.

Chapter 9

Structuring and governance

The New Power University will need to adapt its structures and governance to flourish within a broader ecosystem

In his book *The Australian Idea of a University*, Glyn Davis worries how alike higher education institutions are in Australia and how this creates a risk to the sector from external shocks. His main explanation for this homogeneity is the path dependency created by the foundation of The University of Sydney in 1850, which provided the blueprint for subsequent Australian universities.

This idea of path dependency also applies to universities beyond Australia. It is extraordinary how universities across the world are still broadly modelled on the structures developed at the University of Bologna and the other 'confessional universities' in the middle ages (as discussed in Chapter 2). At that time, faculties were organised into four disciplines – Arts, Law, Medicine and Theology – focused on the delivery of teaching. Today, most universities follow this model with cognate disciplines grouped into faculties such as health, humanities, social sciences and the physical and engineering sciences, albeit they have expanded their purpose to include research. Although the number of faculties and departments or schools may vary between institutions, broadly speaking, the majority of universities follow this model.

As Davis examines, the reason for this type of path dependency is because 'the creation of new universities is a rare and expensive act' and that 'it becomes costly to contemplate major change in direction, and may be challenging conceptually because the original form and mission of the organisation seem comfortable and apparently logical'.[292] As Davis goes on to describe, the QWERTY keyboard is an often used example of path dependency. Originally developed in the 19th century to overcome the jamming of mechanical typewriters by separating commonly used letters, today, with electronic keyboards, it is both inefficient and no longer required. Nevertheless, QWERTY remains the standard, with competitors, such as the Dvorak and Colemak layouts, seen as niche despite being more efficient, ergonomic and apparently easier to learn.

The question for the New Power University is whether its organisational form should be dictated by the path that originated in Bologna or if the benefits of a new structure, to meet its evolving mission and values, outweigh the costs and risks of moving away from this. In *New Power*, Timms and Heimans (2018) examine this issue through the lens of leadership, drawing out an alliteration of signalling, structuring and shaping.[293] Signalling, as noted briefly in Chapter 7, is the way new power leaders use rhetoric to empower supporters with a sense of ownership, giving people 'permission to dance'.[294] Structuring is how leaders organise and conduct the dance, putting in place practices to enable participation and agency, as we saw with Parent Power in Chapter 8. Shaping is how the new power leader models overall norms and behaviours that are then upheld by the crowd or social movement.

Applying this thinking to the New Power University means challenging the current structures of higher education institutions, considering how best to design an organisational form that delivers on its purposes – learning, research and social responsibility – and best supports its people – students, staff and communities. In this chapter, we explore this by examining alternative structures, how they would fit into broader systems approaches to policy design and, finally, how to provide practical and effective oversight of the New Power University through appropriate forms of governance.

---

[292] Davis (2017), pp. 31–2.

[293] Timms and Heimans (2018), p. 175.

[294] Using this analogy developed by Derek Sivers, described in Chapter 1.

The organisational design for a New Power University should follow its strategy

A common mistake is to create organisational structures before having a clear idea of strategy. Parts Two and Three of this book proposed a high-level strategy for the New Power University. This is the starting point from which we need to identify the most appropriate organisational design. In doing so, we should be mindful that New Power Universities need not be homogenous in either strategy or structure. Put another way, it is likely that different institutions will put different emphases on different elements of the New Power University, meaning that they will have different strategies and thus different structures.

What are the alternative organisational designs for a university? Clearly, there is the status quo – the 'Bologna model', if you like – but there are others. David Staley sets out some of these in his book *Alternative Universities: Speculative Design for Innovation in Higher Education*. In the introduction of the book, he notes how he wishes 'to present alternatives to existing institutional forms of the university as a way to critique current practices . . . In the realisation . . . that there is little appetite for developing universities that deviate so dramatically from the norm'.[295] In Table 9.1, I have tried to summarise the 10 'speculative designs' that Staley proposes and then evaluate them against the strategic needs of the New Power University.

Staley clusters his 'designs' into four groups: organisation, apprenticeship, technology and attributes. The first group is characterised by the organisational structure and 'by their difference from the way most universities are organised today'.[296] The two apprenticeship models look to substitute classroom teaching with real-world experience. The technology designs, not surprisingly, envisage technology as a key role in education but not as the system of delivery. The final two attribute designs focus on the transformative experience of the student.

It is interesting how a number of these alternatives resonate with some of the ideas already explored for the New Power University. For example, the idea of a Platform University sits nicely with the discussion in Chapter 3 about allowing students to 'pick and mix' modules across a number of different providers, 'stacking' credentials to build up a bespoke undergraduate course. Likewise, the Micro College is similar to the idea floated for 'gig academics'

---

[295] Staley (2019), pp. 18–9.

[296] Staley (2019), p. 15.

Table 9.1 Alternative university designs

	Speculative design	Description
Organisation	Platform University	An agnostic platform that is organised and managed organically, connecting teachers and students.
	Micro College	One professor with approximately 20 students. Faculty establishes a range of micro colleges in different locations with different pedagogical approaches.
	Humanities Think Tank	Research-focused institute that mobilises the humanities to contribute to policy development and broader public discourse.
Apprenticeship	Nomad University	The university is organised like a series of gap-year experiences with the physical location shifting around the world for different courses and years.
	Liberal Arts College	Centred on skills rather than subjects, such as complex problem solving, imagination and cross-cultural competency.
Technology	Interface University	Based on the idea that the future cognition will be a hybrid of artificial and human intelligence. Students learn to think with and through algorithms and computers through an otherwise traditional curriculum.
	University of the Body	Focus on developing students' literacy skill so they can take in and analyse more and more information.
Attributes	Institute of Advanced Play	Generation of new and novel knowledge through imagination and play, leading to unplanned and unexpected insights.
	Polymath University	Students major in three different disciplines – one in science, one in arts or humanities and the other a professional discipline.
	Future University	As the case study is the basis of traditional business skills, future scenarios are used to examine how the future might unfold.

in Chapter 7, who develop and own their course content in selling it into a market of higher education providers. The Liberal Arts College has a focus on graduating the 'world ready' student, as discussed in Chapter 3, while the Polymath University echoes the benefits of an interdisciplinary approach, as explored in Chapter 4.

Building on Staley's ideas, a further feasible model for the New Power University could be to design its organisational form around a series of 'grand challenges' in areas such as sustainable energy, ageing and urban living. This is an idea that Geoff Mulgan and colleagues put forward in a paper for the innovation think tank Nesta in 2016[297] and uses the challenges as the pedagogical basis for structuring learning and, to a lesser extent, as the focus for research.

This 'problem-based' approach has been adopted by a number of medical schools globally and has also been applied to other disciplines such as engineering. One example that Mulgan, *et al.* use to illustrate their case is the Olin College of Engineering, a private undergraduate teaching college located in Massachusetts, USA. Olin was founded in 1997 with a large endowment from the eponymous FW Olin Foundation. The vision of the trustees was to radically change engineering education with a focus on the 'needs of real people' to 'solve the world's complex future challenges'. As its website states, 'Olin "engineer-innovators" envision and deliver products, services and systems that transform the way people live on this planet.'[298] Interestingly, Olin had no departments or tenured faculty, basing its academic approach on the 'philosophy . . . that learning should be taken out of the world of academic theory and practised in context. Tasks are designed to model real-life constraints such as finance and personnel, so that students learn the skills which are required to cope in a professional environment. All students complete a yearlong capstone project that gives them the opportunity to implement what has been learned in the real world.'[299]

For the New Power University, the problem with the approaches of both Staley and Mulgan is that they focus primarily on new forms of education and not on how to combine learning, research and social responsibility into a single academic mission, perhaps its single most important defining characteristic. Interestingly, this is also the case for some of the innovative research

---

[297] Mulgan, *et al.* (2016).

[298] http://www.olin.edu/about/.

[299] Mulgan, *et al.* (2016), p. 5.

institutes such as Howard Hughes Medical Institutes' Janelia Research Campus[300] and The Francis Crick Institute in London.[301] The Crick, for example, has adopted a structure with no departments but where staff can move from one area to another depending on the research project they are working on. It has also adopted an innovative '6+6 model' where young scientists coming into the Crick have a maximum of two six-year terms at which point they are expected to establish themselves in a university or other research institute, mirroring, in a way, the ideas put forward in Chapter 7 for tenure for early career researchers.

In the USA, Arizona State University (ASU) goes some of the way in addressing these issues. Michael Crow (its president) and William Dabars, in their book *Designing the New American University*, quote a 2004 ASU White Paper that sets out design principles calling for a future institution that:

> **measures its academic quality by the education that its graduates have received rather than the academic credentials of its incoming freshman class; one at which researchers, while pursuing their scholarly interests, also consider the public good; one that does not just engage in community service, but rather takes on major responsibility for the economic, social, and cultural vitality of its community.[302]**

Through a process that has taken over a decade, Crow has not only focused ASU's mission on these principles but has aligned its structure through a 'federation of unique transdisciplinary . . . schools and colleges . . . through the consolidation of academic departments which . . . no longer serve as the sole institutional locus of a given discipline'.[303] 'These new academic entities ("new schools") have been established to both advance teaching and engender research, both fundamental and applied, that possesses the interdisciplinary breadth to address large scale "grand challenges".'[304] One example of this would be the Global Institute of Sustainability, which brings together a range of experts – from built environment to human evolution – in a school that offers 'transboundary'[305] undergraduate and postgraduate degrees along with

[300] https://www.janelia.org.

[301] https://www.crick.ac.uk.

[302] Crow and Dabars (2015), p. 242.

[303] Crow and Dabars (2015), p. 246.

[304] Crow and Dabars (2015), p. 277.

[305] https://sustainability.asu.edu/people/.

'use-inspired research with purpose and impact'[306] in climate change adaptation, biodiversity, behavioural change, urbanisation and future and system thinking, to name a few.

The Institute also has a programme of 'partnership'[307] activities that comfortably align with the social responsibility agenda of the New Power University. For example, it has teamed up with the City of Phoenix and Arizona Public Service (APS) to launch 'Energize Phoenix', a project to create thousands of jobs while transforming neighbourhoods and commercial districts along the light rail line into a 'Green Rail Corridor'. ASU worked with the City of Phoenix and APS to retrofit homes and businesses to increase energy efficiency and to reduce carbon emissions in the community.[308]

Olin and ASU, as innovators in the higher education sector, both go some way in pointing to a complete solution for the appropriate organisational form of the New Power University – with Olin not having departments and ASU focusing on transdisciplinary institutes and schools while moving power away from academic departments. However, as with the theoretical models of Staley and Mulgan, neither are complete. Olin is predominantly an educational institution that does undertake some research but, at least on its website, does not major on social responsibility. ASU gets a step closer but it still has more traditional academic departmental forms that sit within the transdisciplinary institutes and schools.

Nonetheless, the idea to use societal challenges as a primary organisational principle is one that can be adopted by the New Power University. Certainly, there is no lack of challenges facing the world today: what if the New Power University was organised around these? Imagine a Faculty for Climate Change Adaptation. This would blend learning, research and social responsibility in its core academic mission, with academics and third space professionals from a range of disciplines and practices – history, sociology, geography, meteorology, instructional design, consultancy, policy analysis – either on contract or tenured at an early part of their careers. Research agendas would reflect societal need, with the faculty operating in a socially responsible way and mobilising assets to deliver social good. Disciplinary identity could, if needed, be organised along horizontal interest groups, either as part of a networked organisation

---

306 https://sustainability.asu.edu/research/.

307 https://sustainability.asu.edu/partnerships/.

308 https://sustainability.asu.edu/news/archive/city-of-phoenix-receives-25-million-grant-to-create-energize-phoenix-in-partnership-with-arizona-state-university-and-arizona-public-service/.

or as communities of practice. Although this type of organisational structure is common in the private sector, it is less common in public sector institutions, especially universities. However, in reviewing the concept and applicability of networked organisations to universities, Lewis, *et al.* (2005) note that:

> **somewhat ironically, while universities have been remodelling themselves along orthodox corporate lines, many management theorists are becoming increasingly critical of top-down corporate styles of management and organisational structure.**[309]

Despite the merits of a more multi-disciplinary and networked organisational form for the New Power University, Lewis, *et al.* (2005) do caution against seeing such a model as a panacea for university design. In studying five Australian universities, the 'network organisation model did not supersede previous organisational structures but instead was often articulated in complex ways to existing bureaucratic, collegial and managerial practices within the university setting'.[310] This, then, is yet another challenge for the New Power University, to break free from these old power 'bureaucratic, collegial and managerial practices' in establishing an alternative university design. If the path dependency of the past is broken, and structure follows strategy, then the success of such alternative designs will signal the New Power University is coming of age.

The New Power University will contribute to society as part of an ecosystem that permeates its organisational boundaries

Another paradigm for thinking about the New Power University could be one of an ecosystem. This was an approach adopted by Ron Barnett in his book *The Ecological University: A Feasible Utopia*,[311] where he argues that the university is connected with a number of ecosystems such as knowledge, social institutions, persons, the economy, learning, culture and the natural environment. This biological metaphor has also been widely used as a framework to conceptualise organisational design, both within institutions and between institutions. While not an entirely accurate metaphor, it provides

---

[309] Lewis, *et al.* (2005), p. 64.

[310] Lewis, *et al.* (2005), p. 72.

[311] Barnett (2018).

an interesting way to think about the structure and functioning of universities. Just as the New Power University is likely to be structured around some form of a network, it will also be part of a broader ecosystem that extends beyond its organisational boundaries to informally and formally connect with other key civic institutions.

The idea of ecosystems has been around for a long time in policy analysis and has been applied to education, healthcare and innovation on a regular basis. As Mars, *et al.* (2012) point out, the adoption of such a framework provides an 'operating logic . . . as actors and the organisations they create become more interconnected in an increasingly networked global economy and society'[312] but there are 'critical differences between biological and organisational ecosystems' not least the 'misguided assumption . . . that biological ecosystems are both communal (supported by individual commitments to the greater good) and stable'.[313] Their point is that individual species are working to maximise their success (as measured by staying alive and reproducing) and thus an 'innovation in nature happens mostly by accident and typically confers an advantage to a particular unit rather than to the system as a whole'. Likewise, they conclude that there is 'no firm evidence that biological ecosystems become stable over time . . . for example, an organism that innovates in such a way that it can no longer be eaten by a predator disrupts the established food web and thereby causes a ripple effect across the entire ecosystem'. Notwithstanding these caveats, they do conclude that 'the conceptual merits of the organisational ecosystem metaphor are such that it should certainly be retained'.

In cautiously adopting an ecosystem paradigm, it seems to me there are three ways in which the New Power University can engage: the first is as a key civic institution in a local economy; the second is as part of a 'vertically integrated' education system, which may or may not be geographically defined but would provide education across all age groups; the third is as a 'horizontally integrated' system of universities, which, again, need not be geographically defined. There may well be others, but below I explore the key characteristics of these three models to illustrate how the New Power University can help further contribute to society beyond its organisational boundaries.

In exploring the social responsibility of the New Power University (Chapter 5) and how it engages with its communities, both locally and virtually (Chapter 8), we explored the idea of a university as a civic institution. At the

---

[312] Mars, *et al.* (2012), p. 280.

[313] Mars, *et al.* (2018), p. 279.

same time, in Chapter 8, I expressed my concern about the parochial way 'civicness' is being framed in contemporary policy debates about higher education as a university-led, top-down, agreement-driven process, rather than one that is driven by local communities, through listening exercises as nicely encapsulated through the Aboriginal term *Bala lili* (which, you will recall, means 'to give and take, listening and understanding'). In my idealised world, I would see the New Power University as an indispensable partner in a civic ecosystem; a partner that neither dominates nor is dominated but is able to work effectively with a range of different organisations, from small community-based groups through to large businesses. As a result, the New Power University is seen to be contributing to the local economy through procurement, employment and the purchasing power of students, it partners with local companies through research and innovation, it supports local education by sponsoring schools, it engages with and contributes to local authorities and it enables the social cohesion of local communities. I suspect, in reading that list, many colleagues would say that is what they are already doing and, to a degree, it is, but it is often through the lens of old power transactional values, that is 'if we sponsor a local school that will get us reputational credit with the local politicians which will ease our next planning application'. To avoid this pitfall means investing in relationships, actively listening and shaping practice to be a full and active member of the local community. This, as we have seen throughout this book, has not been the historical way that universities have operated but can be achieved through adopting the new paradigm I am arguing for. That said, I have also cited a number of examples of extraordinary practice – the Social Justice Leave at the University of Technology Sydney, Australia, The Works at The University of Manchester, UK, and the international consortium running the PADILEIA programme for refugee students in the Middle East – which demonstrates what is possible. The challenge for the New Power University will be to move from these examples of civic engagement to one where such engagements are connected and stewarded as part of a wider ecosystem of socially attuned civic institutions.

The second type of ecosystem I identified above is one that is 'vertically integrated'. In the language of economics, that is an organisation that 'owns' its own 'supply line'. When applied to education, this would mean the New Power University taking on some form of responsibility for schools and colleges in its locality. There are two antecedent ideas for this. The first, as noted in Chapter 3, is the analogous development of academic health science centres (AHSCs) where universities and health authorities have come together to create a health ecosystem, often stretching from primary care through to that provided in hospitals.[314] The advantage of such partnerships is that patients – the local community – are getting the most cutting-edge care as it is provided by doctors who also work as researchers in the university, and that researchers get access to patients for their research. While the latter point may come across as transactional, it is worth noting that health outcomes are often better for patients that participate in research studies.[315]

The second antecedent is that a number of universities already have relationships with schools in their locality – we saw that with Widener University in Pennsylvania where they founded the state's first university-based charter school as well as with Prepanet in Mexico, which the Tecnológico de Monterrey established an online accessible high school. There are a number of examples of this type of relationship, including, in the UK, formal sponsorship of schools.[316] But, as we saw in Chapter 5, when this was raised as a policy, it was quickly knocked down by the old power establishment as being 'a distraction'.

Combining these two ideas – that of an AHSC and the sponsorship of schools – leads you to envisage an ecosystem where a New Power University works in partnership with other education providers in its locality – from primary/elementary schools, secondary/high schools through to post-16 further education colleges and other local universities. In the same way that AHSC has shared objectives to improve patient and population health outcomes, you could envisage a New Power University taking up the stewardship for an 'academic education system' with the objective of improving educational outcomes for a community. As we will discuss below, there are challenges with this type of model in terms of governance (who is in charge and what are the organisational boundaries?), but it is also worth noting that such issues arise in AHSC and have been resolved. Indeed, in a commentary piece informed by a literature review on AHSC,[317] Catherine French and Naomi Fulop comment:

Many AHSCs have changed governance arrangements over time . . . less because of inherent faults in governance arrangements and more because of financial issues and conflicts between senior executives . . . Whether an AHSC is successful in achieving its mission or not depends more on the abilities of its people and their relationships

---

[314] French, *et al.* (2014).

[315] Boaz, *et al.* (2015).

[316] For example, the Exeter Maths School (https://www.exetermathematicsschool.ac.uk/our-story/) and King's Maths School (https://www.kingsmathsschool.com) are sponsored by the University of Exeter and King's College London respectively.

[317] French, *et al.* (2014).

with each other than how they are governed. Governance models are shaped by the individuals who operate them and there are no ideals – they are influenced by local context and personalities.[318]

The final form of ecosystem is potentially more ambitious and will, no doubt, be 'shaped by the individuals who operate them', and that is to imagine an ecosystem that is 'horizontally integrated', to go back to the economics jargon. That is to formalise relationships between an ecosystem of universities. This could be defined geographically but also need not be. One historical example would be the University of London, which was founded in 1836 as a degree-awarding examination board for students holding certificates from University College London and King's College London. Today, it is a 'loose federation' of 17 independent member institutions (who now award their own degrees) who share a number of resources, including the delivery of online education.[319] Another innovative and geographically defined example would be the Universities of Nottingham initiative cited in Chapter 8, that is a 'pioneering collaboration which brings together the strength and civic missions of Nottingham's two world-class universities'. The focus of Nottingham Trent University and the University of Nottingham is 'transformative change for the people and place of Nottingham and Nottinghamshire' and thus is clearly embedded with a civic and regional focus.[320]

Circle U – the European University Alliance – is another example of a horizontal federation.[321] A pilot initiative in response to French President Emmanuel Macron's proposal for a European University,[322] its vision is to be 'an inclusive, research-intensive and interdisciplinary European university. Students, staff and partners from civil society, businesses and the public sector collaborate to jointly develop competencies and solutions for keeping Europe and our planet healthy, peaceful, democratic and prosperous.' This will include developing new models of virtual joint learning among students from seven universities across Europe. The challenge for this new type of arrangement is old power universities have tended to resist partnerships with 'lesser'

---

[318] https://www.academichealthsolutions.com/thought-leadership/academic-health-science-centres-learning-social-sciences.

[319] It is also noteworthy that, in its original form, it acted as the type of accreditation function we explored in Chapter 3, when we discussed the 'stacking' of credits in a pick and mix degree offering.

[320] https://www.universitiesfornottingham.ac.uk/about.

[321] https://www.circle-u.eu.

[322] https://www.daad-brussels.eu/en/eu-higher-education-policy/european-universities/.

institutions. They are more likely to partner in dual and joint degrees with the 'highest ranking', 'world class' universities as measured through the league tables, which, as we saw in Chapter 2, ironically are based on research outputs.

A non-geographically defined ecosystem would be the PLuS Alliance, established by Arizona State University, USA, King's College London, UK, and the University of New South Wales, Australia. It derives its name from the location of each institution – Phoenix, London and Sydney – and describes its vision as 'global communities empowered through innovative and accessible education and research'.[323] Focused on tackling a number of global challenges, the Alliance aims to increase the flow of students and staff between the partner institution and to co-market online qualifications. This is an interesting innovation with Mark Lester, former head of global partnerships at Future-Learn, an online platform, drawing parallels with the airline industry in an interesting article in *Inside Higher Education*. As Lester argues:

Major national airlines, when faced with regulatory and cost barriers to international expansion, have formed alliances to open up new markets. Through alliance networks, individual airlines have been able to:

- **Offer their passengers a larger and denser global network of destinations with smoother connections.**
- **Sell tickets to destinations across the entire alliance network, increasing the utility of the airline to their customers.**
- **Offer valuable frequent-flier programs, which benefit their own customers and also bring alliance partner customers to the airline.**
- **Win new customers and improve their quality perception from alliance promotion.**

Universities might be able to secure some of the same benefits from alliance formation. This has already happened in research as universities pooled resources to win a larger share of research grants and for sharing services. This could now be about to happen in the online qualification space.[324]

---

[323] https://plusalliance.org/about.

[324] https://www.insidehighered.com/digital-learning/views/2018/06/27/what-online-education-can-learn-airline-industry-opinion.

Putting aside the environmental impact of the airline industry, and the fact that universities are not selling a service or product in quite the same way, the analogy between oneworld[325] and the PLuS Alliance is an interesting one that would allow the application of a number of the new power values and practices across a diverse range of New Power University strategies and structures under different national regulatory regimes. It is possible, for example, to imagine a shared platform that provided access to the same online material accessed by members of a global ecosystem where students come together for virtual education but may physically meet at different campuses worldwide; research would be focused on global challenges through collaborative networks forming within the ecosystem; while social responsibility would be delivered through the institutional being of the member universities as well as, say, making a targeted effort to reduce international travel within the ecosystem. Third space and professional staff could be employed by the member universities, or through the alliance, while academic staff would either be affiliated with member universities or be engaged on a 'gig' basis by the system. The bulk purchase of modules would both benefit the gig academic (by securing a bigger market) and allow costs to be managed and shared across the ecosystem. A focus by the horizontally integrated alliance on the social purpose of higher education would deliver social good to both the physical communities where the New Power Universities are located and to a virtual community online.

More varied and fluid forms of governance and oversight will allow the New Power University to adapt and flourish

As Peter Eckel and Cathy Trower emphasise in the introduction of their book *Practical Wisdom: Thinking Differently About College and University Governance*, 'The goal of good governance is to advance colleges and universities, to make them increasingly and steadfastly relevant social organisations that maximise their missions and have lasting positive impact on their students and communities, and to do this in ways that are financially sustainable over the long run.'[326] This goal is clearly applicable to the New Power University but will only be sustained if there is a fundamental rethink of traditional old power structures of governance and oversight.

---

[325] An alliance of 13 airlines (https://www.oneworld.com).

[326] Eckel and Trower (2019), p. 3.

The governance of overcentralised managerial regimes of old power university is complicated by 'bicameralism', a word that typically is used to describe the separation of powers between two legislative chambers: in the UK, the House of Commons and the House of Lords or, in the USA, the House of Representatives and the Senate. In the university context, especially those in the old power Anglo-Saxon tradition, this bicameralism is found between a governing board and the senate (or academic board, as termed in some universities). As Jones (2002) argues, 'Bicameralism represented a governance structure that attempted to balance the need for external accountability to the state which financially supported the institution with the need for the participation of the professoriate in decisions that focused on academic standards.'[327] The trouble with this structure is that it reinforces the 'academic apartheid' referred to in Chapter 7, by excluding key members of the New Power University, that is professional staff, third space professionals, students and affiliated communities.

Even though many universities have addressed these issues of participation by inviting faculty, staff and student representatives to sit on both governing boards and senates (and their equivalents), these old power bicameral structures still tend to inhibit new power approaches of informal networks and conditional affiliation in getting things done. Indeed, I don't think it is an exaggeration to suggest that, in many universities, old power resides in those who are expert in routing decision-making processes through the byzantine committee structures, rather than those with the most innovative, creative and impactful ideas for change.

So, what does governance look like in the New Power University? Part of the change will be structural – removing the old power bicameralism and replacing it with networked modalities for shared decision making. Jones (2002) draws on the concept of policy networks while Eckel and Trower (2019) talk about shared governance. Neither are new and both exist in old power universities but need to be simplified and amplified, while becoming more inclusive. If we go back to first principles and consider the roles and responsibilities of an old power governing board, they can be summarised into four areas:[328]

1 (Re)-stating the university's mission and purpose.

2 Monitoring university performance.

---

[327] Jones (2002), p. 218.

[328] As paraphrased from Eckel and Tower (2019), p. 18.

3 Safeguarding the university's assets (financial, physical and reputational).

4 Being the 'eyes and ears' between the university and its external world.

One possible model would be to consider the New Power University as a cooperative, that is an organisation that is 'controlled and run by and for their members to realise their common economic, social and cultural needs and aspirations',[329] and to adopt and re-purpose some of the governance principles applied by such institutions. As noted in an article in *The Guardian* on the corporate governance of cooperatives, the 'movement periodically wrestles with the question of how to relate member engagement and (at least in legal terms) democratic control of co-op societies to the way that boards of directors and senior managers strategically manage their businesses'.[330]

Drawing from the experience of co-operatives, one approach applicable to the New Power University would be a single governing body with an executive team who have the authority to manage the university, but who do this by applying the mantra 'management is not a status but a process'.[331] The challenge, however, will be to avoid the type of producer capture where governance ends up serving the interests of the governors, rather than the broader social interests or purposes of the New Power University.

This raises the question, however, of how to define 'membership', whether that membership bestows democratic rights to elect the governing body and, if it does, whether a system of 'one member one vote' applies. There is almost certainly no single answer to this question – and there may, indeed, not be an answer, given differences in standing and status within universities and the ambiguity about ownership for public institutions – but, assuming there is an answer, it should be up to each individual New Power University to decide. At one extreme, you could have a system of self-referential nomination to a governing board that decides on who to elect as future members. At the other extreme, all stakeholders in the university could have a vote and there is a democratic process. It may be that, for example, alumni have a vote, but it is weighted in such a way that those who graduated a number of

---

[329] https://www.ica.coop/en/cooperatives/what-is-a-cooperative.

[330] https://www.theguardian.com/social-enterprise-network/2012/may/24/cooperatives-tackle-corporate-overnance.

[331] https://www.ica.coop/en/cooperatives/what-is-a-cooperative.

years ago have less influence than, say a student studying today. An 'outside-the-box' idea would be to look at the fan-based ownership of football clubs. In Spain, four teams (Real Madrid, Barcelona, Athletic Club Bilbao, and Club Atlético Osasuna) are legally constituted as member-owned non-profit sports associations. Members have a number of rights, including electing the president of the club and getting discounts on season tickets, etc. Advocates claim that this model 'develops, fosters and perpetuates close social and economic bonds with the community',[332] a key focus of the New Power University, while detractors are concerned about the politicisation of sport and the lack of transparency, especially regarding finance. For the New Power University, what seems most critical is to ensure that the governing board has the diverse range of voices represented on it – students and staff, local and international communities, executive and non-executive, alumni, etc. – and that it operates to an informal and opt-in set of values and way of working.

A closing reflection on the inward practices of the New Power University

This chapter has consciously been less definitive in setting out the structural and governance practices of the New Power University than Part Two (on purpose) and Part Three (on people). This is for three reasons. First, it is important that the organisational structure, the role within ecosystems and governance models, align first and foremost to strategy. I have set out some of the key characteristics of a New Power University but, as noted above, they will rightly be mixed in different ways, not least to minimise any future risk of establishing unhelpful path dependency. It would, therefore, be inappropriate to proscribe both governance and organisational structures until that vision is determined. Second, the values of new power demand a more organic, participatory approach to decision making, so it feels appropriate to put forward ideas to stimulate the thinking while being comfortable that these will evolve over time. Finally, while I have been very critical of the way old power universities have narrowed their purpose and have treated their people, I am less critical of the *theoretical* aspects of university governance, other than, perhaps, the more

---

[332] https://bleacherreport.com/articles/404511-cure-or-curse-socio-club-ownerships-in-spanish-la-liga.

undesirable effects of bicameralism. As Eckel and Trower (2019) conclude in their chapter on shared governance:

> **In many ways the characteristics and contributions of shared governance are appearing in corporate America. *Harvard Business Review*, the exemplar of contemporary management thought, is rife with articles that promote flat hierarchies, shared decision-making, devolved or employee-driven strategies, knowledge workers and the creative class, and self-managed teams. 'Progressive management thinkers have been talking about worker empowerment for decades.'[333] Higher Education has been using it for centuries. In today's world of expected revolution and change, universities continue to be extremely resilient.[334]**

To create a forward-looking institution fit for the 21st century, the challenge is putting these new power values into practice, at the expense of the corporate instrumentalised managerialism, satirised by Stefan Collini[335] in Chapter 2, that has defined the HiEdBizUK university of the past 30 years. Or, as the Spanish philosopher José Ortega y Gasset put it in his pamphlet *Mission of the University*, 'Any reform movement which is limited to correcting slovenly or slipshod abuses in our university will lead inevitably to a reform which is equally slovenly . . . An institution is a machine in that its whole structure and functioning must be devised in view of the service it is expected to perform. In other words, the root of university reform is a complete formulation of its purpose. Any alteration, or touching up, or adjustment about this house of ours, unless it starts by reviewing the problem of its mission – clearly, decisively, truthfully – will be love's labour lost.'[336]

---

[333] Citing Martin (2010), p. 71.

[334] Eckel and Trower (2019), p. 172.

[335] Collini (2012), p. 153.

[336] Ortega y Gasset (1946), p. 36. It is worth noting that this pamphlet was based on a series of lectures given in 1930.

Chapter 10

The advocate for change

The New Power University must be an advocate for the social good

Throughout this book, I have followed Ortega y Gasset's advice in seeing 'the root of university reform [as] a complete formulation of its purpose'. I have made the case that the social purpose of the New Power University in the 21st century must be focused on the triad of learning, research and social responsibility. This mission is not only delivered by the power of students, staff and communities but it is also enabled through the conduct of the New Power University. In building this case, I have highlighted a number of contradictions that riddle old power universities, including: monopolistic and self-regulated powers to award degrees; perverse incentives to invest in discovery research so as to drive rankings in global league tables, at the expense of applied impactful research; low-paid outsourcing of staff; limited support to help students through a delayed transition to early adulthood; continued defence of tropes like tenure, academic freedom and institutional autonomy; and disengagement from local communities and the political and social issues that matter most to them. Partly, these tensions exist because of a long, unchanged and unchallenged history and, partly, because of the introduction of unreflective managerialism.

The biggest contradiction of them all, however, is the idea that the university is a neutral actor when it comes to political and social issues. The principle that 'the university is the home and sponsor of critics; it is not itself a critic' (to quote The University of Chicago's Kalven Committee report, more below) is both hypocritical and wrong. Self-evidently, a university is willing to be a critic when it comes to matters affecting its own interests, for example funding, student fees, planning decisions, and such like. So, why does it argue that it should not be a critic on the political and social issues of the day? This 'in-your-face' inconsistency is one of the many reasons that the social contract between universities and wider society is broken, as discussed in Chapter 1.

To make matters worse, while claiming this neutrality, in practice, universities are actually taking positions quite regularly on social issues such as marriage equality (in Australia) and Brexit (in the UK). Again, this muddled thinking is understandably feeding anti-university sentiment, as this form of exceptionalism consciously distances universities from their societal obligations.

The old power arguments that have led to this position are now both unsustainable from an intellectual perspective and unacceptable in terms of the consequences that arise from the way universities contribute to division in today's societies. A New Power University must ditch the notion of political neutrality to become a clear and powerful advocate for issues that matter to its students, staff and communities. Two case studies in particular – marriage equality and Brexit – hold lessons for how this should work, how the risks involved must be navigated and point towards how universities can become better at being advocates for social good.

Old power interests in protecting position and privileges have underpinned universities not taking a stance on political or social issues

As we saw in Chapter 7, the idea of academic freedom arose when Emperor Barbarossa granted sanctuary for scholars visiting Bologna in the 11th century. This 'freedom' was extended over time as the church, monarchies and governments granted various privileges to universities and their academic staff, as was the case for the University of Cambridge in the middle ages and, more recently, the introduction of the concept of tenure at the turn of the 19th century in the USA. This nexus of academic freedom, institutional autonomy and professorial tenure has, understandably, been robustly defended by university leaders and academics alike ever since.

A key part in protecting the position and privileges of universities has been the avoidance of conflict around strongly contested societal issues that are generally seen as the purview of the political world. Probably the strongest argument for this stance is the 'Report on the University's Role in Political and Social Action', published in 1967 by a faculty committee chaired by Harry Kalven, the Harry A. Bigelow Professor of Law at The University of Chicago Law School.[337] The case made in the three-page 'Kalven Report', as it is known today, is best summarised by this lengthy, but abridged, quote:

> **A university has a great and unique role to play in fostering the development of social and political values in a society. The role is defined by the distinctive mission of the university and defined too by the distinctive characteristics of the university as a community . . . To perform its mission in the society, a university must sustain an extraordinary environment of freedom of inquiry and maintain an independence from political fashions, passions, and pressures . . . Since the university is a community only for these limited and distinctive purposes, it is a community which cannot take collective action on the issues of the day without endangering the conditions for its existence and effectiveness . . . Our basic conviction is that a great university can perform greatly for the betterment of society. It should not, therefore, permit itself to be diverted from its mission into playing the role of a second-rate political force or influence.**

As Boyer (2015), in his book *The University of Chicago: A History*, notes, 'The Kalven report gave Chicago a sturdy stake in the ground of ideological neutrality as it sought to ward off unwanted political interventions and partisan temptations from outside the University's walls.'[338] This ideological neutrality was reaffirmed by the outgoing president, Robert Zimmer, in a speech he gave in 2009 (as cited by Boyer), where he argued:

> **The commitment to maintain open, rigorous, intense inquiry in an environment of maximal intellectual freedom is not a simple one. It is difficult and to succeed demands a culture and community that will support it. The University of Chicago holds these as its highest values, and we seek to reinforce them at every turn. The Kalven report is a**

---

[337] http://www-news.uchicago.edu/releases/07/pdf/kalverpt.pdf.
[338] Boyer (2015), p. 501 (online version).

component of this culture. Many other institutions push other values forward as legitimate competing interests, and their culture may not support such a strong position on this particular set of values. Every institution needs to come to its own conclusion as to what it is and what it wants to be. It needs to decide how much weight to give to various competing interests. Kalven only works at the University of Chicago because of these common values at the University, and can only be fully understood as a part of the realization of these values.[339]

However, even with this explicit commitment to 'sustain an extraordinary environment of freedom of inquiry and maintain an independence from political fashions', The University of Chicago has, in fact, shown it is willing to take a position on a political and social issue of the day, namely freedom of expression (as discussed in Chapter 6). Importantly, Zimmer acknowledges that 'every institution needs to come to its own conclusion' and any student, member of faculty or staff who goes to The University of Chicago should know that they have a strong and consistent position on freedom of expression. So, put bluntly, if you don't agree with that position, then don't go there and, if you are there and don't like it, then leave.

In fact, this ability to advocate on an issue and speak out seems to be supported by Kalven himself. At the end of his eloquent exposition in favour of neutrality, he goes on to make the case for such exceptionalism:

From time to time instances will arise in which the society, or segments of it, threaten the very mission of the university and its values of free inquiry. In such a crisis, it becomes the obligation of the university as an institution to oppose such measures and actively to defend its interests and its values.

Beyond this justification for universities to advocate on an issue that directly affects their interests, the position and privileges enjoyed by universities provide an obligation to go further in speaking out on contested issues of wider societal importance that will, almost inevitably, have a political dimension.

Having institutions that are able to 'speak truth to power' is a key characteristic of a civilised society. Universities and academics do not have a monopolistic right to this role but, as independent centres of knowledge curation and

---

[339] https://president.uchicago.edu/page/address-delivered-columbia-university.

creation, their contribution in doing so is critical. Moreover, if they are unable to speak truth to power for fear of the repercussions, the principle of academic freedom turns out to be toothless and, in turn, unravels the reasons for institutional autonomy and tenure. This is what we see from Amy Buller's account of 1930s Germany, where 'professors [were too] remote from life'[340] to effectively speak truth to the Nazis, or about the Nazis to others. Rather, universities should be willing to take a stance on the important issues happening in the societies of which they form a part, as with the Central European University announcing the relocation of its campus from Budapest in Hungary to Vienna in Austria, as it was unwilling to abide by new laws inhibiting free speech.[341]

New Power Universities should take positions on the contested political or social issues of the day

In exploring the issues on which universities and university leaders should consider taking a position, it is helpful to think of these in terms of two dimensions: whether the issue is driven by self-interest or is of wider societal interest and whether the issue is contested or not (Figure 10.1). Clearly, neither dimension is mutually exclusive. There are issues where the interests of the university overlap with the society's and there is, of course, some degree of judgement involved as to how contested an issue is by those concerned. Nevertheless, this framework helps think through the 'what, why and how' of the way universities take a position on social and political issues.

The 'Protectionist' quadrant in the top left of Figure 10.1 focuses on contested issues, such as the direction of higher education policy, that affect the viability of universities in terms of both their purpose and as businesses. As Glyn Davis, the former vice-chancellor of The University of Melbourne, put it in an all-staff email in 2014, titled 'Who speaks for the University', 'The institution cannot be silent when matters of higher education policy are to be settled.' He goes on to ask, 'Who then speaks for the university', suggesting that, 'The answer . . . is both general and specific. Every member of the university community has a right to express their views . . . [but] . . . since

---

[340] Buller (1943), p. 136.

[341] https://www.theguardian.com/world/2019/nov/16/ceu-classes-move-to-vienna-orban-hungary-ousts-university.

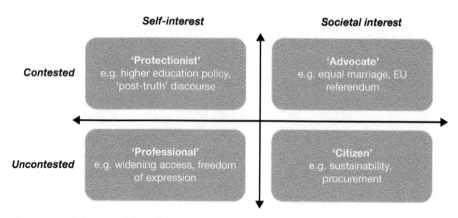

Figure 10.1 Types of political and social issues where universities take a position

Melbourne must also offer a view as an institution, the specific responsibility to speak falls to the governing body, the University Council . . . Faced with questions for the institution, the Council debates principles, settles disagreement where necessary by vote, and shares its decision in public statements.' This email was circulated in the context of some radical proposals for higher education policy in Australia, which included cuts to funding and an increase in interest rates for student loans. Both issues affected the self-interest of the university as they would impact on its ability to generate revenues.

What about more nebulous issues such as advocating against public discourse based on 'alt-facts' and 'post truth'? Davis' successor as vice-chancellor at The University of Melbourne, Duncan Maskell, picked up on this issue in one of his first press interviews for *The Age* in February 2020, when he described Michael Gove, the British politician who infamously said, 'I think people in this country have had enough of experts', as a 'fool'.[342] Maskell points out, 'If I tell you something about salmonella . . . you need to bloody well listen to me because I spent my entire career trying to understand this thing . . . But, that's not how the world works anymore. Some commentator can say well I don't believe that, actually it's like this.' Maskell connects this behaviour to what he labels the 'politicisation of knowledge', whereby objective facts are not accepted by partisans. 'So, if you come out and say something that you earnestly believe, based on the scientific evidence about climate change, for example, somebody else comes along and says you're part of a left-wing conspiracy . . . No, I'm not. I'm just giving you the data, mate.' This was a point

---

[342] https://www.theage.com.au/politics/victoria/tthey-re-definitely-not-cash-cows-lunch-with-university-of-melbourne-vice-chancellor-duncan-maskell-20200205-p53xwl.html.

that Amy Buller made in the 1930s in *Darkness Over Germany*, and one that I already quoted in Chapter 1, when she noted that:

You will find it is not essential to them to know what is the scientific explanation of these problems in detail, for they say what is essential, is that our experience is the basic experience of historic reality.[343]

I share these concerns and, indeed, in an article I wrote for the online magazine *Encompass* immediately after the Brexit referendum in the UK, I also took on the anti-intellectualism or anti-expert vibe of Gove's comments.[344] In that piece I pointed out that:

Both sides of the referendum argument were guilty of undermining the role of the expert with very loose use of facts and a dishonesty in not saying 'we don't know'. Some did their best to challenge this – for example Full Fact[345] and UK in a Changing Europe[346] – but were drowned out by lie and counter lie from both sides.

This is bad news for universities. As Maskell notes, 'If society decides it's not going to operate on the basis of knowledge, the universities are really challenged in terms of why we are here.' It is, therefore, appropriate and right that universities advocate and defend the idea of critical and reasoned thought and reflection and means it is in their self-interest to stand up to ideologies that undermine knowledge, evidence and facts. This was the case in the 1930s in Germany and, sadly, also seems to be increasingly the case in today's 'in-between time'.

Moving onto the 'Professional' quadrant in Figure 10.1, this deals with the social and political issues in everyday university life, which are still in the university's self-interest but are largely uncontested. The two examples cited are social mobility (having policies in place that encourage young people from disadvantaged groups to apply to university) and freedom of expression (that is supporting the principle of free speech).

Both these issues have already been touched on earlier in this book. Chapter 3 examined the 'graduation gap' between rich and poor that, while participation in higher education has significantly increased over the past 30 years

---

[343] Buller (1943), p. 152.

[344] https://encompass-europe.com/comment/i-am-an-expert-and-i-care.

[345] https://fullfact.org.

[346] https://ukandeu.ac.uk.

in the UK, the proportion of young people who graduated from university increased by 12 percentage points for the poorest fifth of households, compared to 35 percentage points for the richest fifth. In Chapter 8, I described how a community-led project called Parent Power is trying to address this gap. The issue of under-representation of disadvantaged groups in higher education is clearly a society-wide issue of equity but it is also in a university's self-interest to make progress on this as it helps generates additional fees (albeit at times with discounts through scholarships) and contributes to student, staff and community satisfaction and sense of being and purpose.

The issue of freedom of expression is a bit more nuanced. As we noted above, The University of Chicago has made this a cause célèbre and, as such, may have positioned it in one of the two 'contested' cells because of the political and societal context of that institution. However, for the majority of universities, policies around freedom of expression are largely 'hygiene matters'. As we saw in Chapter 6, the number of events where free speech is threatened is very small, and research also shows that 80% of students and the general public think that freedom of expression is more important than ever. As such, despite the heated debate it generates, for the majority of universities, most of the time, the protection of free speech is an uncontested issue, albeit one of deep self-interest, given they are meant to be places where ideas are debated and shaped.

The 'Citizen' quadrant at the bottom right of Figure 10.1 contains wider societal issues that are generally considered uncontested at this time. Again, the cited examples of sustainability and procurement have already been commented on. In Chapter 5, I reviewed procurement policies to support local jobs, reduce academic travel to cut pollution and carbon, and the divestment of endowments from fossil fuel companies to reinvest into ventures with a strong social purpose. Although these policies have not been wholly adopted by all universities, they are, nonetheless, common and often uncontested. In my own university, the chief procurement officer, Veronica Daly, introduced a policy that preferentially bought goods and services from local and social enterprises. There was no resistance to the idea, rather it was enthusiastically welcomed. Indeed, people reacted by saying, 'Why did we not think of that earlier?' Interestingly, these policies go beyond what is in the university's self-interest to consider the wider societal interests. Or, to put it another way, they are implicitly making the university a 'critic' of current accepted practices.

It is in the quadrant labelled 'Advocate' that the real problems arise, when universities are faced with societal issues that are (often strongly) contested.

While we have seen that universities are willing to voice opinions or even criticism around uncontested social and political issues, things get very uncomfortable when moving into areas where there is open and vocal disagreement. It is this variability in response, left unexplained to the wider political and public audiences, that can come across as being self-serving or hypocritical: universities take positions on matters that are either in their self-interest or are uncontested but, when it really matters to society at large, they hide or sit on the fence.

It is this quadrant that the Kalven Committee seems to be most concerned about when commenting that universities cannot 'take collective action on the issues of the day without endangering the conditions for its existence and effectiveness'. The context of that conclusion was a debate about divesting Chicago's endowment from apartheid South Africa. That was at the end of the 1960s but it still resonates today. Indeed, as quoted above, one of the reasons for adopting this position was the view that the university would be 'diverted from its mission into playing the role of a *second-rate* political force or influence' (my italics).

But what if universities were a first-rate political force and saw that as part of their mission? This, for me, becomes one of the core characteristics of the New Power University. It is an institution that embraces the idea of being a 'critic' deliberately, taking positions on the social and political issues of the day. To illustrate how this might work, including how to avoid the risks it raises, I will explore two contrasting case studies involving national debates not directly connected with higher education policy. The first is around equal marriage in Australia and the second is around Brexit in the UK.

On 9 December 2017, an amendment to the federal Marriage Act in Australia gave same-sex couples the same right to marry as heterosexual couples.[347] It was the culmination of decades of campaigning by the LGBTQIA+[348] community and their supporters, including rallying against the explicit prohibition of same-sex marriage in an earlier amendment in 2004. The 2017 change followed a commitment the previous year by the Liberal-led Coalition government to hold a national plebiscite.[349] In effect, the government kicked the issue into the long grass during the election by saying it would only change the law if there was public support for same-sex marriage. In making this

---

[347]   For more detail, see: https://www.nma.gov.au/defining-moments/resources/marriage-equality.

[348]   Lesbian, gay, bisexual, transgender, queer, intersex and asexual.

[349]   In Australia, unlike a referendum, a plebiscite is used to test the public's views on an issue, while a referendum is used to change the Constitution.

electoral commitment, the government was neutralising a toxic issue that divided its supporter base, some of whom were socially conservative and against 'gay marriage'. Ironically, it was unable to get support for the formal plebiscite from the Senate, so took the unusual step of holding a voluntary postal survey.[350] A staggering 80% of eligible Australians participated in the survey, with the Australian Bureau of Statistics announcing, on 15 November 2017, that 61.6% of participants had answered yes to the question, 'Should the law be changed to allow same-sex couples to marry?'

Just over two years later, on 31 January 2020, the EU (Withdrawal Agreement) Bill finally passed the House of Commons, paving the way for the UK's exit from the European Union on 31 December 2020. Like the equal marriage debate in Australia, it followed years of efforts by (largely but not exclusively) Eurosceptics in the Conservative Party, then joined by the UK Independence Party (UKIP) and, later again, the Brexit Party. Again, as with the equal marriage debate, Brexit originated in a manifesto commitment during the 2015 General Election when the Conservative Party said they would hold 'an in-out referendum by the end of 2017'.[351] This fulfilled a promise made by the Prime Minister of the Conservative-led Coalition, David Cameron, in January 2013, to allow the British people to 'have their say' on Europe[352] and was also an attempt to neutralise a divisive issue that had split his party since the election of Margaret Thatcher in 1979. Seventy-two per cent of eligible voters[353] took part in the referendum on 23 June 2016, with 51.9% voting 'to leave the European Union' (as the referendum question was phrased).

In both of these cases, universities took a position on the issue concerned. In Australia, while some offered no institutional position, others aligned with the majority view in supporting equal marriage. With Brexit, all the UK universities were on the 'wrong side of history', as many commentators put it, in backing the Remain campaign, largely as a unified sector under the auspices of Universities UK (UUK), their representative body. What is interesting, in both cases, is not what positions were ultimately chosen, but how universities ended up taking a position in the first place when, on other contested political and social issues, they sit on the fence.

---

[350] Gravelle and Carson (2019).

[351] See http://ucrel.lancs.ac.uk/wmatrix/ukmanifestos2015/localpdf/Conservatives.pdf (p. 72).

[352] https://www.bbc.co.uk/news/uk-politics-21148282.

[353] It is worth noting that a number of groups were excluded from voting, such as European citizens who had settled in the UK.

In examining this question, it is important to acknowledge that there was considerable debate as to whether it was appropriate to take a position and, even to this day, there are different views. Interestingly, as far as I can tell in my research, there was little dissent as to what that position should be, if taken: that is to support equal marriage in Australia and remain in the EU in Britain.

In Australia, 65 'academic organisations' including, by my counting, about a quarter of universities, came out 'in support for Marriage Equality' by endorsing the Australian Marriage Equality campaign.[354] Academic organisations can be departments or student unions, which is importantly different from the university taking an institutional view, as defined by Glyn Davis above. But it is also worth noting that a number of leading universities invoked the Kalven Committee line in refusing to take a position. For example, Michael Spence, the vice-chancellor of The University of Sydney at the time, is reported in the *Sydney Morning Herald* as saying that advocating a 'yes' vote would have 'a potentially chilling effect on debate'.[355] In a statement, he went on to argue:

I do not believe it appropriate for us to adopt an institutional position. In saying so I want to stress that I do not mean to sound insensitive to the very real pain experienced by those currently unable to marry under Australian law. But I think the issue goes to [the] heart of the function of the university as an institution . . . universities in the secular liberal tradition are essentially for a debate in which ideas can be freely expressed and discussed.

By contrast, Monash University – a peer of The University of Sydney[356] – came out in support for marriage equality with its vice-chancellor, Margaret Gardner, noting that:

Since it was founded, Monash has stood for the principles of fairness, tolerance and diversity. Support for marriage equality is consistent with these values and our commitment to championing those values.

---

[354] http://www.australianmarriageequality.org/academic-support/.

[355] https://www.smh.com.au/national/nsw/university-of-sydney-staff-call-on-management-to-publicly-support-samesex-marriage-20171102-gzdj14.html.

[356] Both institutions are members of the Group of Eight (along with Melbourne, also referred to). The Group of Eight 'is a coalition of world-leading research-intensive Australian universities'. See https://go8.edu.au.

I managed to arrange a call with Gardner, as I was interested in understanding why Monash was so unequivocal in its support for marriage equality. Interestingly, Gardner said it was not a point of contention. The principle of equity was deeply embedded within the Monash culture and, while the position was discussed at various governance committees, there was a general consensus that supporting a 'yes' vote was appropriate and the right thing for a university like Monash to do.

Other leading universities, such as The University of Melbourne, did not publicly endorse the Australian Marriage Equality campaign but came out in support of a yes vote. They did this by passing a resolution at their Academic Board to support marriage equality. But, in speaking to people from The University of Melbourne, it is clear that the argument put forward by Michael Spence was deeply interrogated with full knowledge of the risks of adopting an institutional position to academic freedom. Nevertheless, in having this debate, they concluded, 'This [resolution] was based on the values of the University that include upholding fundamental human rights and respecting the freedoms and rights of all members of the University community.'[357]

In contrast, the UK university sector adopted a largely unified stance in its opposition to Brexit. In the summer of 2015, a year before the EU referendum, UUK launched the 'Universities for Europe' campaign. At the launch, the then president-elect of Universities UK, and vice-chancellor of the University of Kent, Julia Goodfellow, said:

> **It is abundantly clear that the UK's membership of the European Union has an overwhelmingly positive impact on our world-leading universities, enhancing university research and teaching. By supporting collaboration and breaking down international barriers, the EU helps universities to carry out cutting-edge research and make discoveries that improve people's lives and enhance the UK's global influence.[358]**

This view was widely held within the higher education sector, with a survey undertaken a couple of weeks before the referendum suggesting that 90% of

---

[357] https://about.unimelb.edu.au/newsroom/news/2017/september/university-of-melbourne-academic-board-supports-marriage-equality.

[358] https://www.independent.co.uk/news/uk/politics/eu-referendum-brexit-would-harm-higher-education-and-research-universities-claim-10417379.html.

university staff would support Remain.[359] This position was endorsed by university leaders, when a letter published days before the vote in *The Independent*, and signed by vice-chancellors from almost every major higher education institution in the country, said they were 'gravely concerned' about the impact of Brexit.[360]

But not everyone was happy. My colleague Anand Menon is director of the ESRC[361] UK in a Changing Europe initiative, which is tasked with 'promoting rigorous, high-quality and independent research into the . . . relationship between the UK and the European Union (EU) . . . and providing . . . an authoritative, non-partisan and impartial reference point for those looking for information, insights and analysis about UK-EU relations'.[362] In a strongly-worded piece for *The Conversation* a few months after Universities in Europe was launched, he, like Spence in Australia, invoked the Kalven Committee line:

> I think there is a danger that, by taking such a clear stand on such a hotly debated political issue, universities may make it harder for their staff to foster precisely those sorts of debates that universities are meant to encourage . . . There should be no doubt about what the stance adopted by UUK means. Its members are the heads of universities in the UK, not the staff of these institutions. So it is not the case that 'universities' have expressed a preference. Rather, their vice chancellors and principals have . . . To see them adopt such a definitive position on an issue that goes far beyond the world of higher education might potentially compromise their ability to act as such.[363]

Menon's main contention was that the position taken by UUK risked undermining the impartiality of the UK in a Changing Europe. As he wrote in a reflective piece three years later, 'The aggressively pro-Remain stance of Universities UK did not really help us. Attempting to underline our impartiality, while representing a sector whose leadership were far too quick to become

---

[359] https://www.timeshighereducation.com/news/european-union-referendum-nine-out-of-ten-university-staff-back-remain.

[360] https://www.independent.co.uk/news/uk/politics/leaders-of-100-top-uk-universities-warn-of-brexit-risk-to-global-standing-a7092516.html.

[361] Economic and Social Research Council – the main funder of social science research in the UK.

[362] https://ukandeu.ac.uk/about-us/.

[363] https://theconversation.com/universities-uk-is-wrong-to-take-sides-on-question-of-eu-membership-47385.

cheerleaders for the Remain cause, presented an interesting challenge.'[364] Of course, it is also the case that the universities were not an uninterested party in the Brexit debate. They receive over a £1 billion of European Commission research funding, enrol students from the European Union and, for the research universities, recruit about a fifth of their staff from European countries, under visa-free freedom of movement regulations. So, many onlookers thought universities were acting in their own self-interest, despite using arguments based on the interests of society. As Menon noted in the earlier piece, 'Many of those who favour British exit are already inherently suspicious of universities – an "EU funded conspiracy" – as one Eurosceptic put it to me well before the launch of the UUK campaign.' Thus, rather than been seen as 'Advocates', this perception would put them in the 'Protectionist' quadrant in Figure 10.1.

It is, perhaps, the reality of this collective self-interest, and certainly the wider perception of that by politicians and public alike, that differentiates the two case studies: the Australian universities, in each independently advocating for equal marriage, did so explicitly to uphold values that they considered to be essential for the society they are part of. The UK universities supporting Remain came across as a self-serving lobby group acting in concert.

These examples again underline that universities already do take positions, not just on uncontested issues, such as environmental sustainability or the divestment of endowments, but also on those contested societal issues, either where they consider there is a strong self-interest to do so or where fundamental values are at stake. So that I am not misunderstood on this point, I am not suggesting that universities should adopt party political positions nor am I suggesting that they need to adopt positions on all issues. What I am saying, however, is that for university leaders to continue saying that it is not 'appropriate . . . to adopt an institutional position' on the important social and political matters of the day creates confusion and serves to undermine the social contract between universities and wider society.

A stronger, consistent and more defensible position for the New Power University would be to acknowledge that they can act as advocates. Crucially, though, the arguments around any given issue must be openly debated by students, staff and their communities, through the necessary networked governance structures discussed in Chapter 9. Based on that free and open debate, a position can then be taken, which is transparently published, so everyone knows where different universities lie on different issues (or, put another way, there need not be

---

[364] Menon (2018).

conformity across the sector). New Power Universities might well have different positions on different issues and that market of ideas will attract or repel students and staff based on the values of the institution. This, to me, seems a far more coherent proposition than pretending that the university 'is itself not a critic'.

What's the story? The New Power University as a first-rate advocate

A few years ago, I was told an anecdote about Boris Johnson, now Prime Minister of the UK. Apparently, when Mayor of London (between 2008 and 2016), Johnson had the habit of randomly asking employees the question 'What's the story?' while roaming around City Hall. At first, this clearly rattled those he questioned but, as time went by, everyone came to know how to respond: they had to be able to rattle off a 30-second 'elevator pitch' to the Mayor, which explained the most interesting things about their respective portfolios. I've no idea whether this tale is genuine and have been unable to validate the story but it does ring true and provides a useful framing for how the New Power University can become more effective in engaging, shaping and influencing social and political issues of the day.

It is an inability to tell the story that Mark Leach, the founder and editor-in-chief of Wonkhe,[365] highlighted in a controversial but accurate article in 2018, where he argued, 'The higher education sector, for all its strengths, has lost its ability to tell a coherent story about itself. The sector and its leadership are now suffering a collective crisis of moral authority, a crisis of leadership, and a crisis of identity.'[366] He goes on to argue:

> **Too often wonks forget the reality of politics today and that it is not about bureaucrats, technocrats and managers. Or carefully, evidenced, incremental reform. Or even perfectly crafted policy . . . It is about power, legitimacy and survival and how to harness the public support to secure it . . . Telling the right story, at the right point and in the right way. A story that makes sense of the world around us – our families, our homes, our workplaces and our communities. A story which connects emotionally to our passions, aspirations and ambitions, for good and for ill.**

---

[365] https://wonkhe.com.

[366] https://wonkhe.com/blogs/the-enemy-within-why-the-narrative-about-universities-and-students-went-so-wrong/.

Telling this story is best done by applying the new power approaches to community organising discussed in Chapters 5 and 8 and which are used in creating social movements. As the Harvard academic Marshall Ganz put it in an interview with the American journalist and political commentator Bill Moyers in 2003:

> **Movements have narratives. They tell stories, because they are not just about rearranging economics and politics. They also rearrange meaning. And they're not just about redistributing the goods. They're about figuring out what is good.**[367]

I have already referenced the work of Ganz in Chapter 7, where I recommended his 'head, hearts and hands' framework as a model for leaders of the New Power University. As I argued, 'The new power leader has to have a strong social purpose with a supporting narrative, has to be deeply analytical, supported by data and a strategic outlook and, critically, has to get their 'hands dirty' – that is demonstrate the ability to deliver on the missions of the New Power University be that through directly supporting learning, through their research and through being personally socially responsible.'[368] To help develop the 'public narrative', as Ganz calls it, he suggested another framework that comprises three stories: the story of 'self', the story of 'us' and the story of 'now'.[369] The story of self is about your personal values and journey that led to the call of action – your lived experience. The story of us defines and distinguishes a community through shared values, experiences and aspiration – it creates a collective identity. The story of now communicates why that urgent change and a call to action is needed at this particular moment in time.

In the following box, I have developed a public narrative for this book, which appropriately draws from *my* lived experience, articulates a collective identity for a hypothetical university in the UK, and creates a call for action that redefines the social purpose of universities for the 21st century. Each New Power University will need to develop its own narrative that describes its social purpose and that speaks to the identities and motivations of those in its communities. Only then can you begin to engage effectively with and

---

[367] https://billmoyers.com/segment/marshall-ganz-on-making-social-movements-matter/.

[368] Chapter 7, p. 129.

[369] Ganz (2010).

influence the social and political issues of the day, especially for those that are more strongly contested.

At the same time, universities do need to be mindful of Kalven's exhortation to avoid 'playing the role of a second-rate political force' and have to work hard to become 'first-rate' advocates. How to be a first-rate advocate is a topic that is explored in an excellent book edited by Ant Bagshaw and Debbie McVitty, *Influencing Higher Education Policy: A Professional Guide to Making an Impact*.[370] Bagshaw works at the higher education consultancy Nous, McVitty is a colleague of Leach at Wonkhe where she is the editor, and the contributors to the book largely come from a public affairs background, working in higher education. As such, the book is a deeply practical set of reflections and ideas on how to shape policy and influence politics. In the opening chapter, McVitty cites Timms and Heimans' (2018) *New Power*, in noting how 'social media give individuals a voice and the capability to publish an opinion and organise action'[371] and combines this with the rise of populism. Critically, in my view, she concludes, 'Populist politics and social media are clearly not going anywhere. Nor are they an unmitigated negative. Populism speaks to the desire for accountability; social media gives ordinary people a platform.'[372]

The public narrative for the New Power University

I am a privileged member of the metropolitan liberal elite. I live and work in cities; my personal values can best be described as being socially liberal; and, across the UK population, I am in the top decile in terms of income and educational attainment. I am the third generation of my family to go to university. Like many, I found my undergraduate education at the LSE eye-opening. I learnt to learn. I discovered how energising it is to acquire new knowledge and to challenge existing orthodoxies. Sadly,

▶

---

[370] Bagshaw and McVitty (2020).

[371] Bagshaw and McVitty (2020), p. 4.

[372] Bagshaw and McVitty (2020), p. 12.

I also learnt how power is collected and then kept hold of. As my journey unfolded, I could see how the hoarding of power negatively impacted on decisions to fund research, the effectiveness of public services and, most recently, the purpose of higher education.

Although, over my lifetime, we have seen global improvements in life expectancy, poverty and wellness, this has been interleaved with several historical shocks: 9/11, the global financial crash, the recent COVID pandemic, and a continuing climate crisis that seemingly can only get worse. The dynamic tension of good and bad – the way positive and negative trends and events come together to present us with potentially very different futures based on the choices we make now – illustrates to me that we are living through a unique 'in-between time'. A time when universities have a duty to play a hugely important role in shaping a 'positive moment of uncertainty . . . to emerge into a less ideological and more humanitarian era'.[373]

Throughout their long and resilient history, universities have evolved with the times, reshaping not only their purpose and how they work but also the social contract with the communities they exist within. Now is one of those evolutionary moments where those who share my optimism for the New Power University must come together to redefine the social purpose of higher education. Remaining 'remote from life'[374] is not an option, as it will have a profoundly negative impact, not only on the institution of the university but also on the communities they serve.

This means sharing and distributing institutional and individual privilege and power, foregoing the exclusive model of the old power university and adopting a new inclusive paradigm. It is through new power that we can reshape and energise the mission of universities for the future. It is through new power that more effective forms of learning emerge. It is through new power that research will focus on need. It is through new power that universities become socially responsible. The New Power University is a rearticulation of the social purpose of the university that is fit for the 21st century.

---

[373] Saul (2005), p. 6.
[374] Buller (1943), p. 136.

So, how does the New Power University practically engage with policy and political issues? There is a mass of literature on how to do this from a range of disciplinary perspectives, dating back to some seminal work by Carol Weiss in the 1970s.[375] There are hundreds of different frameworks that have been developed and tested by academics and policymakers.[376] When I run workshops on how to communicate with policymakers, I tend to synthesise this literature into the '3Ts' of trust, timing and translation.[377] Trust refers to building coalitions or movements through one-to-one relationships with individuals (using the approach advocated by Matthew Bolton in his book *How to Resist*,[378] which I referred to in Chapter 3). Timing is about being agile and exploiting the prevailing political winds. This can be particularly challenging for old power institutions, including universities, where decisions are managed through committee processes, hence the need for a more flexible networked governance approach, as suggested in Chapter 9. Translation is about the public narrative, as already discussed, but it is also about understanding the context within which you are operating. Or, as the writer and philosopher Umberto Eco puts it in his book *Mouse or Rat? Translation as Negotiation*:

Translation is always a shift, not between two languages but between two cultures – or two encyclopaedias. A translator must take into account rules that are not strictly linguistic but, broadly speaking, cultural.[379]

I like the 3Ts as they blend some of the more traditional old power thinking on how to influence policymaking with some of the new power values. Trust, for example, can conjure up an image of an old boys' network but new power is built from trust. As Timms and Heimans (2018) point out, Airbnb's business model is that you trust your home to strangers, and those strangers trust you in presenting your home fairly which, when you think about it, is mind-boggling given you have never met. Timing is about that old power 'window of opportunity' but also plays into the previous discussion on conditional affiliation of students and staff (Chapters 4 and 5) opting in and out of the New

---

[375] Weiss (1979).

[376] It will take us off topic to review them here, but some important papers include: Weiss (1979); Hanney, *et al.* (2003); Lomas (2005); and Oliver, *et al.* (2016).

[377] Hinrichs-Krapels, *et al.* (2020).

[378] Bolton (2017).

[379] Eco (2003), p. 82.

Power University at different times: not taking part need not be a lack of engagement but a new way of participation.[380] Translation is not simply about working out the old power 'line to take' but is about using the right language in the right context to create connections – to create the shared public narrative of the New Power University that has the spreading of ideas at its core. As Timms and Heimans (2018) put it, 'The future will be won by those who spread their ideas better, faster and more durably,'[381] and this is best done through 'a peer connection with people you care about or share values with. Connected ideas bring you closer to other people and make you (feel) part of a like-minded community. This sets off a network effect that spreads the idea further.'[382]

It is worth recalling some of the history from Chapter 2, that from the 11th century until about the 17th (in Europe), universities held primary responsibility for the 'spread of ideas'. That public service was interrupted by the introduction of journals and journalists in the 17th century (made possible for mass consumption by the steam press and the railways for distribution) who replaced the university as the gate-keepers of information. With the emergence of new power, and the associated disruption of the media industry, there is an opportunity for universities to pivot back as the world's trusted provider of high-grade information. Such an endeavour would align nicely with the purpose and values of the New Power University.

Even if the New Power University can 'tell a coherent story about itself' and effectively apply the 3Ts in shaping and influencing policy and political environment, it needs to decide the social and political issues it wishes to advocate for. As Bagshaw notes in the closing chapter of *Influencing Higher Education Policy*, 'Universities should not necessarily engage on all of these matters, or indeed pursue each with equal vigour; external engagement and policy influencing should be seen as both for a corporate benefit, and as a broader mix of civic activities.'[383] He goes on to conclude that:

The traditional model of external policy influence by universities has been a benign amateurism where hope and accident have been primary

---

[380] Timms and Heimans (2018), p. 26.

[381] Timms and Heimans (2018), p. 53.

[382] Timms and Heimans (2018), p. 38.

[383] Bagshaw and McVitty (2020), p. 164.

tools for policy influence. That is no longer acceptable. Universities should accept that external policy influence is core business, both to further their own institutional success and as a tool for effective positive outcomes as part of their wider mission to do good in society.[384]

This 'mission to do good in society' is precisely why the New Power University should take a position on political or social issues of the day.

---

[384] Bagshaw and McVitty (2020), p. 169.

Postface

What looks like a crisis today is actually an equivalent opportunity.
John Ralston Saul (2005), p. 295

I was half-way through writing this book when the world was confronted with, in the words of the UN Secretary-General Antonio Guterres, the 'most challenging crisis we have faced since the Second World War'.[385] The COVID-19 pandemic disrupted virtually all aspects of life and mobilised nations globally on a scale not seen since that conflict. A new infectious virus that caused a severe acute respiratory disease, especially in the elderly, killed half a million people and infected over seven million worldwide, within six months of it emerging in the Chinese City of Wuhan in December 2019.[386] There was no treatment nor vaccine, meaning that the only intervention available to governments was to 'lock down' society – shops were closed, factories mothballed, schools shut and normal university activity suspended. The lockdown prevented the transmission of the disease from person-to-person by restricting their movement and confining people to their homes. As the historian Lawrence Freedman pointed out, it was a truly unprecedented moment with it being 'unusual to have so many countries, varying in size, demography, socioeconomic structures and politics, addressing the same challenge at the same time'.[387]

Like all sectors, universities have been profoundly impacted by the pandemic. In the short term, they pivoted to a new way of working, with students

---

[385] https://www.un.org/en/un-coronavirus-communications-team/time-science-and-solidarity.

[386] https://coronavirus.jhu.edu/map.html.

[387] Freedman (2020), p. 26.

returning (where possible) home to continue their education online and staff asked to work remotely using video-conferencing technology. Critically, they did not shut. Universities around the world contributed extraordinary efforts to fight the virus – testing existing medicines, developing novel vaccines, creating apps for population health surveillance, building new, easy-to-manufacture ventilators – as well as supporting their local communities through the redeployment of clinical staff, student volunteering, providing food parcels, bridging grants to local small businesses and not-for-profits, and protective ware such as gloves, masks and gowns to community partners.

Despite leaning into the crisis in this way, many universities faced, and continue to face, a short-term existential threat. The business model in Anglo-Saxon universities, where high-margin international students cross-subsidise loss-making activities, such as research and the fulfilment of social responsibilities, has been hugely challenged with a significant anticipated decline in student enrolments. This creates a liquidity crisis for universities that could become a solvency issue if extended over the mid-term (that is the next two to three years). Requests from university leadership for bailouts from government fell on deaf ears. Frankly, this did not surprise me. As we discussed in the early parts of this book, the social contract that gives universities their licence to operate is broken and, in a long queue of special pleading, universities were always going to be near the bottom of the politician's in-tray.

As I write, university leadership and commentators are, understandably, focused on the near-term horizons to ensure the viability of their institutions into the future. However, decisions that are made today will shape what is possible tomorrow and so it is important to have line of sight to where on the horizon institutions aspire to get to in a Post-COVID (Po-Co) environment. It is almost certainly the case that the demand for universities that can offer high-quality learning and research coupled with committed social responsibility will increase, nationally and internationally. As such, and as noted in the preface, the arguments I put forward for the New Power University are both accelerated and amplified by the COVID-19 pandemic.

In fact, the immediate response to the pandemic illustrates what is possible. Shifts to online learning, the challenge to find a vaccine and the mobilisation of students and staff volunteers are all ideas put forward in earlier chapters. More profoundly, across society, we have, arguably, seen a shift to a new form of collectivism where society has come together in some extraordinary ways that were, frankly, unimaginable a year ago. As Charles Leadbeater put it in a recent pamphlet:

> **The threat posed by COVID-19 brought about an abrupt change in our priorities, the tone of public discourse and our sense of ourselves. Saving lives and supporting health care workers became the absolute priority rather than making profits. Generosity has become more important than selfishness. Our response has been a collective expression of love combined with power.** [388]

Leadbeater argues that we should learn this profound lesson and apply 'love + power' to 'tackle deeply entrenched and emerging social challenges'. As such, he is building on the work of social movements and notions of new power that have heavily shaped my thinking about the social purpose of the university. Not only is this about a renewed Po-Co understanding of purpose but it is also about a way of working. Leadbeater quotes Martin Luther King in this regard, noting that 'such work should be long, because it takes time; broad because it reaches out; deep because it is about what matters in life; and tall, because it aims for higher goals'. A perfect note to end this book.

---

[388] https://www.tacsi.org.au/wp-content/uploads/2020/06/TACSI_LovePower_Report.pdf.

Appendix 1

Analysis of Gen Z students and non-students

As noted in Chapter 6, I undertook a small bit of research to determine the differences between Gen Z students and non-students, using data collected from the Community Life Survey for the UK for 2017–18,[389] European Social Survey for 2017[390] and the International Social Survey Programme for 2014.[391] A King's student – Klaudia Stanoch – under the supervision of my colleague Bobby Duffy supported me in this analysis. Generation Z includes people born between 1995 and 2012. With the assumption that people start university from the age of 18, wherever possible, respondents who were 18 to 22 years old at the time when the surveys were conducted were selected for the analysis. The survey questions were then reviewed and a series of potential variables that could describe the attitudes, values and behaviours of Gen Z students and non-students were identified.

Using SPSS (a statistical software programme), cross tabulations were generated to produce a series of graphs that were reviewed. At this stage, a number of variables were dropped as the sample size was deemed to be too small to allow any further analysis or the variable was similar to another that was examined across the three surveys. Ten variables were further analysed to see whether there were any statistical differences between the student and non-student groups using a Chi-square test of independence. From this, five of the results were deemed to be statistically significant at the $p = < 0.05$ level and four of these are presented in Chapter 6 (Figure 6.2). It should be stressed

---

[389] https://www.gov.uk/government/collections/community-life-survey.

[390] https://www.europeansocialsurvey.org.

[391] http://w.issp.org/menu-top/home/.

that this approach can be critiqued as 'p-hacking', that is looking for and only presenting statistically significant associations in data but, for the purposes I wanted to explore, seems appropriate and defensible. As also noted in Chapter 6, the effect size – which determines how much student status influences the outcome of the variable – was relatively small for all the variables. Finally, and again as noted in Chapter 6, what this analysis does not tell us is whether there is a selection effect – that is if individuals with a certain set of attitudes, values and behaviours are more likely to go to university – or whether the attitudes, values and behaviours are shaped by the experience of a university education.

Appendix 2

Responses from non–Anglo countries to the challenge of current university staffing, and the proposed solutions

	Cameroon	Nigeria	Spain 1	Spain 2	Romania
Is there a divide between academic and professional staff and, if so, does that divide impact on the function and culture of the university?	Yes, there is a divide between academic and professional staff. This divide impacts on the function and culture of the university. The university is increasingly unable to innovate and even efficiently perform current missions because of the limited collaboration between these two groups, which is critical. Instead of collaboration, they are also almost always suspicious of each other. This mutual suspicion has serious implications on performance.	Yes. The workforce comprises academic and non-teaching professional staff. The core function of the former is to conduct academic research and engage in teaching while the latter are more or less bureaucrats who perform mainly administrative and technical duties. In some way, the structural distribution of roles has affected the culture of the university in Nigeria. For example, it is generally perceived in the Nigerian university system that academic staff are	The academic–professional division is deeply rooted in Spanish universities. Professionals are responsible for the administration and management of services; they are rarely involved in educational or research projects. Some professors (the associates) are professionals hired on an hourly basis and do not participate in government tasks. Few tenured professors make their academic tasks compatible with professional practice. All of this has a negative impact on the social function of universities.	In Spain, the divide between academic staff and administration staff is very strong and very often both groups undervalue each other. Academics feel that administrative staff do not provide the things they need for their job (either teaching or research) which forces them to assume a lot of bureaucratic burden that academics should not do. Administration staff see academics as empowered people that work at their own rhythm and that do not appreciate the labour of administration.	

	Cameroon	Nigeria	Spain 1	Spain 2	Romania
	The limited interaction between academics and professionals means that the university is trapped in a 'frozen culture' considered safe by those who primarily make decisions, albeit being at odds with the current context.	superior to non-teaching professional staff in terms of their status and social relevance. Interestingly, this perception extends beyond the university environment into the larger Nigerian society. Academic staff are, therefore, more respected in both the university system and society.			
Do you have issues of casualisation (where academic staff are employed on short-term contracts with little job security) and, if so, how are you addressing this, if at all?	Yes. Entry-level academic and part-time lecturers fall in this group. These categories are employed on short-term contracts and enjoy very little job security. Part-time lecturers especially can see their contract (though very short term) very easily terminated. These two groups, however, do a greater share of the work.	Yes, but not exactly the form it takes in Western universities. There is no casualisation among academic staff in Nigeria. However, some forms of contract employment exist. First, when an academic member of staff or a higher-level non-academic member of staff retires, he/she may be given contract employment for two years and is subject to renewal for another two years after which the contract ends. This form of contract is being phased out as a result of the recent National Universities Commission's	The problem of temporary contracts in junior academics is serious, although a large majority have no problems with the renewal of their contracts and their promotion to higher levels, subject to an assessment of their merits. Their access to tenure tends to be excessively delayed.	We do have issues of casualisation, usually under the figure called 'profesor asociado' (not to be translated as the 'associated professor' of UK and USA universities). This *profesor asociado* is defined in our law as someone who is a prestigious professional outside the university and collaborates with it by giving some hours of lectures (not well-paid, more as a service or for his/her CV). As a consequence of economic difficulties, especially after the economic crisis, this figure has been used to hire (young) people willing	Short-term contracts do exist and are usually employed when hiring practitioners (usually the term we use to refer to people with no PhD, but extensive knowledge of their field, who may, on occasion, give classes based on their professional experience). However, employing practitioners is considered rather an exception from the rule (with the rule being that only PhDs would teach – or those being doctoral students).

Does tenure – or something equivalent – exist in your jurisdiction and, if so, is it creating the type of perverse behaviour described in the draft text?	Yes, tenure creates such behaviour. The reason is that senior staff in this category (associate professors and professors) have a sense of entitlement and some see themselves as 'untouchable'. This means they seem not to bother about productivity or the consequences of their actions. […] directive that abrogates it. Second, someone working outside of the university system, either in the private sector or the public bureaucracy and has retired from his/her previous employment, may be hired as a contract staff. The contract is renewable every year and may be terminated by the university at short notice.	No. In the Nigerian university system, once an academic member of staff is employed and confirmed, he/she enjoys tenureship until retirement at the age of 65 or 70, if the staff attains professorship before 65. In other words, tenureship is automatic for all academic staff. Consequently, the kind of perverse behaviour experienced in the West does not exist in the Nigerian university system.	In public universities (not private ones) in Spain, most of the permanent teaching staff are civil servants. Their conditions are not regulated by the university but by the State. After passing the entrance exams, they occupy a position from which they cannot be removed, except in exceptional cases; this facilitates some of the negative behaviour described in the text, since the subsequent economic incentives are only linked to evaluations of their research activities. […] to pursue an academic career, that are paid very low (by hours) and have to employ themselves as autonomous (therefore paying part of their own social security) in order to fulfil the legal requirements of the position. They have become known as the 'fake asociados' and universities are designing plans to promote them.	In the Spanish system, permanent positions are most often public servants, therefore almost impossible to remove. We have two categories: Profesor Titular and Catedrático. Since 2007, there is also the position of Profesor Contratado Doctor, that is a permanent position under a labour contract. But it is seen as an intermediate step towards the public servant ones. A problem that we encounter is that the average age of these figures is very high (almost 50 for Profesor Titular and 58 for Catedrático).	Permanent positions in Romanian academia represent the rule. Tenure is associated with all positions (assistant professor, lecturer, senior lecturer and professor) and is linked to the university where one teaches (for example I am currently a senior lecturer in Bucharest; if I want to become a professor, I need to search a vacant position in any university and participate in a public competition).

	Cameroon	Nigeria	Spain 1	Spain 2	Romania
				That means that people do not get a tenure (nor permanent) position until they are in their 40s, which is a big problem.	If I win, then I become a professor in that particular university where the position was vacated).
Would the introduction of an expanded and dominant cohort of third space professionals break down the academic–professional staff dualism in your jurisdiction?	I think that an expanded and dominant cohort of third space professionals will break down the academic–professional staff dualism in my university. It is, however, not possible to imagine this happening in the near future as this will be a very 'radical' change, given the current situation.	Yes. The superiority status enjoyed by academic staff in relation to the non-teaching staff and its associated social identities and some discriminatory practices will naturally break down.	The massive introduction of professionals from the third space would largely break the professional–academic dualism in Spanish universities.	Certainly, these third space professionals do exist already (invisible by now) and their formal recognition and development could be interesting. In many meetings, we mention the need of a hybrid profile: not a pure academic nor a pure administrative but both of them. Probably, this is also forced by the bureaucracy that takes many hours of academic staff and also the technification of some support administrative positions (project managers, managers of research labs, quality assessments and evaluation).	

Would the introduction of UON Academy-type function/ department help to address the issues around the casualisation of academic staff and to reset the psychological contact?	The University of Newcastle approach can help address the issues around casualisation and reset the psychological contract. The main challenge is that it, however, will appear too radical for the university to consider implementing such now.	Not really, since about 98% of academic staff are on full-time employment and also enjoy tenureship.	Specific programmes to support the integration of temporary staff and their 'psychological contract' with the university would be very beneficial.	I do not see it right now in Spain.
Would the ending of tenure for senior academics – and the introduction of tenure for junior academics – be a viable solution for the management of academic careers?	This can be a solution. It will, however, require that the conditions that have made casualisation an option in UON or similar are met. This is because I think very few academics are able to function in this way in developing countries such as Cameroon. The reason is that skill levels and individual objectives for a good number mean they would not be competitive or, worse, will be redundant if such a change occurred today. Introduction of tenure for junior academics is easy to achieve and will be a good solution.	This currently does not apply in Nigeria. All academic staff enjoy automatic tenureship as noted above.	The extension of the periods of stability proposed in the text for young teachers would be very positive. On the other hand, it does not seem feasible in Spanish public universities to end the tenure of senior academics. It would require major legislative reforms, as tenured professors and lecturers are civil servants, and it would be necessary to count on the opposition of these who govern the universities.	I do think that tenure should be introduced for junior academics (although a good point is how early should they be 'forced' to stay some years of postdoc or not?). As I pointed out before, in Spain, tenure arrives, nowadays, too late, which is what makes an 'academic career' not very attractive among the young. But I do not agree with the idea of ending tenure for senior academics and, legally, it would be impossible right now (since we are public servants). But also, in my experience, senior professors either are active in research and they continue with their regular tenure life or they become

	Cameroon	Nigeria	Spain 1	Spain 2	Romania
				more involved in administration, falling, in a natural way, into the category of the third space. Ending tenure for seniors in Spain will be unthinkable and, in my opinion, socially regrettable and will make academic careers less attractive. I do not see the point of it. Probably, it is easier to make more flexible the bridges between universities and enterprises or shared positions between two universities.	
Would the explicit acceptance of a 'gig academic' model address some of the challenges currently faced by universities in your jurisdiction?	The explicit acceptance of this model will address some of the challenges faced by universities in my jurisdiction. The lack of compensation of some form of security for academics on short-term contracts and the near absence of collaboration between third space professionals and academics, in particular, will be addressed. These two issues will be very relevant in improving the academic performance in my jurisdiction.	No, since both junior and senior academics enjoy tenureship.	The 'gig academic' model could only be partially applied in our universities because the Spanish university system is quite closed and has little room for the mobility of interuniversity teaching and research groups. In particular, there are still many difficulties and limitations to the autonomous recruitment of foreign academics.	No, I do not see that. Probably I do not understand enough the concept of gig-academic. If it can be seen as a 'star' among academics that goes from one place to another giving lectures, I do not see it as a real alternative for a significant part of the senior academic staff. I would rather go in the direction of making more common the shared positions I already mentioned above.	

References

Baer, U. (2019) *What Snowflakes Get Right: Free Speech, Truth, and Equality on Campus*. Oxford: Oxford University Press.

Bagshaw, A. and McVitty, D. (eds) (2020) *Influencing Higher Education Policy: A Professional Guide to Making an Impact*. London: Routledge.

Barber, M., Donnelly, K. and Rizvi, S. (2013) 'An avalanche is coming: higher education and the revolution ahead'. London: IPPR. Available from: https://www.ippr.org/publications/an-avalanche-is-coming-higher-education-and-the-revolution-ahead. [Accessed August 2020.]

Barnett, R. (2018) *The Ecological University: A Feasible Utopia*. London: Routledge.

BIS (2015) 'The effect of higher education on graduates' attitudes: secondary analysis of the British Social Attitudes Survey', BIS research paper no. 200. London: Department for Business Innovation & Skills. Available from: https://assets.publishing.service.gov.uk/government/uploads/system/uploads/attachment_data/file/474228/BIS-15-89-the-effect-of-higher-education-on-attitudes.pdf. [Accessed August 2020.]

Boaz, A., Hanney, S., Jones, T. and Soper, B. (2015) 'Does the engagement of clinicians and organisations in research improve healthcare performance: a three-stage review', *BMJ Open* 5: e009415. Available from: https://bmjopen.bmj.com/content/bmjopen/5/12/e009415.full.pdf. [Accessed August 2020.]

Bolton, M. (2017) *How to Resist: Turn Protest to Power*. London: Bloomsbury.

Boyer, J.W. (2015) *The University of Chicago: A History*. Chicago: University of Chicago Press.

Brennan, J., Durazzi, N. and Séné, T. (2013) 'Things we know and don't know about the wider benefits of higher education: a review of the recent literature', BIS Research Paper, URN BIS/13/1244. London: Department for Business, Innovation and Skills. Available from: http://eprints.lse.ac.uk/55427/1/__libfile_REPOSITORY_Content_Durazzi,%20N_Durazzi_Things%20we%20know_2014.pdf. [Accessed August 2020.]

Brooks, D. (2015) *The Road to Character*. London: Allen Lane.

Buller, A. (1943) *Darkness Over Germany*. London: Longmans Green & Co.

Bush, V. (1945) 'Science: The Endless Frontier', a report to the President on a programme for post-war scientific research. Washington, DC: US Office of Scientific Research and Development, Government Printing Office. Available from: https://www.nsf.gov/od/lpa/nsf50/vbush1945.htm#ch1. [Accessed August 2020.]

Byrne, E. and Clarke, C. (2020) *The University Challenge: Changing Universities in a Changing World*. London: Pearson.

Calderon, A.J. (2018) 'Massification of higher education revisited'. Melbourne: RMIT University. Available from: http://cdn02.pucp.education/academico/2018/08/23165810/na_mass_revis_230818.pdf. [Accessed August 2020.]

Camerer, C.F., Dreber, A., Forsell, E., Ho, T-H, Huber, J., Johannesson, M., et al. (2016) 'Evaluating replicability of laboratory experiments in economics', *Science*, 351, 1433–6. Available from: https://science.sciencemag.org/content/sci/351/6280/1433.full.pdf. [Accessed August 2020.]

Chalmers, I. and Glasziou, P. (2009) 'Avoidable waste in the production and reporting of research evidence', *Lancet*, 374, 86–9. Available from: https://www.thelancet.com/journals/lancet/article/PIIS0140-6736(09)60329-9/fulltext. [Accessed August 2020.]

Chesbrough, H. (2020) *Open Innovation Results: Going Beyond the Hype and Getting Down to Business*. Oxford: Oxford University Press.

Chesbrough, H., Vanhaverbeke, W. and West, J. (eds) (2003) *Open Innovation: Researching a New Paradigm*. Oxford: Oxford University Press.

Civic University Commission (2019) 'Truly Civic: strengthening the connection between universities and their places'. London: UPP Foundation. Available from: https://upp-foundation.org/wp-content/uploads/2019/02/Civic-University-Commission-Final-Report.pdf. [Accessed August 2020.]

Collini, S. (2012) *What Are Universities For?* London: Penguin Books.

Comroe, J.H. and Dripps, R.D. (1976) 'Scientific basis for the support of biomedical science', *Science*, 192, 105–11. Available from: https://science.

sciencemag.org/content/192/4235/105?ijkey=4a5cf139236072ae6324c5af6 637a5c3471dcd69&keytype2=tf_ipsecsha. [Accessed August 2020.]

Contopoulos-Ioannidis, D.G., Nitzani, J.P., Ioannidis, J.P.A. (2003) 'Translation of highly promising basic science research into clinical applications', *The American Journal of Medicine*, 114, 477. Available from: https://www.amjmed.com/article/S0002-9343(03)00013-5/pdf. [Accessed August 2020.]

Crawford, T. and Germov, J. (2015) 'Using workforce strategy to address academic casualisation: a University of Newcastle case study', *Journal of Higher Education Policy and Management*, 37 (5), 534–44. Available from: https://www.tandfonline.com/doi/abs/10.1080/1360080X.2015.1079394?journalCode=cjhe20. [Accessed August 2020.]

Crow, M. and Dabars, W. (2015) *Designing the New American University*. Baltimore: Johns Hopkins University Press.

Davis, G. (2017) *The Australian Idea of a University*. Melbourne: Melbourne University Press.

De Vries, W. and Slowey, M. (2012) Concluding reflections. Between Humboldt and Newman: marketization and global contributions to contemporary higher education. In Schuetze, H.G. and Álvarez Mendiola, G. (eds) *State and Market in Higher Education Reforms: Trends, Policies and Experiences in Comparative Perspective*. Rotterdam: Sense Publishers, pp. 215–23.

Dickens, C. (1858) *Household Words*. Vol. XIX, p. 58. Available from: http://www.djo.org.uk/household-words/volume-xix/page-58.html. [Accessed August 2020.]

Donovan, C. (2016) From multiversity to postmodern university. In Cote, J.E. and Furlong, A (eds) *Routledge Handbook of the Sociology of Higher Education*. London: Routledge.

Douglas, D., Grant, J., Wells, J. and Nous Group (2020) 'Advancing University Engagement: University Engagement and Global League Tables'. London/Chicago/Melbourne: King's College London/University of Chicago/University of Melbourne. Available from: https://www.kcl.ac.uk/policy-institute/assets/advancing-university-engagement.pdf. [Accessed August 2020.]

Eckel, P. and Trower, C. (2019) *Practical Wisdom: Thinking Differently about College and University Governance*. Sterling: Stylus Publishing.

Eco, U. (2003) *Mouse or Rat? Translation as Negotiation*. London: Weidenfeld & Nicolson.

Elliot Major, L. and Machin, S. (2018) *Social Mobility: And Its Enemies*. London: Pelican.

Europe Engage (2017) *Europe Engage: Developing a Culture of Civic Engagement through Service-learning within Higher Education in Europe*. Brussels: European Union. Available from: https://europeengagedotorg.files.wordpress.com/2018/09/libro-1.pdf. [Accessed August 2020.]

Freedman, L. (2020) 'Strategy for a pandemic: the UK and COVID-19', *Survival*, 62, 25–76. Available from: https://iiss.tandfonline.com/doi/full/10.1080/00396338.2020.1763610#.Xt83-i2ZP64. [Accessed August 2020.]

French, C.E., Ferlie, E. and Fulop, N.J. (2014) 'The international spread of Academic Health Science Centres: a scoping review and the case of policy transfer to England', *Health Policy*, 117, 383–91. Available from: https://www.sciencedirect.com/science/article/pii/S0168851014001705?via%3Dihub. [Accessed August 2020.]

Fund, S., Mosterd, M. and Godek, P. (2019) *Open Access Monographs in the UK: A Data Analysis*. Berlin: fullstopp Gmbh.

Furedi, F. (2018) *What's Happened to the University? A Sociological Exploration of Its Infantilisation*. London: Routledge.

Fyfe, A., Coate, K., Curry, S., Lawson, S., Moxham, N. and Røstvik, C. (2017) 'Untangling academic publishing: a history of the relationship between commercial interests, academic prestige and the circulation of research', Zenodo. Available from: https://zenodo.org/record/546100#.XjP-dC2cbm0. [Accessed August 2020.]

Ganz, M. (2010) Leading change: leadership, organization, and social movements. In Nohria, N. and Khurana, R. (eds) *Handbook of Leadership Theory and Practice: A Harvard Business School Centennial Colloquium*. Boston: Harvard Business Press. Available from: http://marshallganz.usmblogs.com/files/2012/08/Chapter-19-Leading-Change-Leadership-Organization-and-Social-Movements.pdf. [Accessed August 2020.]

Ganz, M. and Lin, E.S. (2011) Learning to lead: pedagogy of practice. In Snook, S., Nohria, N. and Khurana, R. (eds) *Handbook for Teaching Leadership: Knowing, Doing, and Being*. Los Angeles: SAGE, pp. 353–66. Available from: https://dash.harvard.edu/bitstream/handle/1/29314926/Chapter_8_Ganz-Lin.pdf?sequence=1&isAllowed=y. [Accessed August 2020.]

Gavazzi, S.M. and Gee, E.G. (2018) *Land-grant Universities for the Future: Higher Education for the Public Good*. Baltimore: Johns Hopkins University Press.

Goddard, J. (2009) 'Re-inventing the civic university'. London: Nesta. Available from: https://www.nesta.org.uk/report/re-inventing-the-civic-university/. [Accessed August 2020.]

Grant, J. and Buxton, M.J. (2018) 'Economic returns to medical research funding', *BMJ Open*, 8. Available from: https://bmjopen.bmj.com/content/8/9/e022131.info. [Accessed August 2020.]

Grant, J., Cottrell, R., Cluzeau, F. and Fawcett, G. (2000) 'Evaluating the "payback" on biomedical research by characterising papers cited on clinical guidelines: applied bibliometric study', *BMJ*, 320, 1107–11. Available from: https://www.bmj.com/content/320/7242/1107.long. [Accessed August 2020.]

Grant, J., Green, L. and Mason, B. (2003) 'Basic research and health: a reassessment of the scientific basis for the support of biomedical science', *Research Evaluation*, 12, 217–24.

Grant, J., Hewlett, K., Nir, T. and Duffy, B. (2019) 'Freedom of expression in UK universities', Policy Institute at King's, London. Available from: https://www.kcl.ac.uk/policy-institute/assets/freedom-of-expression-in-uk-universities.pdf. [Accessed August 2020.]

Gravelle, T. and Carson, A. (2019) 'Explain the Australian marriage equality vote: an aggregate-level analysis', *Politics*, 39 (2), 286–301. Available from: https://ac437174-476e-4b37-8c1f-688348853686.filesusr.com/ugd/d49f5d_4c4e59cb159d4ba5b58a820e69a95c62.pdf. [Accessed August 2020.]

Guest, D. (2004) 'Flexible employment contracts, the psychological contract and employee outcomes: an analysis and review of the evidence', *International Journal of Management Reviews*, 5/6 (1), 1–19. Available from: https://www.uv.es/psycon/documentacion/IJMR_002.pdf. [Accessed August 2020.]

Guest, D. and Isaksson, K. (2019) 'Temporary employment contracts and employee well-being during and after the financial crisis: introduction to special issue'. *Economic and Industrial Democracy*, 40 (2), 165–72. Available from: https://journals.sagepub.com/doi/10.1177/0143831X18804706. [Accessed August 2020.]

Habib, A. (2019) *Rebels and Rage: Reflecting on #FeesMustFall*. Jeppestown: Jonathan Ball Publishers.

Halpern, D. (2005) *Social Capital*. Cambridge: Polity Press.

Hanney, S.R., Gonzalez-Block, M.A., Buxton, M.J. and Kogan, M. (2003) 'The utilisation of health research in policy-making: concepts, examples and methods of assessment', *Health Research Policy and Systems* 1, 2. Available from: http://www.health-policy-systems.com/content/1/1/2. [Accessed August 2020.]

Harris, J.T. and Karkavy, I. (2003) 'Colleges, universities and communities advancing social and economic justice', *Journal of Poverty Law and Power*, July–August, 149–53.

Hearnshaw, F.J.C. (1929) *The Centenary History of King's College London*. London: Harrap.

Hinrichs-Krapels, S., Bailey, J., Boulding, H., Duffy, B., Hesketh, R., Kinloch, E., Pollitt, A., Rawlings, S., van Rij, A., Wilkinson, B., Pow, R. and Grant, J. (2020) 'Using Policy Labs as a process to bring evidence closer to public policymaking: a guide to one approach', *Palgrave Communication*, 6 (101). Available from: https://doi.org/10.1057/s41599-020-0453-0. [Accessed August 2020.]

HMSO (2003) 'The Future of Higher Education'. White Paper. London: HMSO. Available from: http://www.educationengland.org.uk/documents/pdfs/2003-white-paper-higher-ed.pdf. [Accessed August 2020.]

Horne, J. and Sherington, G. (2012) *Sydney: The Making of a Public University*. Carlton: The Miegunyah Press.

Ipsos MORI (2018) 'Beyond binary: the lives and choices of Generation Z'. London: Ipsos MORI. Available from: https://www.ipsos.com/ipsos-mori/en-uk/ipsos-thinks-beyond-binary-lives-and-choices-generation-z. [Accessed August 2020.]

Jansen, J. (2019) *Decolonisation in Universities: The Politics of Knowledge*. Johannesburg: Wits University Press.

Jones, G.A. (2002) The structure of university governance in Canada: a policy network approach. In Amaral, A., Jones, G.A. and Karseth, B. (eds) *Governing Higher Education: National Perspectives in Institutional Governance*. Dordrecht: Kluwer Academic Publishers, pp. 213–34. Available from: https://link.springer.com/chapter/10.1007/978-94-015-9946-7_11. [Accessed August 2020.]

Jose, V.S. and Nameer, P.O. (2020) 'The expanding distribution of the Indian Peafowl (*Pavo cristatus*) as an indicator of changing climate in Kerala, southern India: a modelling study using MaxEnt', *Ecological Indicators*, 110. Available from: https://www.sciencedirect.com/science/article/abs/pii/S1470160X19309252. [Accessed August 2020.]

Kennie, T. and Middlehurst, R. (2021) *Leadership Transitions in Universities. Arriving, Surviving and Thriving at the Top*. London: Routledge.

Kerr, C. (1963) *The Use of the University*. Cambridge: Harvard University Press.

King's College London (2018) 'Service Strategy: a framework for delivery, 2018–2023'. King's College London. Available from: https://www.kcl.ac.uk/aboutkings/strategy/kings-service-strategy.pdf. [Accessed August 2020.]

King's College London and Digital Science (2015) 'The nature, scale and beneficiaries of research impact: an initial analysis of Research Excellence

Framework (REF) 2014 impact case studies'. King's College London: The Policy Institute at King's. Available from: https://www.kcl.ac.uk/policy-institute/assets/ref-impact.pdf. [Accessed August 2020.]

Knights, B. (1978) *The Idea of the Clerisy in the Nineteenth Century*. Cambridge: Cambridge University Press.

Kramer, M.E. and Porter, M.R. (2011) 'Creating shared value. How to reinvent capitalism and unleash a wave of innovation and growth', *Harvard Business Review*, 89 (1–2), 62–77.

Larivière, V., Haustein, S. and Mongeon, P. (2015) 'The oligopoly of academic publishers in the digital era', *PLoS ONE*, 10 (6): e0127502. Available from: https://journals.plos.org/plosone/article/file?id=10.1371/journal.pone.0127502&type=printable. [Accessed August 2020.]

Levitt, T. (2015) *Welcome to GoodCo: Using the Tools of Business to Create Public Good*. New York: Routledge.

Lewis, T., Marginson, S. and Snyder, I. (2005) 'The network university? Technology, culture and organisational complexity in contemporary higher education', *Higher Education Quarterly*, 59 (1), 56–75. Abstract available from: https://onlinelibrary.wiley.com/doi/abs/10.1111/j.1468-2273.2005.00281.x. [Accessed August 2020.]

Lichten, C., Ioppolo, R., D'Angelo, C., Simmons, R.K. and Morgan Jones, M. (2018) 'Citizen science: crowdsourcing for research'. Cambridge: THIS Institute. Available from: https://www.thisinstitute.cam.ac.uk/wp-content/uploads/2018/05/THIS-Institute-Crowdsourcing-for-research-978-1-9996539-0-3.pdf. [Accessed August 2020.]

Lifshitz-Assaf, H., Tushman, M.L. and Lakhani, K.R. (2018) 'A study of NASA scientists shows how to overcome barriers to open innovation', *Harvard Business Review*, reprint H04CII. Available from: https://hbr.org/2018/05/a-study-of-nasa-scientists-shows-how-to-overcome-barriers-to-open-innovation. [Accessed August 2020.]

Lomas, J. (2005) 'Using research to inform healthcare managers' and policy makers' questions: from summative to interpretive synthesis', *Healthcare Policy*, 1, 55–71. Available from: https://www.ncbi.nlm.nih.gov/pmc/articles/PMC2585236/. [Accessed August 2020.]

Ludlum, R.P. (1950) 'Academic freedom and tenure: a history', *The Antioch Review*, 10 (1), 3034. Available from: https://www.jstor.org/stable/4609390?seq=1. [Accessed August 2020.]

Lukianoff, G. and Haidt, J. (2015) 'The coddling of the American mind', *The Atlantic*. September. Available from: https://www.theatlantic.com/

magazine/archive/2015/09/the-coddling-of-the-american-mind/399356/. [Accessed August 2020.]

Lukianoff, G. and Haidt, J. (2018) *The Coddling of the American Mind. How Good Intentions and Bad Ideas Are Setting Up a Generation for Failure.* London: Penguin.

Mars, M.M., Bronstein, J.L. and Lusch, R.F. (2012), The value of the metaphor: organizations and ecosystems', *Organizational Dynamics*, 41, 271–80. Available from: https://www.sdlogic.net/uploads/3/4/0/3/34033484/mars_bronstein_lusch_og_dyn.pdf. [Accessed August 2020.]

Martin, R.L. (2010) 'The execution trap', *Harvard Business Review*, 86, 64–71. Available from: https://hbr.org/2010/07/the-execution-trap. [Accessed August 2020.]

Mason, P. (2015) *PostCapitalism: A Guide to Our Future.* Bristol: Allen Lane.

Menon, A. (2018) 'Academic engagement in febrile times: the case of the UK in a changing Europe', *Political Insight*, June, 15. Available from: https://journals.sagepub.com/doi/10.1177/2041905818779328. [Accessed August 2020.]

Mulgan, G., Townsley, O. and Price, A. (2016) 'The challenge-driven university: how real-life problems can fuel learning'. London: Nesta. Available from: https://media.nesta.org.uk/documents/the_challenge-driven_university.pdf. [Accessed August 2020.]

Naidoo, R. and Williams, J. (2014) 'The neoliberal regime in English higher education: charters, consumers and the erosion of the public good', *Critical Studies in Education*, 56 (2). Available from: https://www.tandfonline.com/doi/abs/10.1080/17508487.2014.939098. [Accessed August 2020.]

National Academies of Sciences, Engineering, and Medicine (2018) *Learning through Citizen Science: Enhancing Opportunities by Design.* Washington, DC: The National Academies Press. Available from: https://www.nap.edu/catalog/25183/learning-through-citizen-science-enhancing-opportunities-by-design. [Accessed August 2020.]

Newman, J.H. (1852/2008) *The Idea of a University Defined and Illustrated: In Nine Discourses Delivered to the Catholics of Dublin.* Available from http://www.gutenberg.org/files/24526/24526-pdf.pdf. [Accessed August 2020.]

Odgers, C.L. and Jensen, M.R. (2020) 'Annual Research Review: adolescent mental health in the digital age: facts, fears, and future directions', *Journal of Child Psychology and Psychiatry*, 61 (3). Available from: https://doi.org/10.1111/jcpp.13190. [Accessed August 2020.]

Oliver, K., Innvar, S., Lorenc, T., Woodman, J. and Thomas, J. (2016) 'A systematic review of barriers to and facilitators of the use of evidence by policymakers', *BMC Health Services Research*, 14 (2). Available from: https://bmchealthservres.biomedcentral.com/articles/10.1186/1472-6963-14-2. [Accessed August 2020.]

Olonisakin, F. (2021) 'Global leadership at King's: a framing paper'. [In preparation.]

Orben, A. (2020) 'Teenagers, screens and social media: a narrative review of reviews and key studies', *Social Psychiatry and Psychiatric Epidemiology*, 55, 407–414. Available from: https://doi.org/10.1007/s00127-019-01825-4. [Accessed August 2020.]

Orr, D.W. (1994) *Earth in Mind: On Education, Environment, and the Human Prospect*. Washington, DC: Island Press.

Ortega y Gasset, J. (1946). *Mission of the University*. Abingdon: Routledge.

Oswald, J. (2012) 'The Spinning House girls: Cambridge University's distinctive policing of prostitution, 1823–1894', *Urban History*, 39 (3), 453–70. Available from: https://www.cambridge.org/core/journals/urban-history/article/spinning-house-girls-cambridge-universitys-distinctive-policing-of-prostitution-18231894/580D69C95551D8877B32A698534EE7DC. [Accessed August 2020.]

Patalay, P. and Gage, S.H. (2019) 'Changes in millennial adolescent mental health and health-related behaviours over 10 years: a population cohort comparison study', *International Journal of Epidemiology*, 48 (5), 1650–64. Available from: https://academic.oup.com/ije/article-abstract/48/5/1650/5366210?redirectedFrom=fulltext. [Accessed August 2020.]

Pearson (2019) 'The Global Learner Survey'. London: Pearson. Available from: https://www.pearson.com/content/dam/global-store/global/resources/Pearson_Global_Learner_Survey_2019.pdf. [Accessed August 2020.]

Pietsch, T. (2019) Transformations to higher education. In Fitzgerald, T. (ed) *Handbook of Historical Studies in Education*. Springer International Handbooks of Education. Singapore: Springer. Available from: https://link.springer.com/referenceworkentry/10.1007%2F978-981-10-0942-6_47-1#citeas. [Accessed August 2020.]

Piwowar, H., Priem, J., Larivière, V., Alperin, J.P., Matthias, L., Norlander, B., Farley, A., West, J. and Haustein, S. (2018) 'The state of OA: a large-scale analysis of the prevalence and impact of Open Access articles', *PeerJ*

6: e4375, 13 February. Available from: https://peerj.com/articles/4375/#. [Accessed August 2020.]

Putnam, R.D. (2000) *Bowling Alone*. New York: Simon & Schuster.

Robbins, L. (1963) 'Higher Education Report of the Committee appointed by the Prime Minister under the Chairmanship of Lord Robbins 1961–63'. The Robbins Report 1963, Committee on Higher Education. London: HMSO. Available from: http://www.educationengland.org.uk/documents/robbins/robbins1963.html. [Accessed August 2019.]

Rodin, J. (2007) *The University & Urban Revival: Out of the Ivory Tower and Into the Streets*. Philadelphia: University of Pennsylvania Press.

Rosenfeld, M., Thomas, R.J. and Hausen, S. (2019) 'Disintermediating your friends: how online dating in the United States displaces other ways of meeting', *Proceedings of the National Academy of Science*, 116 (36), 17753–8. Available from: https://www.pnas.org/content/116/36/17753. [Accessed August 2020.]

Røttingen, J.A., Regmi, S., Eide, M., Young, A.J., Viergever, R.F., Årdal, C., Guzman, J., Edwards, D., Matlin, S.A., Terry, R.F. (2013) 'Mapping of available health research and development data: what's there, what's missing, and what role is there for a global observatory?' *The Lancet*, 382, 1286–307. Available from: https://www.thelancet.com/journals/lancet/article/PIIS0140-6736(13)61046-6/fulltext. [Accessed August 2020.]

Saul, J.R. (1973) The evolution of civil military relations in France after the Algerian War. PhD Thesis. London: King's College London, University of London.

Saul, J.R. (1977) *The Birds of Prey*. New York: HarperCollins.

Saul, J.R. (2005) *The Collapse of Globalism: And the Rebirth of Nationalism*. New York: Harry N. Abrams.

Sight Loss and Vision Priority Setting Partnership (2013) 'Setting priorities for eye research: final report'. London: Sight Loss and Vision Partnership. Available from: http://www.jla.nihr.ac.uk/priority-setting-partnerships/sight-loss-and-vision/downloads/SLV-PSP_Final_Report_v111.pdf. [Accessed August 2020.]

Smith, R. (1987) 'Comroe and Dripps revisited', *BMJ*, 295, 1404–7. Available from: https://www.ncbi.nlm.nih.gov/pmc/articles/PMC1248552/. [Accessed August 2020.]

Staley, D.J. (2019) *Alternative Universities: Speculative Design for Innovation in Higher Education*. Baltimore: Johns Hopkins University Press.

Stuart, M. and Shutt, L. (2019) 'The permeable university: the purpose of universities in the 21st century: a manifesto'. Lincoln: University of Lincoln. Available from: https://21stcenturylab.lincoln.ac.uk. [Accessed August 2020.]

Thunberg, G. (2019) *No One is Too Small to Make a Difference*. London: Penguin.

Timms, H. and Heimans, J. (2018) *New Power: How It's Changing the 21st Century – And Why You Need to Know*. New York: Macmillan.

Trow, M. (1973) *Problems in the Transition from Elite to Mass Higher Education*. Berkeley: The Carnegie Commission on Higher Education. Available from: https://eric.ed.gov/?id=ED091983. [Accessed August 2020.]

Tushman, M., Lifshitz-Assaf, H. and Herman, K. (2014a) 'Houston, We Have a Problem: NASA and Open Innovation (A)'. Harvard Business School Case 414-044, May (revised November 2014). Available from: https://www.hbs.edu/faculty/pages/item.aspx?num=47334. [Accessed August 2020.]

Tushman, M., Lifshitz-Assaf, H. and Herman, K. (2014b) 'Houston, We Have a Solution: NASA and Open Innovation (B)'. Harvard Business School Supplement 414-057, May (revised November 2014). Available from: https://www.hbs.edu/faculty/Pages/item.aspx?num=47335. [Accessed August 2020.]

Twenge, J.M. (2017) 'Have smartphones destroyed a generation? More comfortable online than out partying, post-Millennials are safer, physically, than adolescents have ever been. But they're on the brink of a mental-health crisis', *The Atlantic*, September. Available from: https://www.theatlantic.com/magazine/archive/2017/09/has-the-smartphone-destroyed-a-generation/534198/. [Accessed August 2020.]

Twenge, J.M. (2018) *iGen: Why Today's Super-connected Kids Are Growing Up Less Rebellious, More Tolerant, Less Happy – And Completely Unprepared for Adulthood, and What That Means for the Rest of Us*. New York: Atria Books.

Twenge, J.M., Joiner, T.E., Rogers, M.L. and Martin, G.N. (2018) 'Increases in depressive symptoms, suicide-related outcomes, and suicide rates among US adolescents after 2010 and links to increased new media screen time', *Clinical Psychological Science*, 6(1), 3–17. Available from: https://journals.sagepub.com/doi/full/10.1177/2167702617723376. [Accessed August 2020.]

Valero, A. and Van Reenen, J. (2019) 'The economic impact of universities: evidence from across the globe', *Economics of Education Review*, 68, 53–67. Available from: https://www.sciencedirect.com/science/article/pii/S0272775718300414. [Accessed August 2020.]

van Agtmael, A. and Bakker, F. (2018) *The Smartest Places on Earth: Why Rustbelts are the Emerging Hotspots of Global Innovation*. New York: Public Affairs.

van de Werfhorst, H.G. (2019) 'Are universities left-wing bastions? The political orientation of professors, professionals, and managers in Europe', *British Journal of Sociology*. 00:1–27. Available from: https://onlinelibrary.wiley.com/doi/full/10.1111/1468-4446.12716?af=R. [Accessed August 2020.]

Wagner, J., Katz, B. and Osha, T. (2019) 'The evolution of innovation districts: the new geography of global innovation'. The Global Institute of Innovation Districts. Available from: https://www.giid.org/the-evolution-of-innovation-districts-download/. [Accessed August 2020.]

Watson, D., Hollister, R.M., Stroud, S.E. and Babcock, E. (2011) *The Engaged University. International Perspectives on Civic Engagement*. New York: Routledge.

Weiss, C.H. (1979) 'The many meanings of research utilization', *Public Administration Review*, 39, 426–31. Available from: https://www.jstor.org/stable/3109916?origin=crossref&seq=1. [Accessed August 2020.]

Whitchurch, C. (2013) *Reconstructing Identities in Higher Education: The Rise of 'Third Space' Professionals*. New York: Routledge.

Whitchurch, C. (2015) The rise of third space professionals: paradoxes and dilemmas. In Teichler, U. and Cummings, W.C. (eds) *Recruiting and Managing the Academic Profession*. Dordrecht: Springer. Available from: https://www.researchgate.net/publication/293098467_The_Rise_of_Third_Space_Professionals_Paradoxes_and_Dilemmas. [Accessed August 2020.]

White, S. (2018) 'Learning designers and educators in the "third space": the socio-technical construction of MOOCs in UK higher education'. Thesis for the degree of Doctor of Philosophy, University of Southampton, Southampton. Available from: https://eprints.soton.ac.uk/433536/1/S_White_thesis_final.pdf. [Accessed August 2020.]

Willetts, D. (2017) A *University Education*. Oxford: Oxford University Press.

Wilson, P., Mathie, E., Keenan, J., McNeilly, E., Goodman, C., Howe, A., Poland, F., Staniszewska, S., Kendall, S., Munday, D., Cowe, M. and Peckham, S. (2015) 'ReseArch with Patient and Public invOlvement: a RealisT evaluation – the RAPPORT study'. NIHR Journals Library. Available from: https://www.ncbi.nlm.nih.gov/books/NBK316007/. [Accessed August 2020.]

Yousafzai, M. (2013) *I Am Malala: The Girl Who Stood Up for Education and Was Shot by the Taliban*. Boston: Little Brown and Company.

YouthSight (2019) 'How Gen Z will change the world, Vol. 1'. London: YouthSight. Available from: https://www.youthsight.com/blog/how-gen-z-will-change-the-world-vol-one. [Accessed August 2020.]

Index

note: page numbers in *italics* denote figures.

Publisher's acknowledgements

Photo credits:
18 Alamy Stock Photo: MShieldsPhotos/Alamy Stock Photo; **84 Alamy Stock Photo:** Moshe Torgovitsky/Alamy Stock Photo.

Text credits:
1, 12 Macmillan Publishers: Henry Timms and Jeremy Heimans (2018) Understanding "New Power", Macmillan Publishers; **5 Abrams Books:** Saul (2005), The Collapse of Globalism: And the Reinvention of the World, Viking Canada, p. 6; **7 Allianz Global Investors:** Used with permission from Allianz GI Global Capital Markets & Thematic Research Data as of December 2019; **10 Pearson Education:** Buller, E. A. (1944) Darkness Over Germany. Germany: Longmans, Green & Company; **10 Ancient Modern:** A warning from history, Church Times, 5 May 2017; **12 Macmillan Publishers:** Adapted from Timms, H., Heimans, J. (2018) New Power: Why Outsiders are Winning, Institutions are Failing, and how the Rest of Us Can Keep Up in the Age of Mass Participation. United Kingdom: Pan Macmillan; **14 Macmillan Publishers:** New Power: How It's Changing the Course of the 21st Century – and Why You Need to Know, Pan Macmillan; **13 Taylor & Francis Group:** Naidoo and Williams (2014) The neoliberal regime in English higher education: charters, consumers and the erosion of the public good, Critical Studies in Education, Vol. 56 (2); **18 Guardian News & Media Limited:** Jeremy Heimans, New Power author Jeremy Heimans: 'Like it or not, the old world isn't coming back', Decca Aitkenhead, Guardian News & Media; **20 Springer Nature:** Pietsch (2019) Handbook of Historical Studies in Education pp. 1–13; Transformations to Higher Education, p. 3; **21 Pearson Education:** The cumulative line is based on a list of foundation dates of universities in Europe published on Wikipedia; **22 Springer:** De Vries and Slowey (2012) Concluding Reflections. Between Humboldt and Newman, Springer, P.3; **22 Oxford University Press:** Willetts, D. (2017) A University Education. Oxford: Oxford University Press; **23, 27 Johns Hopkins University Press:** Crow and Dabars (2015) Designing the New American University. Published by Johns Hopkins University Press; **23 John Henry Newman:** Newman

(1852) The Idea of a University Defined and Illustrated In Nine Discourses Delivered to the Catholics of Dublin, p. 38; **23 Taylor & Francis Group:** Donovan (2106) Brunel University, pp. 1–2 of https://bura.brunel.ac.uk/bitstream/2438/11902/3/Fulltext.pdf. Accessed 11 November 2019; **24 Melbourne University Press:** Davis, G. (2017) The Australian Idea of a University. Melbourne: Melbourne University Press, p. 39; **26 Sargent Shriver National Center on Poverty Law Publication:** Colleges, Universities and Communities Advanced Social and Economic Justice, Harris and Karkavy (2003), p.152; **27 Johns Hopkins University Press:** Gavazzi and Gee (2018), Land-Grant Universities for the Future, Johns Hopkins University Press, p. 157; **27 United States Congress:** Extract from Morrill Act 1862; **28 Department of Education:** HMSO (2003) 'The Future of Higher Education'. White Paper. London: HMSO; **29 Pearson Education:** Newman, J. H. (1852) Idea of a University: Defined and illustrated. London: Longmans, Green & Co; **29 John Henry Newman:** Newman (1852) The Idea of a University Defined and Illustrated In Nine Discourses Delivered to the Catholics of Dublin, p. 182; **30 Taylor & Francis Group:** Naidoo and Williams (2014) The neoliberal regime in English higher education: charters, consumers and the erosion of the public good in Critical Studies in Education, Vol. 56 (2); **33 University of Pennsylvania:** Amy Gutmann (2017) President University of Pennsylvania; **38 Jonathan Ball Publishers:** Adam Habib (2019) Rebels and Rage: Reflecting on #FeesMustFall, Jonathan Ball Publishers; **38 'Funmi Olonisakin:** Used with permission from 'Funmi Olonisakin; **39 Quillette Pty:** Doug Stokes (2019), Forget About Decolonizing the Curriculum. We Need to Restore the West's Telos Before it's Too Late, Quillette, March 3; **39 Guardian News & Media Limited:** James Muldoon (2019) Academics: it's time to get behind decolonising the curriculum, The Guardian, 20 March; **40 New York University Press:** Jansen (2019) Decolonisation in Universities: The politics of knowledge, NYU Press; **40 Harvard Business Review:** Tomas Chamorro-Premuzic and Becky Frankiewicz (2019) Does Higher Education Still Prepare People for Jobs?, HBR, 14 Jan; **41 Penguin Random House:** Collini (2012), What are Universities For?, Penguin UK, p. 154; **41 Europe Engage:** Europe Engage (2017) Europe Engage: Developing a Culture of Civic Engagement Through Service-learning Within Higher Education in Europe. Brussels: European Union; **43 Institute for Public Policy Research:** Barber (2013) An avalanche is coming: Higher education and the revolution ahead, IPPR, p. 3; **43 The New York Times Company:** D. Brooks (2013) The Practical University, New York Times, 4 April; **43 The New York Times Company:** D.Brooks (2015) The Big University, New York Times, 6 October; **43 John Henry Newman:** Newman (1852) The Idea of a University Defined and Illustrated In Nine Discourses Delivered to the Catholics of Dublin, p. 126; **44 Condé Nast:** S. Leckart (2020) The Stanford Education Experiment Could Change Higher Learning Forever, Condé Nast; **44 UPP Foundation Limited:** Glyn Davis (2017) Professor Glyn Davis Full Speech: "An irredeemable time? The rising tide of hostility toward universities", UPP Foundation, Oct 19; **45 John Henry Newman:** Newman (1852) The Idea of a University Defined and Illustrated In Nine Discourses Delivered to the Catholics of Dublin, p. 126; **47 Twitter Inc:** Nick Hillman, Tweet, March 13, 2019; **47**

ConservativeHome: Nick Hillman (2017) We must continue to expand higher education, ConservativeHome, Sep 30; **48 Government Digital Service:** Education Secretary FE speech with Social Market Foundation, Department for Education, July 9, 2020; **49 Penguin Random House:** Elliot Major and Machin (2018) Social Mobility: And Its Enemies, Penguin UK, pp. 97, 99; **50 Institute of Fiscal Studies:** Line is drawn from different sources. Solid line is from IFS (2010) Working Paper W10/04; **50 Graphreader:** Data extracted from Figure 2 using http://www.graphreader.com so may not be entirely accurate; **50 House of Commons:** Dashed line is from Figure 1 of House of Commons Public Accounts Committee report on Widening Participation; **50 Government Digital Service:** Data estimated by reading graph. Dotted line is from DfS briefing (https://www.gov.uk/government/statistics/participation-rates-in-higher-education-2006-to-2017) using direct data source; **52 Angel Jose Calderon:** Angel Jose Calderon (2018) Massification of higher education revisited, Table 2; **54 Wonkhe Ltd:** Wonkhe (2017) Should universities raise school attainment? Yes, and here's why, June 6; **54 Louise Richardson:** University of Oxford Vice-Chancellor, Louise Richardson; **56 U.S. Government Publishing Office:** A Report to the President by Vannevar Bush, Director of the Office of Scientific Research and Development, July 1945, United States Government Printing Office, Washington: 1945; **58 Pearson Education:** Byrne and Clarke (2019) The University Challenge. Published by Pearson Education; **60 Research Excellence Framework:** "The Case of the Forged Gospel Fragment", Used with permission from REF 2014 IMPACT CASE STUDY; **61 Research Excellence Framework:** Using honey bees as an effective deterrent for crop-raiding elephants, Used with permissions from REF 2014 IMPACT CASE STUDY; **64 Harvard Business Review:** Hila Lifshitz-Assaf, Michael L. Tushman, and Karim R. Lakhani (2018) A Study of NASA Scientists Shows How to Overcome Barriers to Open Innovation, Harvard Business Review, May 29, 2018; **64 National Center for Biotechnology Information:** Wilson et al. (2015) ReseArch with Patient and Public involvement; **64 The College of Optometrists:** Sight Loss and Vision Priority Setting Partnership (2013), p. 26; **65 Elsevier:** Jose and Nameer (2020) Ecological Indicators; **65 Cornell University:** About eBird, https://ebird.org/taiwan/about; **67 Condé Nast:** G. Moody (2016) Open access: All human knowledge is there – so why can't everybody access it?, ARS Technica, 6/17/2016; **70 F1000 Research Ltd:** Used with permission from F1000, About F1000: Who We Are; **74 Financial Times Limited:** Responsible capitalism requires new standards, Financial Times, Oct 27, 2019; **74 The Economist Newspaper Limited:** Social impact: what does it mean, and how should we measure it?, The Economist, Jan 13, 2020; **74 Harvard Business Review:** Kramer and Porter (2011) The Big Idea: Creating Shared Value. How to Reinvent Capitalism – and Unleash a Wave of Innovation and Growth, Harvard Business Review; **75 University of Pennsylvania:** PennCOMPACT2022 Impact, Amy Gutmann; **77 Taylor & Francis Group:** Watson, D., Hollister, R. M., Stroud, S. E. and Babcock, E. (2011) The Engaged University. International Perspectives on Civic Engagement. New York: Routledge; **77 University of Haifa:** Welcome to the University of Haifa, https://www.haifainternational.com/; **78 University of Lincoln:** Stuart and Shutt (2019) The purpose of universities in the 21st century: a manifesto, University of Lincoln, p.16; **78 UPP Foundation Limited:** Truly Civic: Strengthening the connection between universities and their places, UPP Foundation, p. 4; **79 University of London:** Dickens (1858), p. 58 quoted in Hearnshaw (1929), p. 256; **79 Amy Gutman:** Amy Gutmann (2017) President University of Pennsylvania; **82 King's College London:** Meet King's College London, Education Strategy (2017–2022), King's College London (2018), p. 5; **83 Grammarist:** See no evil, hear no evil, speak no evil, Grammarist; **85 Guardian News & Media Limited:** Oliver Milman (2014) Coalition accused of 'bullying' ANU after criticism of fossil fuel divestment, Guardian News, Oct 14; **87 Taylor & Francis Group:** Levitt (2015) Welcome to GoodCo: Using the Tools of Business to Create Public Good, Ashgate Publishing, p. 195; **89 Penguin Random House:** Collini (2012) What are Universities For?, Penguin UK, p. 25; **90 King's College London:** London needs a civic heart, Baroness Deborah Bull CBE Vice-President & Vice-Principal (London), King's College London 2019; **91 Malala Yousafzai:** Malala Yousafzai, Gen Z student and education campaigner; **94 Ipsos:** Ipsos MORI (2018) Data on alcohol consumption taken from p. 37 and is based on a survey of English 13–15 year olds; Data on community citizenship is taken from p. 139 and is based on a survey of UK school children aged 14–16 years; Data on sexual identity and gender neutral bath rooms is taken from pp. 26–29 and is based on UK (sexual identity) and US (gender neutral bathrooms) surveys of 15+ and 13–20 year olds respectively; **96 Centre for Longitudinal Studies:** Depression is on the rise among young people, but antisocial behaviour is down, new research shows, Centre for Longitudinal Studies, 28 Feb 2019; **97 John Wiley & Sons, Inc:** Odgers, C. L. and Jensen, M. R. (2020) Annual Research Review: Adolescent mental health in the digital age: facts, fears, and future directions. Journal of Child Psychology and Psychiatry, Vol. 61: 336–348. doi:10.1111/jcpp.13190; **97 John Wiley & Sons, Inc:** Odgers and Jensen (2020) Annual Research Review: Adolescent mental health in the digital age: facts, fears, and future directions in Journal of Child Psychology and Psychiatry, Vol. 61, Issue 3; **98 The Atlantic:** Twenge, J. M. (2017) 'Have Smartphones Destroyed a Generation? More comfortable online than out partying, post-Millennials are safer, physically, than adolescents have ever been. But they're on the brink of a mental health crisis', The Atlantic, September; **98 Taylor & Francis Group:** Furedi, F. (2018) What's Happened to the University? A Sociological Exploration of its Infantilisation. London: Routledge; **99 The Atlantic:** Lukianoff, G. and Haidt, J. (2015) 'The coddling of the American mind', The Atlantic, September; **99 News Group Newspapers:** Thomas Burrows (2019), CLAPTRAP 'Snowflake' Oxford University students ban clapping and replace it with 'jazz hands' to stop 'anxiety', News Group Newspapers, 24 Oct 2019; **99 The Telegraph:** Don't call us snowflakes – it damages our mental health, say young people, The Telegraph, 6 Dec 2017; **101 John Wiley & Sons, Inc:** van de Werfhorst, H. G. (2019) 'Are universities left-wing bastions? The political orientation of professors, professionals, and managers in Europe', British Journal Sociology; **101 Oxford University Press:** Baer, U. (2019) What Snowflakes Get Right: Free Speech, Truth, and Equality on Campus. Oxford: Oxford University Press; **102 YouthSight:** YouthSight (2019) How Gen Z will change the world, Vol. 1, Youth Thinking: 02 May 2019, p. 4; **104 Malala Fund:** Malala Stories, Malala Fund; **104**

Penguin Random House: Thunberg (2019), No One Is Too Small to Make a Difference, Penguin Books Limited, p. 38; **106 Island Press:** Orr, D. W. (1994) Earth in Mind: On Education, Environment, and the Human Prospect. Washington: Island Press; **112 Chad Wellmon:** Chad Wellon, After the University, Long Live the Academy! Oct 26, 2017; **112 Inside Higher Ed:** Madeline St. Amour (2020), Future of the Academy, Inside Higher Ed, Jan 27 2020; **113 UNESCO:** Recommendation concerning the Status of Higher-Education Teaching Personnel, UNESCO, 11 Nov 1997; **113 International Association of Universities:** Academic Freedom, University Autonomy and Social Responsibility, IAU Policy statement; **114 Merriam Webster:** Used with permission from Merriam-Webster, Inc.; **115 Australia Association for Research in Education:** Paul Richardson and Amanda Heffernan, Our university workforce has become a fragmented, casualised 'gig economy'. The problems we face, EduResearch Matters; **115 University World News:** Brendan O'Malley (2020), 'Dehumanising' impact of casualisation of HE staff exposed, University World News, 21 January 2020; **116 Springer:** Extract taken from C. Whitchurch "The Rise of Third Space Professionals" in Ulrich Teichler, William K. Cummings (2015) 'Forming, Recruiting and Managing the Academic Profession', Springer (2015); **116 Taylor & Francis Group:** Whitchurch (2013) Reconstructing Identities in Higher Education, Routledge, p. 144; **116 University of Southampton:** Steven White (2018) Learning designers and educators in the 'third space': the socio-technical construction of MOOCs in UK higher education; **118 Springer:** Extract taken from C. Whitchurch "The Rise of Third Space Professionals" in Ulrich Teichler, William K. Cummings (2015) 'Forming, Recruiting and Managing the Academic Profession', Springer (2015); **119 Taylor & Francis Group:** Whitchurch (2013) Reconstructing Identities in Higher Education, Routledge, p. 144; **119 Taylor & Francis Group:** Whitchurch (2013) Reconstructing Identities in Higher Education, Routledge, p. 144; **120 Peakon:** R. Brooks (2018) Workplace Spotlight: What Google Gets Right about Company Culture, Peakon, 28 June 2018; **120 Australia Association for Research in Education:** Paul Richardson and Amanda Heffernan, Our university workforce has become a fragmented, casualised 'gig economy'. The problems we face, EduResearch Matters; **121 John Wiley & Sons, Inc:** Guest, D. (2004) 'Flexible employment contracts, the psychological contract and employee outcomes: an analysis and review of the evidence', International Journal of Management Reviews, 5/6, 1–19; **122 The University of Newcastle:** UON ACADEMY, Developing, supporting and engaging our sessional academic staff, Currrent Staff; **124 American Association of University Professors:** 1915 Declaration of Principles on Academic Freedom and Academic Tenure, American Association of University Professors; **124 Freakonomics:** Steven D. Levitt (2007) Let's Just Get Rid of Tenure (Including Mine), Freakonomics, March 3, 2007; **128 Guardian News & Media Limited:** Harriet Swain (2018) Have university leaders changed after the vice-chancellor pay scandal?, The Guardian, 1 Nov 2018; **130 TED Conferences, LLC:** Derek Sivers (2010), How to start a Movement, TED 2010; **132 Cambridge University Press:** Oswald (2012) The Spinning House girls, JSTOR, p. 457; **133 The Monthly:** Megan Davis (2020) Reconciliation and the promise of an Australian homecoming, The Monthly, July 2020; **133 The Chicago Maroon:** Lee Harris (2017), The University and the South Side,

The Chicago Maroon, September 15, 2017; **134 University of Pennsylvania:** Rodin (2007) The University and Urban Revival Out of the Ivory Tower and Into the Streets. Published by University of Pennsylvania Press Incorporated; **134 Guardian News & Media Limited:** Brian Oliver (2018) Town v gown: is the student boom wrecking communities?, The Guardian, 23 Sep 2018; **135 Organisation for Economic Co-operation and Development:** Glossary of Statistical terms, OECD; **135 Polity:** Halpern (2005), Social Capital, Polity Books, p. 1; **136 Wonkhe Ltd:** Deborah Bull (2019) What's wrong with "public engagement"?, Wonkhe, 5 July 2019; **138 University of Pennsylvania:** Rodin (2007) The University and Urban Revival Out of the Ivory Tower and Into the Streets. Published by University of Pennsylvania Press Incorporated; **139 Citizens UK:** Extract taken from Citizens UK-Homepage; **141 Wonkhe Ltd:** Paul Webb (2019) Unleashing the power of parents, Wonkhe, 14 June 2019; **142 UPP Foundation Limited:** Truly Civic: Strengthening the connection between universities and their places, Civic University Commission (2019); **146 The Brookings Institution:** Wagner et al. (2019) New insights on how innovation districts are challenging economic and social divides, The Brookings; **147 Perseus Books Group:** van Agtmael and Bakker (2018), The Smartest Places on Earth, PublicAffairs, p. 253; **147 The New York Times Company:** David Brooks (2005) The Education Gap, New York Times, Sept 25; **148 The New York Times Company:** David Brooks (2005) The Big University, New York Times, Oct 5; **151 José Ortega y Gasset:** José Ortega y Gasset, 1946, Mission of the University; **154 Melbourne University Press:** Davis, G. (2017) The Australian Idea of a University. Published by Read How You Want; **155 Johns Hopkins University Press:** Staley (2019) Alternative Universities, Johns Hopkins, pp.18–19; **157 Olin College of Engineering:** Extract taken from Olin – About. Retreived from http://www.olin.edu/about/; **157 World Bank Group:** Geoff Mulgan, Catching-up Regions Poland Supporting Regional Innovation and Entrepreneurship Lodzkie, Podlaskie and Dolnoslaskie regions Report Annexes May 2019; **158 Johns Hopkins University Press:** Crow and Dabars (2015) Designing the New American University. Published by Johns Hopkins University Press; **160 John Wiley & Sons, Inc:** Lewis et al., The Network University? Technology, Culture and Organisational Complexity in Contemporary Higher Education, Higher Education Quarterly, 0951–5224. Vol. 59, No. 1, January 2005, pp 56–75; **161 Elsevier:** Mars, Matthew M., Judith L. Bronstein and Robert F. Lusch (2012) "The Value of a Metaphor: Organizations and Ecosystems", Organizational Dynamics 41 (4): 271–80; **163 Academic Health Solutions Limited:** Academic Health Science Centres: Learning from the Social Sciences, Academic Health Solutions; **165 PLuS Alliance:** Extract taken from 'About PLuS Alliance', PLuS Alliance; **165 Inside Higher Ed:** Mark Lester (2018) How Online Can Learn From the Airline Industry, Inside Higher Ed, June 27, 2018; **166 Stylus Publishing:** Eckel and Trower (2019) The Pivotal – and Pivoting – Partnership, p. 3; **167 Springer:** Governing Higher Education: National Perspectives on Institutional Governance. (2002) Netherlands: Springer Netherlands; **168 Interactive Co-operative Alliance:** What is a cooperative?, Interactive Co-operative Alliance; **168 Guardian News & Media Limited:** Andrew Bibby (2012) How co-operatives tackle corporate governance, The Guardian, 24 May; **169 Bleacher Report, Inc:** Khalid Khan (2010) Cure or Curse: Socio Club

Ownerships in Spanish La Liga, Bleacher Report, 11 June; **170 Harvard Business Review:** Citing Martin (2010) The Execution Trap, Harvard Business Review, p. 71; **170 José Ortega y Gasset:** Ortego y Gasset (1946), p. 36. It is worth noting that this pamphlet was based on a series of lectures given in 1930; **173 University of Chicago Press:** Boyer (2015) The University of Chicago: A History. Published by University of Chicago Press; **174 The University of Chicago:** Robert J. Zimmer (2009) Address Delivered at Columbia University, Office of the President, The University of Chicago, October 21; **175 Pearson Education:** Buller, E. A. (1943) Darkness Over Germany. Germany: Longmans, Green and Company; **175 Glyn Davis:** Glyn Davis, the former Vice Chancellor of the University of Melbourne; **176 Duncan Maskell:** Duncan Maskell, Vice-Chancellor of Melbourne University; **177 Pearson Education:** Buller, E. A. (1943) Darkness Over Germany. Germany: Longmans, Green and Company; **180 Conservative Party:** 'Strong Leadership, A Clear Economic Plan, A Brighter, More Secure Future', The Conservative Party Manifesto 2015; **181 The Sydney Morning Herald:** Andrew Taylor (2017) University of Sydney staff call on management to publicly support same-sex marriage, The Sydney Morning Herald, Nov 2; **182 University of Melbourne:** University of Melbourne Academic Board Supports Marriage Equality, University of Melbourne, 18 Sep 2017; **182 Independent Digital News and Media:** Nigel Morris (2015) EU referendum: 'Brexit' would harm higher education and research, universities claim, The Independent, 27 July; **183 UK Changing Europe:** Extract taken from 'About the authoritative source for independent research on UK–EU relations', UK in a Changing Europe; **183 The Conversation Media Group Ltd:** Universities UK is wrong to take sides on question of EU membership, The Conversation, Sep 17, 2015; **183 SAGE Publication:** Menon (2018) Academic Engagement in Febrile Times: The Case of the UK in a Changing Europe; **185 Wonkhe Ltd:** Mark Leach (2018) The Enemy Within – why the narrative about universities and students went so wrong, Wonkhe, March 9; **186 Schumann Media Center, Inc:** Marshall Ganz on Making Social Movements Matter, Moyers on Democaracy, May 10, 2013; **187 Taylor & Francis Group:** Bagshaw and McVitty (2019) Influencing Higher Education Policy: A Professional Guide to Making an Impact. Published by Routledge; **188 Abrams Books:** Saul (2005), The Collapse of Globalism: And the Rebirth of Nationalism, Harry N. Abrams, p. 6; **189 Orion Publishing Group:** Eco (2003), Mouse Or Rat?: Translation as Negotiation, Weidenfeld & Nicolson, p. 82; **190 Penguin Random House:** Timms and Heimans (2018) New Power: How Power Works in Our Hyperconnected World – And How to Make It Work for You. Published by Penguin Random House, LLC pp. 53, 38; **191 Taylor & Francis Group:** Bagshaw and McVitty (2019) Influencing Higher Education Policy: A Professional Guide to Making an Impact. Published by Routledge, pp.164, 169; **193 Penguin Random House:** John Ralston Saul (2005) The Collapse of Globalism: And the Reinvention of the World, Penguin Canada, p. 295; **193 Johns Hopkins University Press:** COVID-19 Dashboard by the Center for Systems Science and Engineering (CSSE) at Johns Hopkins University (JHU); **193 Taylor & Francis Group:** Freedman, L. (2020) Strategy for a Pandemic: The UK and COVID-19 in Survival 62(3). Published by Taylor & Francis; **195 TACSI:** Charles Leadbeater, Power Meets Love, TACSI, 2020.